Battleground Europe

The Dunkirk Perimeter and Evacuation 1940

Battleground Series

Stamford Bridge & Hastings by Peter Marren
Wars of the Roses - Wakefield/Towton by Philip A. Haigh
Wars of the Roses - Barnet by David Clark
Wars of the Roses - Tewkesbury by Steven Goodchild
Wars of the Roses - The Battles of St Albans by Peter Burley, Michael Elliott & Harvey Wilson
English Civil War - Naseby by Martin Marix Evans, Peter Burton and Michael Westaway
English Civil War - Marston Moor by David Clark
War of the Spanish Succession - Blenheim 1704 by James Falkner
War of the Spanish Succession - Ramillies 1706 by James Falkner
Napoleonic - Hougoumont by Julian Paget and Derek Saunders
Napoleonic - Waterloo by Andrew Uffindell and Michael Corum
Zulu War - Isandlwana by Ian Knight and Ian Castle
Zulu War - Rorkes Drift by Ian Knight and Ian Castle
Boer War - The Relief of Ladysmith by Lewis Childs
Boer War - The Siege of Ladysmith by Lewis Childs
Boer War - Kimberley by Lewis Childs

Mons by Jack Horsfall and Nigel Cave
Néry by Patrick Tackle
Retreat of I Corps 1914 by Jerry Murland
Aisne 1914 by Jerry Murland
Aisne 1918 by David Blanchard
Le Cateau by Nigel Cave and Jack Shelden
Walking the Salient by Paul Reed
Ypres - 1914 Messines by Nigel Cave and Jack Sheldon
Ypres - 1914 Menin Road by Nigel Cave and Jack Sheldon
Ypres - 1914 Langemarck by Jack Sheldonand Nigel Cave
Ypres - Sanctuary Wood and Hooge by Nigel Cave
Ypres - Hill 60 by Nigel Cave
Ypres - Messines Ridge by Peter Oldham
Ypres - Polygon Wood by Nigel Cave
Ypres - Passchendaele by Nigel Cave
Ypres - Airfields and Airmen by Mike O'Connor
Ypres - St Julien by Graham Keech
Ypres - Boesinghe by Stephen McGreal
Walking the Somme by Paul Reed
Somme - Gommecourt by Nigel Cave
Somme - Serre by Jack Horsfall & Nigel Cave
Somme - Beaumont Hamel by Nigel Cave
Somme - Thiepval by Michael Stedman
Somme - La Boisselle by Michael Stedman
Somme - Fricourt by Michael Stedman
Somme - Carnoy-Montauban by Graham Maddocks
Somme - Pozières by Graham Keech
Somme - Courcelette by Paul Reed
Somme - Boom Ravine by Trevor Pidgeon
Somme - Mametz Wood by Michael Renshaw
Somme - Delville Wood by Nigel Cave
Somme - Advance to Victory (North) 1918 by Michael Stedman
Somme - Flers by Trevor Pidgeon
Somme - Bazentin Ridge by Edward Hancock
Somme - Combles by Paul Reed
Somme - Beaucourt by Michael Renshaw
Somme - Redan Ridge by Michael Renshaw
Somme - Hamel by Peter Pedersen
Somme - Villers-Bretonneux by Peter Pedersen
Somme - Airfields and Airmen by Mike O'Connor
Airfields and Airmen of the Channel Coast by Mike O'Connor
In the Footsteps of the Red Baron by Mike O'Connor
Arras - Airfields and Airmen by Mike O'Connor
Arras - The Battle for Vimy Ridge by Jack Sheldon & Nigel Cave
Arras - Vimy Ridge by Nigel Cave
Arras - Gavrelle by Trevor Tasker and Kyle Tallett
Arras - Oppy Wood by David Bilton
Arras - Bullecourt by Graham Keech
Arras - Monchy le Preux by Colin Fox
Walking Arras by Paul Reed
Hindenburg Line by Peter Oldham
Hindenburg Line - Epehy by Bill Mitchinson
Hindenburg Line - Riqueval by Bill Mitchinson
Hindenburg Line - Villers-Plouich by Bill Mitchinson
Hindenburg Line - Cambrai Right Hook by Jack Horsfall & Nigel Cave
Hindenburg Line - Cambrai Flesquières by Jack Horsfall & Nigel Cave
Hindenburg Line - Saint Quentin by Helen McPhail and Philip Guest
Hindenburg Line - Bourlon Wood by Jack Horsfall & Nigel Cave
Cambrai - Airfields and Airmen by Mike O'Connor
Aubers Ridge by Edward Hancock
La Bassée - Neuve Chapelle by Geoffrey Bridger
Loos - Hohenzollern Redoubt by Andrew Rawson
Loos - Hill 70 by Andrew Rawson
Fromelles by Peter Pedersen
The Battle of the Lys 1918 by Phil Tomaselli
Accrington Pals Trail by William Turner
Poets at War: Wilfred Owen by Helen McPhail and Philip Guest
Poets at War: Edmund Blunden by Helen McPhail and Philip Guest
Poets at War: Graves & Sassoon by Helen McPhail and Philip Guest
Gallipoli by Nigel Steel
Gallipoli - Gully Ravine by Stephen Chambers
Gallipoli - Anzac Landing by Stephen Chambers
Gallipoli - Suvla August Offensive by Stephen Chambers
Gallipoli - Landings at Helles by Huw & Jill Rodge
Walking Gallipoli by Stephen Chambers
Walking the Italian Front by Francis Mackay
Italy - Asiago by Francis Mackay
Verdun: Fort Douamont by Christina Holstein
Verdun: Fort Vaux by Christina Holstein
Walking Verdun by Christina Holstein
Verdun: The Left Bank by Christina Holstein
Zeebrugge & Ostend Raids 1918 by Stephen McGreal

Germans at Beaumont Hamel by Jack Sheldon
Germans at Thiepval by Jack Sheldon

SECOND WORLD WAR

Dunkirk by Patrick Wilson
Calais by Jon Cooksey
Boulogne by Jon Cooksey
Saint-Nazaire by James Dorrian
Walking D-Day by Paul Reed
Atlantic Wall - Pas de Calais by Paul Williams
Atlantic Wall - Normandy by Paul Williams
Normandy - Pegasus Bridge by Carl Shilleto
Normandy - Merville Battery by Carl Shilleto
Normandy - Utah Beach by Carl Shilleto
Normandy - Omaha Beach by Tim Kilvert-Jones
Normandy - Gold Beach by Christopher Dunphie & Garry Johnson
Normandy - Gold Beach Jig by Tim Saunders
Normandy - Juno Beach by Tim Saunders
Normandy - Sword Beach by Tim Kilvert-Jones
Normandy - Operation Bluecoat by Ian Daglish
Normandy - Operation Goodwood by Ian Daglish
Normandy - Epsom by Tim Saunders
Normandy - Hill 112 by Tim Saunders
Normandy - Mont Pinçon by Eric Hunt
Normandy - Cherbourg by Andrew Rawson
Normandy - Commandos & Rangers on D-Day by Tim Saunders
Das Reich – Drive to Normandy by Philip Vickers
Oradour by Philip Beck
Market Garden - Nijmegen by Tim Saunders
Market Garden - Hell's Highway by Tim Saunders
Market Garden - Arnhem, Oosterbeek by Frank Steer
Market Garden - Arnhem, The Bridge by Frank Steer
Market Garden - The Island by Tim Saunders
Rhine Crossing – US 9th Army & 17th US Airborne by Andrew Rawson
British Rhine Crossing – Operation Varsity by Tim Saunders
British Rhine Crossing – Operation Plunder by Tim Saunders
Battle of the Bulge – St Vith by Michael Tolhurst
Battle of the Bulge – Bastogne by Michael Tolhurst
Channel Islands by George Forty
Walcheren by Andrew Rawson
Remagen Bridge by Andrew Rawson
Cassino by Ian Blackwell
Anzio by Ian Blackwell
Dieppe by Tim Saunders
Fort Eben Emael by Tim Saunders
Crete – The Airborne Invasion by Tim Saunders
Malta by Paul Williams
Bruneval Raid by Paul Oldfield
Cockleshell Raid by Paul Oldfield

Battleground Europe

The Dunkirk Perimeter and Evacuation 1940

France and Flanders Campaign

Jerry Murland

Series Editor
Nigel Cave

Pen & Sword
MILITARY

First published in Great Britain in 2019 by
Pen & Sword Military
an imprint of
Pen & Sword Books Ltd,
47 Church Street
Barnsley,
South Yorkshire, S70 2AS

ISBN 978 147385 223 5

A CIP catalogue record for this book is
available from the British Library.

Typeset in Times New Roman by Chic Graphics

Printed and bound in England by
TJ International Ltd, Padstow, Cornwall

Pen & Sword Books Ltd incorporates the imprints of
Pen & Sword Archaeology, Atlas, Aviation, Battleground, Discovery,
Family History, History, Maritime, Military, Naval, Politics,
Railways, Select, Social History, Transport, True Crime,
Claymore Press, Frontline Books, Leo Cooper, Praetorian Press,
Remember When, Seaforth Publishing and Wharncliffe.

For a complete list of Pen & Sword titles please contact
PEN & SWORD BOOKS LIMITED
47 Church Street, Barnsley, South Yorkshire, S70 2AS, England
E-mail: enquiries@pen-and-sword.co.uk
Website: www.pen-and-sword.co.uk

Contents

List of Maps

Series Editor's Introduction

It often appears that the British have a particular approach to their twentieth century military history; for they seem to retain in popular memory significant defeats or set-backs more than others. One only has to think of Mons, the first day of the Somme and Passchendaele. Apart from D-Day, in the Second World War the most remembered – and commemorated – land/sea engagement is Dunkirk.

Dunkirk is popularly considered as a purely Anglo-German event, which took place on the beaches immediately around that town; the photographs most associated with it are of long lines of British soldiers waiting to board an eclectic range of shipping, or portray exhausted, bedraggled evacuated soldiers in these vessels. It is often thought that the evacuation was completed in a day or two and from a very limited beach area.

The reality of the events surrounding the Dunkirk Evacuation is clearly laid out in this latest book by Jerry Murland, part of his Battleground Europe series on the France and Flanders Campaign 1940. Although it can obviously stand on its own, to get a complete idea of the evacuation it is necessary to put it in the context of the outstandingly successful German *blitzkrieg* offensive of May 1940, described in the other books. Just because we know it happened and we have become so used to it that it is taken almost casually, it was a brilliant feat of arms; given the potential military capability of its foes, the German army performed efficiently at all levels. The only significant criticism that can be held against the operation is that it could – probably should – have been even more decisive. It remains a, if not the, textbook example of the optimum deployment of force in order to achieve a decisive and likely war-winning victory in the face of a potentially superior enemy.

Although some of the failings that resulted in the incomplete German military victory were self-inflicted, it is also true that the retreat was accomplished in a way that certainly ensured that it was not a complete walk over and certainly was a significant reason for the German failure not only to prevent the evacuation but the sheer scale of it.

A key reason for the retention of military defeats as part of the British 'myth' is that they are perceived as triumphs of the human – or national – spirit in the face of adversity. There is no good military reason not to see Dunkirk as a military disaster that was only partially mitigated by the numbers of troops who were ferried across the Channel to Britain. Examined objectively, the BEF lost huge quantities of badly needed military equipment and stores. France was left on the verge of a decisive military defeat. Britain was soon to lose any point of entry on the continent from which to take on the enemy. Since early May all of her allies and the neutral countries facing her on the continental land mass had been overrun. The threat of a hostile invasion was greater than at any point since Napoleon gathered his Grand Army around Boulogne at the start of the nineteenth century; and the ability to defend against it had been severely compromised.

Yet the events at Dunkirk had an unexpected consequence. After months of a 'Phoney War', the stark realities of the situation came home to the nation. Inspired by a war leader whose political moment had come and supported by an extraordinarily effective propaganda machine, Dunkirk was transformed into a national rallying point whose impact is difficult to underestimate. The international community would have been quite secure in assuming that Britain would be forced, sooner rather than later, to accept an imposed settlement, possibly even a full blooded German occupation.

So those images from the evacuation were twisted around so that they supported the idea of fortitude, determination, of making do, of challenging the Teutonic machine, of standing for principles of democracy and freedoms. They provided the foundations for the resolute reaction to the flawed German strategy of concentrating on the bombing of cities once Goering, in the early autumn of 1940, had decided, rightly or wrongly, that the battle against the RAF had failed. Imperceptibly almost, and despite further military set-backs in places as far afield as North Africa and Crete, Britain was seen as the bastion of democracy in a world dominated by dictatorship and repressive governments; this was perceived nowhere greater than in the United States, a nation that had for some twenty years been dominated by isolationism.

The evacuation of British and French troops from the beaches marked a moment of German triumph; but it also marked the genesis of a British fightback, a fightback that was the first stage of the total commitment of a nation to fight a war that seemed hopeless. This is not to suggest that there were not prominent politicians who felt that a settlement with Germany should be reached, given the seemingly impossible military prospects. The national genius needed to be channelled to face this situation; and Britain was blessed with the inspiring political leadership of Winston Churchill, supported by the understated figure of the leader of the Labour Party, Clement Atlee.

Dunkirk was a disaster; but from the ashes of this military cataclysm rose a united nation that came through all the future reverses to win a victory that was so decisive that it has consequences that have lasted almost eighty years and will continue beyond the present day.

Nigel Cave

Ratcliffe College. Autumn 2018.

Author's Introduction

Dunkerque in Flemish means church of the dunes - a name likely to have been lost on the soldiers assembled on the beaches in May and June 1940. Like many British visitors, I have always been drawn to Dunkerque and the famous evacuation that took place from its sandy beaches in May and June 1940. It was only recently that I discovered that Lieutenant James 'Mick' Murland, an officer in the Royal Inniskilling Dragoon Guards, was evacuated on 2 June from the East Mole at Dunkerque, providing me with a personal aspect to the evacuation. This initial fascination led to several exploratory visits to the flat and rather featureless landscape that surrounds the town and the realization that the evacuation could not have been as successful as it was if a perimeter had not been established with British and French troops deployed to defend it. We can only imagine what *really* went through the mind of Sir Ronald Adam when he was instructed on 26 May to prepare for the evacuation of the BEF and hand over command of III Corps; but it is likely he shared the view of Lieutenant General Alan Brooke, commanding II Corps, who expressed

Dunkirk is France's most northerly seaport and is today France's third largest commercial port after Marseille and Le Havre.

the view in his diary that only twenty-five per cent of the BEF was likely to be saved.

What is perhaps not always appreciated is that the perimeter itself initially ran for some thirty miles from Gravelines to Nieuport and it was not until the evening of 1 June that the eastern sector of the perimeter was abandoned as the BEF came under increasing pressure from the enemy. As far as this book is concerned I have only managed to portray a fleeting glimpse of the confusion and vulnerability that surrounded the evacuation and have focussed on the British sector of the perimeter and the evacuation of British troops, which took place from 26 May to 4 June 1940.

Where further or additional information is required, the author has used square brackets and has adopted the French spelling of place names throughout the text, the only exception being where a quote, book title or cemetery has used the Anglicised form of 'Dunkirk'. Apart from recognising that the 1940 France and Flanders campaign ended in defeat, the reader will soon arrive at the conclusion that not all troops were evacuated from the beaches allocated to them, a situation that also became obvious to Rear Admiral Wake-Walker on 30 May, when he realised the scene that greeted him was entirely different to the three orderly evacuation beaches he had been shown at Dover. This was certainly the experience of Private Alwyn Ward, Royal Army Ordnance Corps (RAOC), who arrived first at Bray-Dunes on 28 May and was then ordered to march to Zuydcoote and Malo-lés-Bains before he and his company were finally lifted from the East Mole three days later. In addition, there is conflicting information in some contemporary accounts regarding the deployment of units along the perimeter as well as some mismatch in regimental histories and war diaries as to the date particular units arrived at Dunkerque and the time at which they were evacuated. This is understandable in the confusion that existed amongst the units defending the perimeter; after all, we should remember that the fact they were evacuated at all makes this story so remarkable.

Ranks and Abbreviations

PSM is an abbreviation of Platoon Sergeant Major, an appointment that was short-lived and carried the rank of warrant officer class III (WOIII). Created in 1938, it was designed to give NCOs experience in commanding units formally commanded by commissioned officers. No promotions to the rank were made after 1940. The ranks given to each individual are those that were held in May 1940 and do not reflect any subsequent promotion received by an individual unless stated. When describing the fighting I have often referred to modern day road numbering in order to give the reader using current maps of the area a more precise location. The sharp eyed reader will also notice that, apart from a few occasions, I have not mentioned any decorations received previously or as a result of the circumstances described in the book. When describing units and formations I have used a form of abbreviation; for example, after its first mention in the text, the 1st Battalion Royal Irish Fusiliers becomes 1/RIF and the 2nd Battalion Bedfordshire and Hertfordshire Regiment becomes 2/Beds and Herts. Infantry battalions were generally divided into four companies and an HQ Company that included the battalion signallers, dispatch riders and medical staff.

German army units are a little more complex. Within the infantry regiment there were three battalions – each one approximately the size of a British battalion – and again, I have abbreviated when describing these units, thus the 151st Infantry Regiment becomes IR 151, while the second battalion within that regiment is abbreviated to II/IR 151; or, in the case of panzer regiments, II/Pz5.

Early History

Inhabited since prehistoric times, the Nord-Pas-de-Calais region has always been one of the most fought-over areas of Europe. Over the centuries, it has been conquered in turn by the Celtic Belgae, the Romans, the Germanic Franks and the English, along with the Spanish, Austrian Netherlands and the Dutch Republic. Dunkerque was originally a small fishing village and held by the Counts of Flanders, who were vassals of the French Crown. In 960AD Count Baldwin III had a town wall erected in order to protect the settlement against Viking raids and the surrounding wetlands were drained and cultivated by the monks of the nearby Bergues Abbey. The early history of Dunkerque highlights its strategic importance and its place in the struggle for possession of Flanders by the great powers of the day, a struggle that was exemplified by the Eighty Years' War (1568-1648). During this period, Dunkerque was briefly in the hands of the Dutch rebels before Spanish forces, under Duke Alexander Farnese of Parma, re-established Spanish rule in 1583, when it became a base for the notorious *Dunkirkers,* who briefly lost their home port when the city was captured by the French in 1646.

In 1658, as a result of the long war between France and Spain, Dunkerque was captured after a siege by Franco-English forces following the Battle of the Dunes. The town, along with Fort-Mardyck, was awarded to England as agreed in the Franco-English alliance against Spain. It came under French rule when King Charles II sold it to France in October 1662. The French government developed the town as a fortified port and the town's existing defences were adapted to create ten bastions. The port itself was expanded by the construction of a basin that could hold up to thirty warships and linked to the sea by a channel dug through coastal sandbanks secured by two jetties - the forerunner of the modern day port of Dunkerque.

During the reign of King Louis XIV, a large number of commerce raiders once again made their base at Dunkerque, Jean Bart being the most famous. It is said that the main character, and possibly the real prisoner, in the famous novel *Man in the Iron Mask* by Alexandre Dumas, was arrested at Dunkerque. He was thought, by some, to be the Count of Vermandois, Louis XIV's illegitimate son. The Treaty of Paris (1763), between France and Great Britain, ended the Seven Years War (1756-1763), and included a clause restricting French rights to fortify Dunkerque, to allay British fears of it being used as an invasion base to cross the English Channel.

The Dunkerque Carnival and the Giants

Each year between January and March, the Dunkerque Carnival sweeps through the whole town. The origins of the carnival date back to the early 17th century, when fishermen went to sea for many months to fish for cod near Newfoundland and Iceland. The highlight of the modern carnival week is Shrove Tuesday, when carnival-goers parade to the sound of an orchestra of sixty musicians dressed as fishermen and led by the drum major. As it passes in front of the *Mairie*, smoked herrings are thrown down from the balcony. Since 1999, giants, big wicker mannequins, have paraded along with the Dunkerque bands, accompanied with great pomp by fifes, drums and members of the public. This Flemish tradition dates back to the early 16th century, when Flanders was part of the Spanish Netherlands, and the Catholic church sought to ward off the threat of Protestantism.

The First World War

Dunkerque remained behind allied lines for the whole of the war and became one of the ports where supplies and material were landed. In January 1916, spy hysteria broke out in the town; the writer and poet Robert Service, then a war correspondent for the *Toronto Star*, was mistakenly arrested for spying and narrowly avoided being executed. The town also suffered extensive damage from the German long range gun, *Lange Max*, which fired heavy shells, weighing approximately 750kg, from Koekelare, in Belgium. On 1 January 1918, the United States Navy established a naval air station to operate their seaplanes, which closed shortly after the Armistice of 11 November 1918.

Acknowledgements

No book of this nature can be completed without the help and assistance offered by others and in this case I must acknowledge the assistance given by Andy Newson who has been an enormous help in supplying me with some of the relevant war diaries and accounts buried away in regimental histories and in reading the chapter devoted to II Corps. He is also responsible for locating the barn where it is thought Ervine-Andrews and B Company of the Lancashire Fusiliers fought their last stand. To him, and the members of the WW2 Talk Forum, I extend my thanks. Jan Vandervelde and Willy Viaene have been incredibly helpful in pinpointing the position of the former BEF Headquarters and supplying a photograph of the building before it was demolished. Jan also read the text of the De Panne walk and made several useful corrections. Walter Lelievre, the archivist at Nieuwpoort, very kindly sent me a number of photographs of the Langebrug at Nieuwpoort and answered my questions about the bridge and its construction. I must also recognize the assistance given by the PRO at Kew, the Imperial War Museum and the Army Museum. Apart from those photographs which I have privately sourced, the remainder have largely come from my own personal collection.

On the ground I have been accompanied by David Rowland, Paul Webster and Bill Dodds. Their company has made each visit thoroughly enjoyable and has contributed much to the suggested routes found in Chapter 9. Lastly, my thanks must go to my wife Joan, who has tolerated my absence across the water with her usual understanding and tolerance.

All mistakes in the text are entirely mine and while I have made every effort to trace copyright holders of the material used, I crave the indulgence of literary executors or copyright holders where these efforts have so far failed and would encourage them to contact me through the publisher so that any error can be rectified.

Jerry Murland
Coventry 2018

Chapter 1

Backdrop to Evacuation

On 10 May 1940 Germany invaded France and the low countries of Holland, Belgium and Luxembourg. The attack involved three Army Groups advancing simultaneously: Army Group B, under *Generaloberst* Fedor von Bock, advanced through north eastern Belgium and a panzer assault, led by *Generaloberst* Gerd von Rundstedt's Army Group A, which attacked through the Ardennes, crossing the Meuse with the intention of cutting through the British and French armies. The third group, Army Group C under *Generaloberst* Wilhelm Ritter von Leeb, was tasked with breaking through the Maginot Line. Dubbed 'the

Fedor von Bock commanded Army Group B.

Gerd von Rundstedt.

The Phoney War was marked by a period of inactivity in France and Belgium. In this photograph cameraman Fred Bayliss (right) and his assistant are preparing to film for Paramount News.

Matador's Cloak' by Basil Liddell Hart, the German plan was masterly in its simplicity and adopted the code word *Fall Gelb*.

Général Georges Blanchard.

Up until 10 May Allied forces, under the overall command of Général Maurice Gamelin, had concentrated on extending the Maginot Line along the Belgian border, a period of some eight months of strategic inactivity that became known as the 'Phoney War'. Gamelin's plan to counter the expected German invasion was for French and British forces to cross the border into Belgium and occupy the line of the River Dyle, which runs roughly north and south about thirty miles east of Brussels. Given the operational code name Plan D, the British Expeditionary Force (BEF) were to deploy between Louvain and Wavre, with the French First Army, under Général Georges Blanchard, on their right in the Gembloux Gap. The Belgians, who were expected to hold their positions for several days, would then fall back into the gap between the left of the BEF and the right of Général Henri Giraud's Seventh Army, who were to link-up with the Dutch via Breda.

Général Henri Giraud.

The BEF Command Structure

In overall command of the BEF was 53-year-old John Vereker, Sixth Viscount Gort. Known more simply as Lord Gort, he was a highly decorated Grenadier Guards officer who had served in the First World War with some distinction; wounded on four occasions, he had been decorated with the Military Cross (MC) and the Distinguished Service Order (DSO) and two bars. His award of the coveted Victoria Cross (VC) came whilst he was commanding the 1st Battalion during the battle on the Canal du Nord in 1918.

Général Alphonse Georges with Lord Gort at Arras in May 1940.

Sir John Dill.

Lieutenant General Michael Barker commanded I Corps after Dill was recalled.

Commanding I Corps was General Sir John Dill, an individual who had served with distinction under Douglas Haig and succeeded General Sir Edmund Ironside as Chief of the Imperial General Staff (CIGS) on 27 May 1940. After Dill's recall, command of I Corps was passed to Lieutenant General Michael Barker. In command of II Corps was the energetic and able Lieutenant General Alan Brooke, a gunner who rose from lieutenant to lieutenant colonel over the four years of the First World War. By the end of 1939 a third regular division had been formed – the 5th Division – and in January 1940 the first of the Territorial divisions arrived, giving rise to the formation of III Corps under Lieutenant General Sir Ronald Adam.

Lieutenant General Sir Ronald Adam.

Lieutenant General Alan Brooke.

The Dyle Line

The German advance of 10 May signalled the end of the 'Phoney War' and the move east by allied forces to the River Dyle. The main fighting force was headed by motorcycle units of the 4/Royal Northumberland Fusiliers and the Morris CS9 Armoured Cars of the 12th Lancers and was carried out with little interference from enemy activity by the troop carrying companies of the Royal Army Service Corps (RASC). Gort's plan was to place the 1st and 2nd Divisions on the right flank and the 3rd Division on the left, astride Louvain. By way of reserve, the 48th (South Midland) Division was ordered to move east of Brussels and the 4th and 50th (Northumbrian) Divisions to the south. In addition, the 44th (Home Counties) Division was under orders to march to the Escaut south of Oudenaarde and the 42nd (East Lancashire) Division placed on readiness to take up station to their right if required.

Events on the Meuse

The campaign was essentially lost on 14 May when German panzer units of Army Group A stormed across the Meuse and headed for the channel ports along a twenty-five mile wide corridor of advance. This was the so-called 'Sickle Cut' through the Ardennes, which reached the Channel coast on 20 May, effectively cutting the Allied armies in two. These German advances late on 13 May had hastened a disorganized French retreat, which twenty-four hours later degenerated into a rout, opening up a dangerous gap that ultimately the French failed to fill. Général Georges Blanchard had little choice but to order a retirement to avoid being outflanked, which, in its turn, involved the British I Corps swinging their line

Général Maxime Weygand replaced Général Maurice Gamelin on 18 May as the Supreme Allied Commander.

back from the Dyle for some six miles to the River Lasane in order to conform to the French retirement. Gamelin was replaced by the 73-year-old Général Maxime Weygand on 19 May, but by then the military disaster of 1940 was almost complete.

A Deteriorating Situation

By 19 May the strategic situation in the French First Army Group had become serious. To the north Allied forces had been forced back to the line of the River Escaut, while in the south the Panzer advance of Army Group A, which had broken through at Sedan, had created a large gap in Général André Corap's Ninth French Army sector. German panzer divisions now threatened the right rear of the BEF, a threat which Gort temporarily countered by the creation of Petreforce in Arras and Macforce, which at the time was thinly spaced along the Haute Deûle and Scarpe Canals. Despite this, German commanders were quite rightly concerned that an Allied counter-stroke from both north and south of the River Somme could in effect turn the tables on the German advance, cut off their supply lines and trap them on the Channel coast.

The Weygand Plan

Weygand announced on 20 May that he was now Commander-in-Chief in all theatres of war and in order to break the German advance he planned a large counter offensive to smash through the panzer corridor and isolate the German armoured divisions on the Channel coast. This would be achieved by an attack from the north linking up with the newly formed French Third Army south of the Somme which, Weygand reported, had already recaptured Péronne, Albert and Amiens. This was blatantly untrue and, according to historian Gregory Blaxland, Weygand was living in a world of fantasy. The demands from Wegand for Gort to support the attack to the south brought the Chief of the Imperial General Staff (CIGS), General Edmund Ironside, to France to assess the situation and pressure Gort into attacking south in conjunction with the French. Convinced that a co-ordinated Allied attack could break the encirclement around the French First Army Group, both Ironside and Gort realised action was needed immediately if there was to be any chance that defeat was to be turned into victory. Gort still firmly believed that the gap in André Corap's Ninth French Army sector must be closed if disaster was to be prevented. But, as he explained to Ironside, this was an undertaking that the French had

General Edmund Ironside.

to initiate from the south, as all the BEF's divisions – except two, which were at Arras with Frankforce - were committed to defending the line of the Escaut.

Frankforce

Frankforce was formed on 20 May [the same day that German forces reached the channel coast] and placed under the command of Major General Harold Franklyn, who commanded the 5th Division. On 21 May a counter-stroke, comprising two infantry battalions from 151 Brigade, 50th Division, and two battalions of tanks from 1 Army Tank Brigade, took place south of Arras against the tightening hold that was surrounding the British garrison. Although the counter-stroke was supported by sixty tanks of the French 3rd Light Mechanized Division (3/DLM) from Général René Prioux's Cavalry Corps, the promise made by Général Gaston-Henri Billotte, who agreed to support the British operation with an attack by two divisions from Général René-Félix Altmayer's V Corps, never materialised.

Whether this was intended to be part of a much larger thrust is still unclear, as it appears that Gort was still harbouring the notion of supporting a French counter attack with the two divisions deployed along the Scarpe valley. That said, the Arras attack did enable the British to tighten their hold on Arras – albeit temporarily – and, as is often cited, built doubts in the minds of German High Command as to the speed of their advance. After the war von Rundstedt admitted that the Arras

The counter-stroke at Arras on 21 May achieved the element of surprise and caused widespread alarm amongst the German High Command. Pictured is the British Matilda Mark 1 tank, which was in production until August 1940.

counter-stroke came at a critical moment and 'for a short time it was feared the panzer divisions would be cut off before the infantry divisions could come up to support them'. The delay imposed by the Frankforce counter-stroke certainly allowed reinforcements to be shipped over to Boulogne on 22 May – a lesson that was repeated at Calais – postponing the move of three panzer divisions towards Dunkerque until 27 May; by which time a more robust defence of the port had been organized to cover the evacuation. In checking the German advance it also added a vital twenty-four hours to the time available for the fortification and defence of the Canal Line. The counter-stroke at Arras is looked at in detail in the Battleground Europe publication, *Frankforce and the Defence of Arras 1940*.

However, in reality the counter-stroke at Arras was much too weak to be a serious threat; but it did delay the German advance and inflicted significant losses on *Generalmajor* Erwin Rommel's 7th Panzer Division. But with Arras still surrounded and likely to fall at any time, Gort gave orders for the British to disengage from Arras on the night of 23 May, an action that must have raised the prospect of an eventual evacuation from the Channel ports.

The Halt Order of 21 May

Certainly Rommel's exaggerated claims of being attacked by five divisions at Arras did much to fuel the expectation of a future allied counter attack within the ranks of German Supreme High Command (OKH) and contributed to two halt orders and, ultimately, the escape of the BEF from Dunkerque. It is highly likely that without this twenty-four hour intervention the famous Hitler Halt Order of 24 May would not have

Erwin Rommel pictured with his driver in France during May 1940.

the effect it did, as Dunkerque would have already been in German hands. It is a sad fact that the Allies were too weak and disorganized to take advantage of the bruised momentum of Rommel's division at Arras. Had they been able to make a combined attack from both north and south of the Somme, the panzers may well have been cut off from their supply lines and become isolated along the Channel coast. Whilst it was clear to a number of allied observers that the counter attack was not going to take place, the *threat* of such an attack led to the order to halt the advance of the panzer divisions on 21 May. However, at this critical juncture in the Dunkerque story, the threat to the panzer divisions no longer came from a counter attack but from the simple fact that the BEF *might* reach the channel ports before the Germans. It was a notion that had already crossed the mind of the British, who responded with a transfer of troops from the British mainland to Boulogne and Calais in order to block the German advance towards Dunkerque.

Boulogne and Calais

It was not until the evening of 21 May that *General der Panzertruppen* Heinz Guderian and his XIX Panzer Corps was ordered to move north and capture the Channel ports. His immediate plan was for the 10th Panzer Division to move on Dunkerque, the 2nd Panzer Division to seize Boulogne and the 1st Panzer Division to advance on Calais. Then, at the crucial moment, perhaps with the taste of the Arras Counter-stroke still in his mind, von Rundstedt held back the 10th Panzer Division, withdrawing them from Guderian's command and placed them in reserve. Although the 10th Panzer Division was restored to Guderian's command on 22 May and redirected to Calais, the damage had already been done and the opportunity of seizing the Channel ports and cutting off the BEF had evaporated. It took the 2nd Panzer Division three days to capture Boulogne, with the infantry finally overwhelming the garrison on 25 May; and even longer to take Calais, which was captured on 26 May.

Heinz Guderian.

The Canal Line

Gort's great fear of the Germans driving forward behind his right flank was becoming a reality and, with the BEF now fighting on two fronts, his answer took the form of a number of *ad-hoc* battle groups, tasked with specific duties of defence. The line to be defended followed the canalized River Aa from Gravelines on the Channel coast, through St-Omer and La

Bassée, to Raches, six miles north east of Douai, and followed the old line of French fortified towns, which had already played a significant part in French military history. The Canal Line was the only natural barrier that stood any possibility of hindering the armoured advance of Army Group A from driving into the rear of the BEF.

Defending the Canal Line

The formation of improvised forces is a feature of Gort's conduct of the campaign and possibly had its origins in the German *Michael* offensive of March 1918, where Grover's Force on the Fifth Army front was one of the first of these *ad hoc* groups to be put into the line in a desperate bid to stem the German advance. Gort's adoption of hastily organised forces came under some criticism as many of the units involved were badly equipped, lacked battlefield experience and had little or no opportunity to make sound administrative arrangements. However, in reality there was little alternative; until the main BEF retired from the Escaut, the regularly organised and equipped infantry divisions were fully committed and none could be freed for the protection of the flank and rear. It was hoped that the defence these groups put up would be enough to deter von Rundstedt by making him hesitate before committing his armour. In the event it was not only the watery Canal Line which delayed the panzers, but the Halt Order of 24 May.

The first of these *ad hoc* forces was the largely ineffective Macforce, under Major General Noel Mason-Macfarlane. Created on 17 May, it was initially ordered to hold the line of the River Scarpe between Raches and St-Amand before it eventually moved north and was disbanded at Cassel on 25 May. Gort created three further formations, under the names of Polforce, Usherforce and Rustyforce, each with specific orders to hold the line of the canals from Gravelines to Raches. His choice of which units to deploy relied very much on availability, hence the mix and match approach to defence that was evident at the main crossing points south of Gravelines. Full details of the intense fighting on the Canal Line can be found in the Battleground Europe volume entitled *The Canal Line 1940.*

Noel Mason-Mcfarlane.

The French First Army at Lille

The defence of the city took place from 28 to 31 May 1940 and involved about 40,000 men of the First Army, under the command of Général Jean-Baptiste Molinié. Fortunately Général Benoît-Léon de la Laurencie

The French First Army at Lille were allowed to keep their weapons in recognition of their courageous stand. Here they march past their German captors, who salute their bravery.

managed to extract the French III Corps and join the British I Corps in their withdrawal to the coast, leaving the French IV and V Corps to fight the 4th Panzer Division, 5th Panzer Division and 7th Panzer Division and four infantry divisions: 11th Division, 217th Division, 253rd Division and 267th Division. The Germans had to fight their way through the suburbs as the French held on in some of the most vicious street fighting of the campaign. The commander of the 40th Artillery Regiment, Lieutenant Colonel Justin Dutrey, committed suicide in the Potié Brewery rather than surrender. In honour of the defenders of Lille and its suburbs, 35,000 men of the garrison were allowed by *General der Infantrie* Alfred Wäger to parade in the main square of Lille with their weapons – without ammunition - on 1 June, where he took the salute. As a consequence of the tenacious French defence of Lille, the BEF and the remaining units of the First Army were able to retreat into the Dunkerque perimeter.

The Halt Order of 24 May

Known more generally as the Hitler Halt Order, which was sent to all German units west of the Canal Line, it remains one of the most hotly debated issues of the Second World War. On 24 May German forces were within ten miles of Dunkerque, the only remaining port north of the Somme River open to the evacuation of the BEF. The leading elements had already crossed the Aa Canal and there were no British or French troops capable of stopping the German panzers from denying the port to the British and trapping about one million Allied troops in a rapidly reducing pocket of resistance. Hitler was on the threshold of a monumental victory and yet, astonishingly, OKH issued the order to halt the advance at 12.45 on 24 May. A furious Heinz Guderian later wrote that:

Adolf Hitler gave his authority to the halt order of 24 May.

> *We were stopped within sight of Dunkerque! We watched the Luftwaffe attack. We also saw the great armada of great and little ships by means of which the British were evacuating their forces.*

Loitering behind the order was the rising crescendo of disagreements between OKH and the officer corps, which escalated on 23 May, culminating in the removal of the Fourth Army from Army Group A and transferring it to Army Group B. In simple terms this meant that from 8.00pm on 24 May all panzer divisions would take their orders from von Bock and von Rundstedt would be concerned only with flank protection along the Somme. Hitler was furious and immediately rescinded the order, his anger focussing not only on the fact it had been made without his approval but because he, too, had feelings of anxiety regarding the exposed nature of the panzer thrust and shared von Rundstedt's desire for the infantry to close the gap between them and the panzers.

Hitler gave von Rundstedt complete freedom with regard to the length of the stop, giving additional weight to von Rundstedt's view that Army Group A would be needed for the eventual swing south of the Somme and the capitulation of the trapped French Army. It was also von Rundstedt's opinion that the remnants of the BEF could in fact be finished off by *Generaloberst* Fedor von Bock's Army Group B and the *Luftwaffe* and it was not until the afternoon of 26 May that Hitler gave permission for the advance on Dunkerque to be continued. Whatever the reasons behind the Halt Order it was a very costly mistake; even though he tried later to put all the blame on Hitler, the chief architect of the order was the wily von Rundstedt, upon whose head must lie the responsibility for

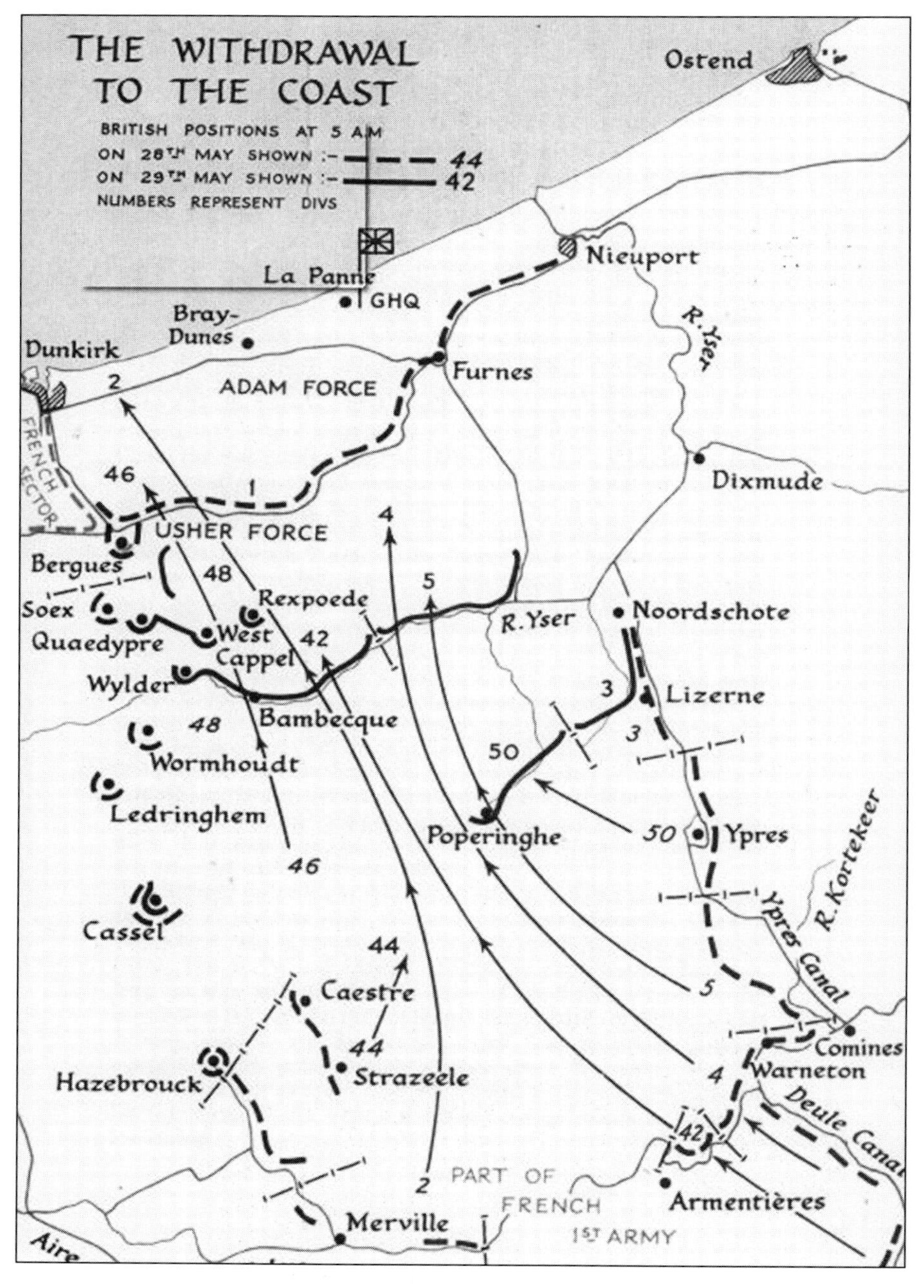

A map illustrating the British withdrawal to Dunkerque.

much of the ultimate failure of German forces to achieve the total destruction of the BEF.

The Dunkerque Corridor

Valuable time was gained from the Hitler Halt Order, giving the Allies the opportunity to create a defensive corridor that the BEF could use to reach Dunkerque. On either side of the corridor, to slow down, and temporarily hold back the German advance, strong points were established in key towns and villages such as Cassel and Wormhout. French support for this plan was essential and it was agreed that the southern end of the corridor would be held by the French First Army. Historians agree that the evacuation would never have been as successful as it was had it not been for the so-called forgotten heroes of Dunkerque – British and French soldiers who were left behind to allow the bulk of the BEF to be rescued. Tragically, only a small proportion of those who stood and fought made it back to the evacuation beaches: most were killed, wounded or taken prisoner.

The Belgian Surrender

The Belgian surrender came into effect at 4.00am on 28 May. Recriminations abounded, with the British and French claiming the Belgians had betrayed the alliance. In Paris, the French Prime Minister, Paul Reynaud, denounced Leopold's surrender, and the Belgian Prime Minister, Hubert Pierlot, informed the Belgians that Leopold had

Leopold III, King of the Belgians.

taken action against the unanimous advice of the government and, as a result, the King was no longer in a position to govern. The argument focussed on the fact that the Belgians had not given any prior warning that their situation was so serious as to capitulate. Such claims were largely unjust. The Allies had known, and admitted it privately on 25 May through their contact with the Belgians, that the latter were on the verge of collapse. But, regardless of who or what was to blame, the Belgian capitulation opened up a large gap on the eastern flank, prompting Gort immediately to dispatch 143 Brigade and the 5th and 50th Divisions to defend his right flank against the inevitable advance of the German Sixth Army. This move finally eradicated any further notion that may have still been lurking in Gort's mind of a counter attack to link up with French forces south of the Somme. Historians feel that this deployment to the Ypres-Comines Canal saved the BEF from a German thrust to take Nieuport [now Nieuwpoort] and La Panne [now De Panne] and ultimately Dunkerque itself. The battle on the Ypres-Comines Canal almost certainly saved the BEF from annihilation.

Chapter 2

The Dunkerque Perimeter

On 23 May it was fast becoming apparent that Dunkerque was the only remaining port that could be used to keep the BEF supplied; particularly as the news that Calais was surrounded, and Boulogne looked very much as if it would also fall, coincided with the RAF and the Navy being unable to guarantee the safety of Ostend [now Oostende]. Although plans for the evacuation of the BEF were only in the preparation stage, it was becoming obvious to a number of senior officers at GHQ that Dunkerque would become the centre of any evacuation should it be deemed necessary. The casual observer could not fail to notice that Dunkerque was one of the most defensible ports in France, being flanked by old fortifications that could stand a substantial bombardment. The port was also home to 61-year-old Admiral Jean-Marie Abrial, the naval and military commander of the Channel ports, and Général Bertrand Fagalde, his deputy, who had their headquarters in the heavily strengthened Bastion 32.

Admiral Jean-Marie Abrial.

General McNaughton's Visit to Dunkerque

Major General Andrew McNaughton, commander of the 1st Canadian Division, arrived at Dunkerque on 24 May and met with Fagalde and Abrial. Fagalde had been appointed by Weygand on 24 May to command the troops in Calais, Boulogne and Dunkerkque, and McNaughton's visit was clearly taken as an indication that a Canadian brigade would soon arrive to strengthen the

Général Bertrand Fagalde inspecting the 5th Battalion Gordon Highlanders. Seen with him is the commanding officer of the battalion, Major Alick Buchanan-Smith.

Dunkerque defences. But McNaughton had other ideas. Once back in England, his report to the CIGS highlighted the need for organisation, not reinforcement, going as far as to say that the area was already congested with troops and the addition of a Canadian brigade would complicate matters even further. He was quite right and one has to question the reasons why he was sent to Dunkerque in the first place. Gort learned of Dill's decision not to send the Canadians to France on 27 May, who expressed his regret in a telegram, citing the 'general situation' as the principal reason.

Major General Andrew McNaughton.

Operation Dynamo

The final decision to evacuate the BEF was taken at a meeting of the War Cabinet on 26 May, two days after McNaughton's visit to Dunkerque. The evacuation, codenamed Operation Dynamo, was given the go-ahead by London at 6.57pm that evening, adopting the name of the dynamo room that produced the electricity for the naval headquarters beneath Dover Castle. Overall command of the operation was given to Vice Admiral Bertrand Ramsey, whose base at Dover Castle became the control centre for the whole evacuation. At 9.00pm that evening Lieutenant General Sir Ronald Adam was summoned to GHQ at Premesques and instructed to assume command of Adamforce and immediately commence the organization of Dunkerque and its beaches for the embarkation of the BEF. He was to hand over command of III Corps to Major General Sydney Wason, who, until that moment, had been on Gort's staff. Adam writes that there was definitely a 'misunderstanding' with regard to the deployment of the guns of 2 Anti-Aircraft Brigade within the perimeter and around the port of Dunkerque. Apparently the orders for the withdrawal and embarkation of specialist personnel ['Useless mouths'] had mistakenly included a number of anti-aircraft units and, assuming the instructions for all gunners to go to the beaches meant the guns must first be put out of action, an order was so given by Major General Hugh

Vice Admiral Bertrand Ramsey masterminded Operation Dynamo.

Martin, the officer with responsibility for anti-aircraft units at GHQ. It was an error that was to cost the evacuation dearly and one that reportedly infuriated Adam.

Adam, in his account of the Adamforce operations, wrote that his role included that of defending the perimeter and that Gort asked him to represent him at Cassel on 27 May, where a meeting had been planned with the French. Giving orders for the main body of his staff to proceed to La Panne and establish his headquarters in the *Mairie*, Adam drove to Cassel, arriving at about 6.30am on 27 May.

The Meeting at Cassel

The meeting took place in the famous Hôtel du Sauvage, situated in the main square of Cassel, and, although the town was under heavy shellfire, it is doubtful if the British garrison defending the hilltop town knew much, or even cared, about the significance of the meeting that was about to take place. It is ironic that, of the officers and men defending Cassel, only a handful would see the evacuation beaches and reach England.

Lieutenant Colonel Viscount Bridgeman arrived in Cassel a short time after Adam:

> *I went across to the Hôtel du Sauvage, which had been hit by a shell. The staff had evidently left the day before, leaving the cloths on the tables in the dining room where the conference was to be*

The Hôtel du Sauvage at Cassel, where the Dunkerque perimeter was agreed.

held ... General Adam had arrived just before me and fortunately Général Fagalde also came early. Armed with my precious map, I got them together on a side table, used by waiters in better times, and they had about ten minutes settling the occupation of the Dunkirk perimeter. It was done in a sensible and friendly way, and fortunately in English.

The main agenda of the meeting actually began about half an hour late, which gave Adam ample time to thrash out the Dunkerque perimeter with Fagalde, and suggest the French should occupy the sector west of Dunkerque and the British the larger sector east of the Dunkerque:

I also asked that the French should, if possible, retire into the sector west of Dunkerque, and that I should like arrangements made for parking of vehicles outside the perimeter and only bringing weapons inside. Orders to this effect had been issued to the British Army.

Rejoining the main meeting, which included Admiral Jean-Marie Abrial, Général Blanchard, commander of the French First Army and Général Louis Koeltz, Weygand's Chief of Staff, there was no difficulty in agreeing the territory to be enclosed within the perimeter. Masterminded by Bridgeman, the line of the perimeter was approximately twenty-five miles long and some seven miles deep and made best use of the canals and waterways around Dunkerkque. Although Adam and Fagalde agreed that Gravelines would be included in the perimeter, pressure from German units had already begun to contract the western edge of the perimeter to the Mardyck Canal.

Général Louis Koeltz, Weygand's Chief of Staff, was also at the meeting at Cassel.

However, much to the consternation and bewilderment of the British, there was a considerable misunderstanding as to the nature of the perimeter. When Blanchard and Gort had met on the morning of 26 May, Gort's Chief of Staff, Lieutenant General Henry Pownall, noted that 'not a word was uttered about moving to the sea', though he strongly suspected that evacuation was on the mind of the French, 'as it was certainly on ours'. Blanchard's orders were to fall back on Dunkerque and defend it, there was certainly no thought of retreating, a notion that was very much to the fore of British thinking. Despite Churchill having informed the French Prime Minister, Paul Reynard, of British intentions, Weygand, for whatever reason, did not pass on this information, leaving Gort, who had been told by London that the French knew of the planned evacuation, embroiled in a rather confusing and embarrassing situation. All of this gave rise to the belief that the British were abandoning the French to their fate.

Fagalde also objected to the fact that Gort had failed to inform him personally of the proposed perimeter around Dunkerque, referring to Adam as 'an intermediary'. Despite Gort's instructions to Adam that he was to act in accordance with French orders, Fagalde remained unconvinced of British intentions and went as far as supporting General Koeltz's proposal for a counter-attack towards St-Omer and Calais! Bridgeman wrote later that, as far as the French were concerned, the main purpose of the meeting appeared to be an opportunity to motivate French forces into some sort of offensive action; particularly as Fagalde agreed with Koeltz and stated loudly that it would be an easy task to take Calais providing he was given some tanks. Whether Sir Robert Adam and the British contingent were by now harbouring any suspicions that the instructions passed on by Reynard did not correspond to those given to Gort by London is anyone's guess as heavy shellfire broke up the meeting prematurely. A flabbergasted Bridgeman recorded Fagalde leaving Cassel, saying he would immediately return to his headquarters and order an attack on Calais! Needless to say, the attack did not take place.

Lieutenant Colonel Viscount Bridgeman.

The Outer Perimeter

As agreed at Cassel, the French line would run from Gravelines, through Mardyck and Spycker to Bergues, with the British sector running through Bergues, Bulskamp, Furnes and Nieuport.The dividing line between the two sectors was the Mardyck Canal. In addition, the low lying areas such as Les Moëres, on the eastern side of the perimeter, were deliberately flooded – referred to as the inundations - in order to impede the German advance. This flooded area extended eastward from Benkies Mille and as far north as Ghyvelde and varied in width from one to three miles. While it certainly posed problems for the enemy, it was not as effective as anticipated, particularly as the depth in some places did not exceed six inches!

To the north of the inundations was low-lying land and the Canal de

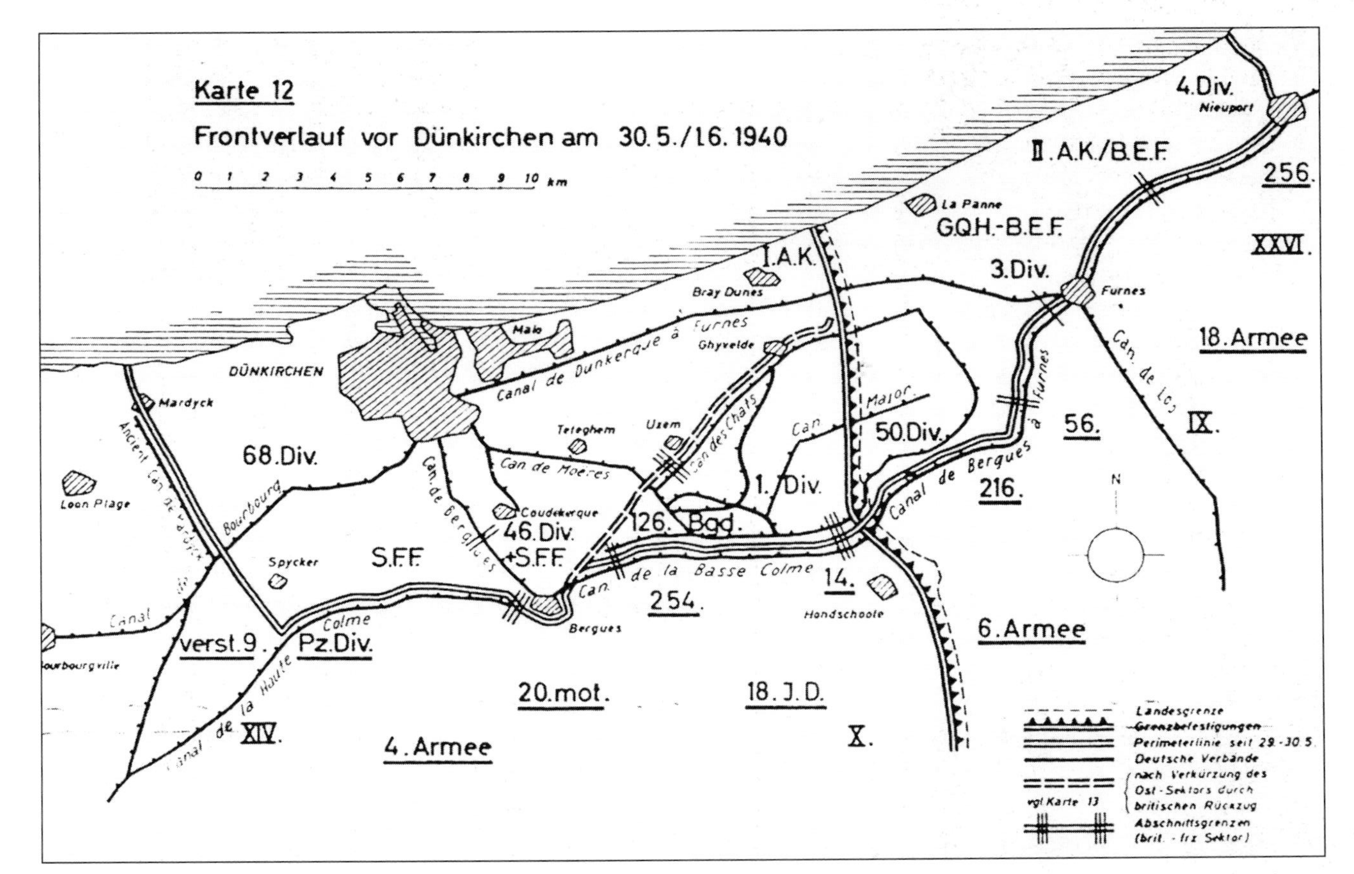

The Dunkerque Perimeter from the German perspective. German and British divisional areas are marked, as is the border between France and Belgium.

The Mardyck Canal marked the western edge of the French sector of the perimeter.

Dunkerque a Furnes, which ran parallel with the railway line and the main road running from Furnes to Dunkerque. Finally, there was the narrow strip of dunes that opened onto a wide sandy beach running along the whole of the perimeter and shelving gently to the sea. While an ideal venue for holiday makers, it was the worst possible venue for evacuating troops: there were no convenient harbours, no piers or jetties except for those at Dunkerque. Positioned along the coast at intervals of three to four miles were the seaside towns of Malo-lés-Bains, Bray-Dunes, La Panne, Coxyde and Nieuport, the last three being in Belgium.

The French Sector

Although the French sector was defended entirely by French troops, there were French units fighting in the British sector of the perimeter. Possibly the most well known to British visitors were the 8th Zouaves, commanded by 47-year-old Lieutenant Colonel Etienne Anzemberger. The Zouaves fought as part of the French 12th Motorised Division, whose headquarters was at the Fort des Dunes, near Leffrinckoucke. Although around one hundred men of the division gathered life rafts from the damaged ships that remained in Dunkerque harbour and paddled to Dover, some 4,000 officers and men surrendered on 4 June. Sadly, Général Louis Janssen, commanding the division, was killed on 2 June. Amongst those who surrendered was Etienne

Lieutenant Colonel Etienne Anzemberger commanded the French 8th Zouaves.

Anzemberger, who was repatriated from Oflag XXB in 1943 and died in 1953. While all French land forces were under the control of Général Fagalde, it was 53-year-old Général Maurice Beaufrère who effectively took control. He commanded the 68th Division in the French sector, a division that was still in good fighting order and was supported by the firepower of its artillery. Nevertheless, it was 137 Infantry Regiment, from the largely destroyed 21st Division, that confronted the 9th Panzer Division and two German infantry regiments (IR 208 and IR 225) – on 30 May and held off the attack on the Haute-Colme Canal, west of Bergues.

The British Sector

Under Bridgeman's plan the British sector was divided into three corps areas or sub-sectors, where dumps of ammunition and rations would be established. III Corps would defend the western end of the perimeter and embark from Malo-lés-Bains, I Corps would hold the centre and use the Bray-Dunes beaches, while II Corps would defend the eastern end and be evacuated from La Panne. In an attempt to avoid the inevitable traffic jams, each corps area would have a collecting point for vehicles outside the perimeter, where all, except fighting vehicles, ambulances and corps and divisional cars, were to be destroyed. Fagalde had agreed to this strict measure at the meeting in Cassel, but it appeared that the French 2nd Division Légère Mécanique (2/DLM) ignored the procedure and completely blocked the road from La Panne to Dunkerque. In the absence of the Military Police, the road was eventually cleared, amidst

All vehicles, except fighting vehicles, ambulances, corps and divisional cars were ordered to be destroyed as they entered the perimeter.

recriminations and loud protests, by sappers using a bulldozer.

Major General Andrew Thorne commanded the 48th Division.

Adam Proceeds to Bergues

On the way to Bergues Adam and his staff were machine-gunned by six Belgian biplanes sporting German markings and Major General Ridley Pakenham-Walsh, the Chief Engineer, was wounded in this attack. At Bergues Adam visited Major General Andrew Thorne, commanding the 48th Division, in the hope of siphoning off some of his reserves for use along the perimeter:

> *While I was there a report arrived that the Germans had broken through the French lines north of Clairmarais Forest, and were advancing north-east and south-east with a number of AFCs. In the circumstances there could be no question of utilising Major General Thorne's reserves. He explained to me his dispositions which I considered admirable, and he offered me the loan of his CRA, Brigadier Hon E F Lawson, whom I instructed to lay out the defence of the perimeter, collecting what troops were available from the organised parties to man these defences, and prevent vehicles entering.*

The dispatch of Andrew Thorne to Bergues was one of the first moves made by Gort in the direct defence of Dunkerque and it was Fagalde's suggestion that the 48th Division covered the defence of the Wormhout area with 144 Brigade, a suggestion that made good sense, particularly

The Dunkerque Gate at Bergues.

as 145 Brigade were defending Cassel and Hazebrouck. Thorne also took Usher under his command and gave him the task of defending Socx as well as Bergues, where Charles Usher had already established his headquarters. As far as the Dunkerque perimeter was concerned, Bergues was an important lynchpin in the defences and marked the boundary between the French and British sectors. The town also had a garrison of French troops and was the headquarters of 59-year-old Général Robert Barthélemy, commander of the Secteur Fortifié des Flandres.

Usherforce

Colonel Charles Usher.

Usherforce was formed on 23 May and placed under Colonel Charles Usher's command. His orders were to take command of all troops in the area, including the remnants of the 23rd Division, and move his headquarters to Bergues. The 49-year-old Usher had been captured at Le Cateau in 1914 while fighting with 1/Gordon Highlanders and spent the remainder of the war as a prisoner. In January 1938 he achieved one of his life's ambitions and took command of the battalion, taking it to France with the 51st (Highland) Division in September 1939. It was to be a short lived tenure, as in February 1940 he handed over to Lieutenant Colonel Harry Wright and embarked on a new role as Area Commandant at St-Malo in Brittany, with the rank of colonel. Usher may have been classed amongst those elderly senior officers who were not up to the rigours of battlefield leadership, but his move to St-Malo did at least avoid another long term of captivity when the survivors of his old battalion were taken prisoner at St-Valery-en-Caux on 12 June. In April 1940 Usher was moved again, this time to take command of X L of C with Major Thomas 'Harry' Jefferies as his Deputy Assistant Quartermaster General (DAQMG). This was intended to be an appointment well in the rear of the fighting but, with the tide of war very much against the Allies, he was destined to be caught up in the fighting as the BEF withdrew towards Dunkerque. Bergues was, at the time, the only place on the British sector of the perimeter that actually contained any troops and to his great credit Usher had organised all available units into an effective and aggressive defence that had so far repulsed all German attempts to take the town. We shall hear more of Bergues in Chapter 6.

The initial Defence of the Perimeter

Brigadier Edward Lawson – known as 'Fred' to his immediate circle – had previously been in command of the short lived X-Force, which came into being on 23 May and was designed to form a temporary defence line along the Canal Line ahead of the infantry, who were *en route* from the Escaut. He was elevated to the peerage on the death of his father in June 1943, becoming the 4th Baron Burnham. On leaving Oxford, Lawson joined the family newspaper, the *Daily Telegraph*, and on the outbreak of war in 1914 he served with the Royal Buckinghamshire Hussars. With his newspaper background, Lawson became Senior Military Adviser to the Ministry of Information and was Director of Public Relations at the War Office from 1943 to 1945. He returned to the *Daily Telegraph* as managing director in 1945, remaining in the post until his retirement in 1961. He died in 1963.

Brigadier Edward Lawson later became the 4th Baron Burnham.

He wrote later that, together with his staff, he was instructed by Adam to organise the defence of the perimeter from Bergues to Nieuport inclusive and was authorised to deploy any troops he found in the area as well as any units or individuals who came in. Selecting Furnes as his headquarters, he set off with his brigade major to have a look, leaving his staff captain to bring on the rest of his staff:

> *I selected my own headquarters at the road junction at the back of the town* [where] *the Germans dropped their two shells every clock hour. The anticipation was worse than their arrival and we always woke up five minutes before they were due ... Obviously, however, this was the best place to find out what was going on and to catch anybody drifting back.*

Lawson had little time to waste. The problem he had was filling the gaps in the line to the right and left of Furnes and creating a mobile force he could use as a reserve:

> *My defence plans were ad-hoc rather than scientific. I divided the front into purely arbitrary sections of equal lengths, lettered from right to left. Sub-units coming in were simple to deal with. They were dispatched to sectors in turn by the brigade major, keeping a record of numbers of men and the names and regiments of sector commanders. Sections without officers, and individuals, were kept 'on ice' until they could be officered and then posted in the same way. All, if hungry, were fed from some mysterious store accumulated by my staff captain.*

Adam's own account refers to Lawson's 'superhuman' efforts in manning the perimeter:

> *From right to left the organisation was roughly - a party of RE, anti-tank gunners and various other units under Lieutenant Colonel Usher in Bergues; various RA parties of 10 to 12 men, a detachment of 68th Field Regiment, an anti-tank battery of 13th Anti-Tank Regiment under Captain M Beresford, 15 Grenadier Guardsmen under Lieutenant Clive between Bergues and Furnes; at Furnes, Major Heard with 12th Searchlight Battery, Lieutenant Colonel Brazier with men of 53rd Medium Regiment, RA, and details of the I Corps Survey Company, RE, about Nieuport.*

Superhuman efforts they may have been but until this jumble of units and men were relieved by more substantial front line troops the defence of the perimeter remained precarious.

The Defences at Nieuport

Brigadier Andrew 'Tommy' Clifton commanded the 2/Light Armoured Reconnaissance Brigade, a unit that, to all intents and purposes, had been reduced to a single composite regiment of light tanks and four dismounted parties. Born in 1887, Clifton spent seven years in the ranks of the Royal Artillery before being commissioned in 1909 into the Durham Light Infantry. He was seconded into the Tank Corps in 1921 and came under the orders of Adamforce early on 28 May, when he was instructed to organise a defensive line from the sea at Nieuport, along the line of the canal to Furnes. After informing II Corps that his headquarters was on the road between Oost-Dunkerke and Wulpen, he was contacted by Fred Lawson:

> [Lawson] *stated that he was already organising the defence of the Wulpen area and we arranged mutually that my responsibility should be from (including) Wulpen through to Nieuport and the sea.*

Reading between the lines, it would appear that Lawson was only too pleased to be relieved of the responsibility of Nieuport and its complex pattern of canal bridges. As Clifton soon discovered, one of the problems facing the defenders was the failure to destroy all the bridges over the canals running from Nieuport to the sea, a problem compounded by the British garrison's inability to stop a determined thrust by German armour with rifle and Bren gun fire.

Gort Moves to La Panne

In the late afternoon of 28 May Lord Gort moved his headquarters from Houtkerque to La Panne, which was in direct communication with London via a submarine telephone cable laid in 1932; a move that technically brought Gort under the command of Admiral Abrial. BEF Headquarters was situated in the *Mairie* on Avenue de la Mer [now called Zeelaan]with the 'Belgian end' of the cable a few yards further on in the

BEF Headquarters was situated in the *Mairie* at La Panne.

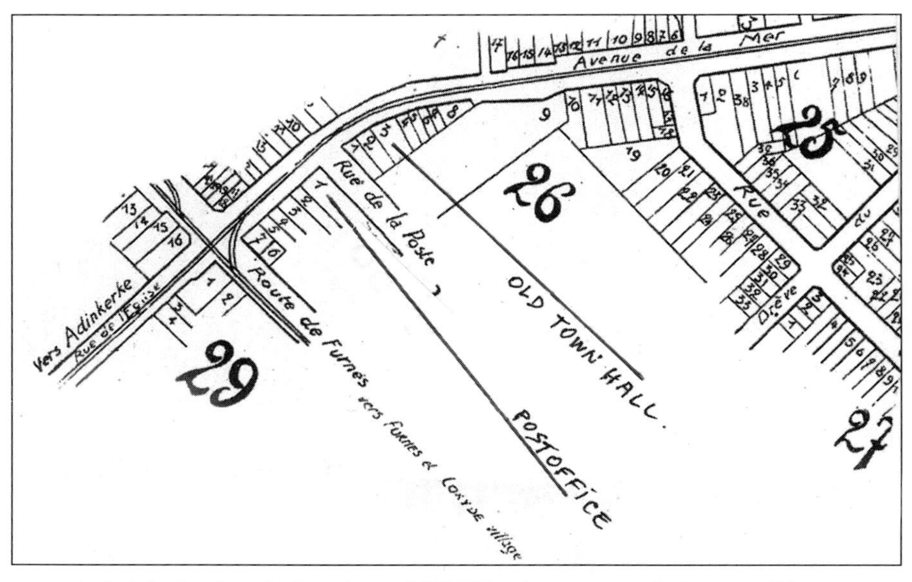

A sketch showing the locations of BEF Headquarters and the post office at La Panne.

post office on the corner of Rue de la Poste [Poststraat]. At La Panne Gort was informed by Sir Ronald Adam that the situation at Dunkerque was grim, with very few of the BEF managing to be evacuated; Gort relayed this assessment to London along with his own view that, should the situation become worse, then surrender might become the only option. This rather gloomy picture was not helped by a telegram from Weygand appealing to Gort to commit the BEF to 'any counter attack thought necessary'. This was a further demonstration, perhaps, of the fantasy world that surrounded Weygand. Nevertheless, it was from La Panne that the order of evacuation was issued: III Corps were to go first; II Corps second and I Corps were to act as rearguard.

Adam and Lawson Leave For England

By 29 May the organization of the perimeter was complete and III Corps' operational duties were passed on to I Corps. Lawson and Adam received orders to move to the beach at La Panne and embark:

> *As we passed down a lane* [sic] *leading to the beach, out of one of the villas stepped Lord Gort. We had a short talk about the war and when I caught up with my party I found them sitting down by a sand dune. For miles, up to Dunkirk, were parties of various strengths presumably with orders similar to ours, and, like us, wondering what the word 'embark' meant.*

HMS *Worcester* transferred Adam and Lawson to England, along with Lieutenant General Alan Brooke. The ship is seen here just after a collision with HMS *Active* in 1937.

Lawson's account, together with that of Admiral Wake Walker, strongly suggests that Gort was in occupation in the centre house of the three royal villas. Wake-Walker's account, in which he describes meeting Gort for dinner in a villa which 'opened directly onto a road running along the top of the sandy slope from the beach' certainly supports this view, as does Major General Montgomery, who refers to Gort's residence being close to his own on the seafront. Gort's residence should not be confused with BEF HQ, which was in the *Mairie* on Zeelaan, about half a mile away

Alexander Appointed to Command the Rearguard

The telegram appointing Major General Barker to the command of the Dunkerque rearguard was in all probability dictated by Churchill and read out by Gort to the assembled officers at the meeting held at La Panne on 30 May. It would appear from Montgomery's memoirs that Gort privately thought the rearguard would not get away and this must have been transmitted to Barker, who received the news with some apprehension. After the meeting Montgomery spoke candidly to Gort regarding Barker's reaction:

> *I told him that we could not yet say it was impossible to get I Corps away; but that it would never get away if Barker was in control, and that the only sound course was to get Barker out of it as soon as possible and give I Corps to Alexander. Gort agreed and Barker was sent away.*

Major General Hon Horace Alexander had, up until 30 May, been in command of the 1st Division and was clearly considered a capable commander by Montgomery. Alexander's move made way for Brigadier Beckwith-Smith to be appointed the acting commander of the 1st Division. Montgomery says he never saw Barker again and that he and Alexander met the next day - presumably after Alexander had been told by Gort of the change of plan - and both men were confident that all would turn out well in the end. Why it took until the afternoon of the next day for Gort to tell Alexander is anyone's guess but, after the news had sunk in, Alexander's reaction was to inform Gort that it was his intention to extricate I Corps from Dunkerque at all costs and not to surrender any part of it. The rearguard was now clearly in the good hands of Alexander; but the intention of the British to evacuate had not been passed on to Fagalde, who was under the impression that the divisions of I Corps were his to integrate with his own troops. Indeed, Fagalde's plan was to hold the perimeter until he was forced to surrender, believing the war was lost; he considered the only moral course of action was to stand and fight. We will hear more of this difference of opinion in Chapter 7.

Major General Hon Horace Alexander.

Major General Bernard Montgomery.

A Shrinking Perimeter

From the evening of 1 June the inner perimeter was defended by I Corps and French units, who utilised the Canal des Moëres and the Canal des Chats as its main defence lines. The last company of Loyals abandoned Bergues at 9.45pm on 1 June and a day later the bridgehead at Hoymille was seized by the enemy. At the eastern end of the perimeter the French 12th Division beat off all incursions by the enemy and a counter attack by the 8/Zouaves and 150th Regiment of Infantry even took sixty prisoners! Units of the French 68th and 32nd Divisions, brought up by Fagalde to reinforce the centre of the perimeter, expelled the enemy incursion at Téteghem and stabilised the line. Thus, at dusk on 2 June, the main line of British defence was between Coudekerque and Zuydcoote – a mile and a half behind the Bergues–Furnes Canal – with German advanced units a mere four miles from Dunkerque.

Throughout 3 June the French put up a heroic resistance but by late in the afternoon the Germans had reached the southern outskirts of

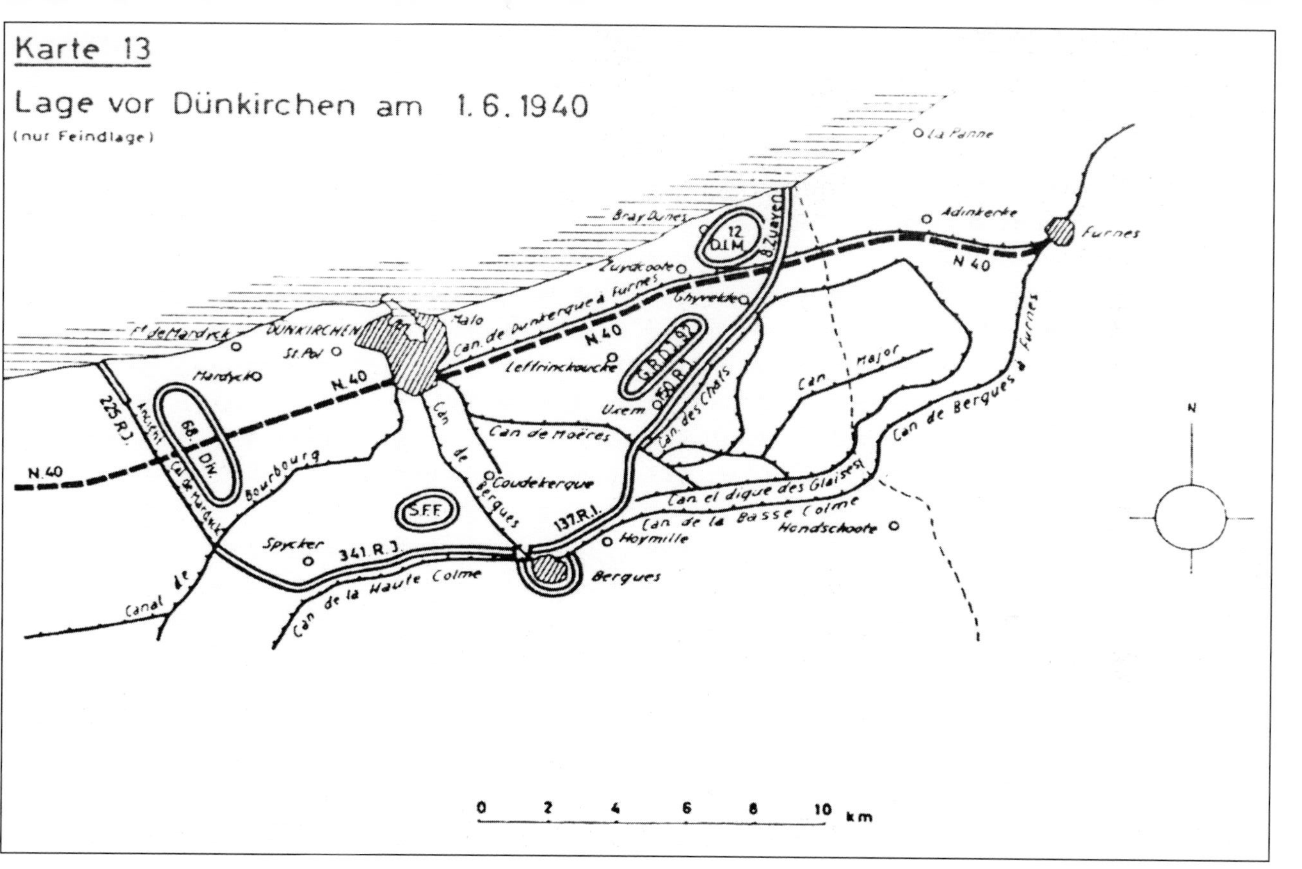

The reduced perimeter at Dunkerque, as seen on 1 June 1940.

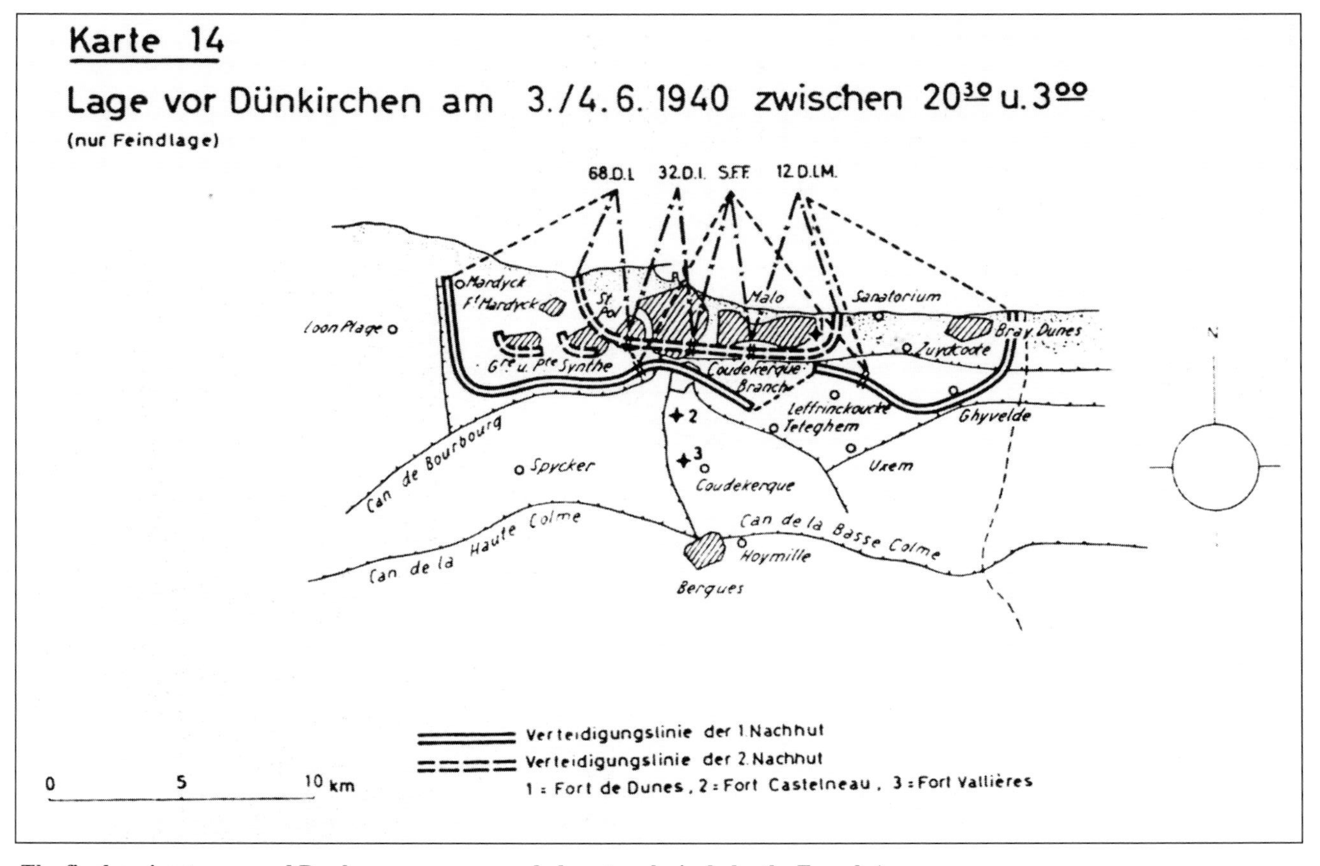

The final perimeter around Dunkerque was manned almost exclusively by the French Army.

Dunkerque. To his credit, Fagalde retained control over the situation and, remarkably, was able to withdraw to a smaller rearguard perimeter, which was held until 2.00am on 4 June by French forces. At dawn on 4 June IR 54, the advanced formation of the German 18th Division, crossed the Canal des Moëres and cautiously continued into Dunkerque. The regiment was the first German unit into Dunkerque on 4 June 1940 and was known thereafter as the Dunkerque Regiment. It was later all but annihilated at Stalingrad. The formal surrender of Dunkerque was made seven hours later at 9.00am (British time) by Général Maurice Beaufrère. The story is told that Friedrich-Carl Cranz, commanding the German 18th Division, asked Beaufrère where all the English were. Beaufrère's s reply to Cranz that they had gone to England was perhaps the final act of defiance from a Frenchman who had commanded a magnificent rearguard action, allowing Alexander and his troops to be evacuated.

The surrender at Dunkerque: Friedrich-Carl Cranz in conversation with a French officer. Général Beaufrère, commanding the French 68th Division, can be seen in the centre.

Chapter 3

German Forces on the Perimeter

The German units that initially lined the French sector of the perimeter in the west were largely drawn from *Generaloberst* Gerd von Rundstedt's Army Group A, while those facing the BEF east of Bergues were almost exclusively from *Generaloberst* Fedor von Bock's Army Group B. Von Bock was destined to be killed near Hamburg by a British fighter aircraft, along with his wife and stepdaughter, in May 1945.

It is interesting to note that up until 31 May there appears to have been a surprising lack of direction given by OKH as to the capture of Dunkerque. Not only was there no apparent co-ordinated plan of attack, but there were a series of disagreements between Günther von Kluge's Fourth Army (Army Group A) and Walther von Reichenau's Sixth Army (Army Group B) as to where the responsibility lay. Finally, Georg von Küchler, commanding the Eighteenth Army (Army Group B), was ordered to destroy or capture all Allied troops in the bridgehead. Of these three men, von Kluge committed suicide in August 1944, having being implicated in the 20 July plot against Hitler, while von Reichenau suffered a stroke in January 1942 and then suffered severe injuries after the flight taking him to Leipzig crashed on landing. Whether he died from his stroke or from injuries sustained in the crash is unknown. Von Küchler survived the war to be tried at

Walther von Reichenau commanded the Sixth Army and died from injuries in 1942.

Günther von Kluge commanded the Fourth Army.

Georg von Küchler, commanded the Eighteenth Army. He committed suicide in 1944.

Nuremberg in October 1948 for crimes committed in the Soviet Union. He was sentenced to twenty-eight years but was released in 1953.

The Panzer Division in May 1940

Alfred Ritter von Hubicki commanded the 9th Panzer Division.

Following the Polish Campaign, all existing light divisions were reorganized into panzer divisions, the 4th Light Division becoming the 9th Panzer Division. **The 9th Panzer Division** had its panzer regiment composed of two panzer battalions and, in addition, each division had a rifle brigade, an artillery regiment [with two battalions], an anti-tank battalion, an anti-aircraft battalion, an engineer battalion, a reconnaissance battalion and a signals battalion. In May 1940 the 9th Panzer Division was fighting under the banner of XIV Corps and commanded by 53-year-old Hungarian born *Generalmajor* Alfred Ritter von Hubicki. The division was the only mechanised armoured division allocated to the German Eighteenth Army during the invasion of France and Flanders and relieved Guderian's 1st and 2nd Panzer Divisions on 29 May.

The German Infantry Division in May 1940

The German infantry soldier, seen here with a K98 Rifle.

The strength of a German infantry division, counting the divisional supply troops, was approximately 17,000 officers and men. The typical German infantry division was made up of three infantry regiments, with each regiment fielding three battalions. Individual battalions contained a headquarters company, a machine gun company and three rifle companies. In addition, the division had on its strength a reconnaissance battalion, a signals and pioneer battalion and an anti-tank battalion. Divisional artillery consisted of four battalions of gunners, each with their own signals platoon.

The Motorised Infantry Division in May 1940

Whereas the standard infantry division in Army Group B relied heavily on horse drawn transport, the motorised division was fully mechanised and able to move at a much greater pace. The internal organisation included six infantry battalions, an artillery regiment, a reconnaissance

The *Panzerabwehrkanone* (Pak 3.7cm).

and a *panzerjäger* [tank hunter] battalion. As with the standard infantry division, it also had its own signals and pioneer battalions. In May 1940 it is likely the *panzerjäger* battalions were equipped with the *Panzerabwehrkanone* [Pak 3.7cm], as the Germans had no self propelled tank hunters at the time.

20th Motorised Division

Commanded by 57-year-old *General der Infantrie* Mauritz von Wikitorin, the division had been present at Arras on 21 May as part of Army Group A before moving north to Dunkerque via Wormhout. However, by the beginning of June the division was reunited with the newly formed Panzer Group Guderian in preparation for the next phase of the German advance. In 1944 age forced Wikitorin's discharge from the army and he died eleven years later, in 1956. In July 1943 the division was redesignated the 20th Panzergrenadier Division.

Mauritz von Wikitorin is seen here on the left standing next to Heinz Guderian at the German-Soviet parade in September 1939.

61st Infantry Division

A reserve division which was raised in 1939, it served for most of the war in Russia. Under the command of *Generalleutnant* Siegfried Haenicke, the division replaced the 20th Motorised Division on the perimeter opposite Bergues. Apart from IR 151 achieving fame on 10 May, by supporting the glider borne infantry of *Sturmgruppe Granit* at the Eben Emael fortress on the Albert Canal, the division had limited combat experience until 27 May. While not exactly its baptism of fire, the fighting on the Ypres-Comines Canal, under Viktor von Schwedler's IV Corps, did prepare the division for operations at Dunkerque. Haenicke surrendered to the Russians in 1945 and died a year later.

Siegfried Haenicke.

XIV Motorised Corps

The corps was under the command of 56-year-old *General der Infantrie* Gustav von Wietersheim and was in action in May 1940, as part of Panzer Group Kleist, relieving XIX Panzer Corps on 29 May. Guderian, in *Panzer Leader*, remarked that six of his units were placed under the command of XIV Corps, including the Infantry Regiment *Grossdeutschland* and the SS Regiment *Liebstandarte Adolf Hitler.* Wietersheim also had under his command the 2nd, 13th and 29th Motorised Divisions. After suggesting a withdrawal to the Don during the Battle of Stalingrad, Wietersheim was relieved of command in 1941 by the commander of the German Sixth Army, Friedrich Paulus, and was subsequently dismissed by Hitler. He died in Bonn in 1974. The corps was renamed XIV Panzer Corps on 21 June 1941.

Gustav von Wietersheim commanded XIV Motorised Corps.

X Corps

The corps was commanded by 55-year-old *General der Artillerie* Christian Hansen, who retired from the Wehrmacht in December 1944 on medical grounds and died in 1972. Of the three divisional commanders on the Dunkerque perimeter in May 1940, two suffered premature deaths: *Generalmajor* Friedrich-Carl Cranz (**18th Division**) was killed in 1941 in a friendly fire incident; and *Generalleutnant* Peter Weyer (**14th**

Friedrich-Carl Cranz commanded the 18th Division and accepted the surrender of Dunkerkque from Général Maurice Beaufrère.

Division) was captured by the Russians and died in captivity in 1947. The third, *Generalleutnant* Walter Behscnitt (**254th Division**), was captured in 1945 and released from captivity by the Allies in 1946. The 14th Division fought on the Escaut and divisional motorcycle units were amongst the first to appear on the River Dyle on 14 May. The division was motorised at the end of 1940. The 18th Division also saw some of its first action in the France and Flanders campaign on the Escaut, becoming motorised in 1941. The 254th Division was destroyed at Vitebsk in June 1944 during Operation Bagration.

Walter Behscnitt.

IX Corps

The corps was commanded by 58-year-old *General der Infantrie* Hermann Geyer, a highly decorated officer who retired in 1943 and committed suicide in April 1946. At Dunkerque the **216th Division** was under the command of *Generalleutnant* Kurt Himer, an interesting individual who was mortally wounded in March 1942, dying of wounds a few weeks later at Simferpol in the Crimea. Also present at Dunkerque was the **56th Division,** commanded by *Generalmajor* Karl Kriebel, who later served as a deputy member on the Court of Military Honour, a drumhead court-martial that expelled many of the Wehrmacht officers involved in the 20 July Plot against Hitler from the army before handing them over to the People's Court. At the end of the war he survived captivity and died in 1961. The division carried the nickname *gekreuzte säbel* – crossed sabres – after the divisional symbol.

Karl Kriebel commanded the 56th Division at Dunkerque.

256th Infantry Division

The division was commanded by *Generalleutnant* Josef Folttmann and attached to XXVI Corps under *General der Artillerie* Albert Wodrig. It was active on the eastern end of the perimeter around Nieuport. Folttmann was taken prisoner by the Americans in 1945 and released in 1947.

Josef Folttmann seen here on the left of the picture.

Chapter 4

Defending the Perimeter – II Corps

II Corps was commanded by 56-year-old Lieutenant General Alan Brooke, who was evacuated from La Panne on HMS *Worcester* during the night of 30 May, the same vessel that carried Sir Ronald Adam and Brigadier Lawson to England. II Corps then came under the command of Major General Bernard Montgomery, while Brigadier Kenneth Anderson was moved from 11 Brigade to command the 3rd Division and Brian Horrocks was elevated from command of 2/Middlesex to that of 11 Brigade. The plain speaking Montgomery was a man that you either liked or disliked. Major Mark Henniker, commanding 253/Field Company, met him near Furnes and immediately became a devotee:

> *He somehow restored my self-confidence and put me back on top of my form. It was an example in good manners for which I have always been grateful.*

Montgomery's combative nature demanded that the Germans were to be aggressively counter attacked whenever they attempted a crossing of the Nieuport-Furnes Canal, an order that may well have contributed to the majority of II Corps being able to break contact and move almost unopposed to the beaches. At 2.30pm on 31 May he moved the corps headquarters to La Panne and established reception areas in the dunes from where troops were summoned by the beach commander for evacuation.

The II Corps' sector of the perimeter ran from Nieuport to the border between Belgium and France. Since the Belgian capitulation, the eastern end at Nieuport was the point of greatest danger to the overall integrity of the perimeter, but fortunately there was a measure of respite for the British. The German 256th Division had been delayed by the French 60th Division, part of which were outflanked and cut off during the morning. Consequently, the first German infantry were not able to reach the canal at Nieuport until later on 28 May, thereby allowing a flimsy defence to be put in place. The 60th Division were attached to the Belgian Army and had been holding a line along the Canal de Dérivation, with its left flank on the sea at Zeebrugge; ordered to fall back, most of the 270th Regiment of Infantry surrendered after being surrounded, leaving the 241st Regiment to reach the coast and eventually Bray-Dunes.

The 12/Lancers

Having been placed under the command of the 3rd Division, Lieutenant Colonel Herbert Lumsden reacted quickly to his gut instinct that the Belgians were no longer in a position to defend the bridges at Dixmude and Nieuport. His instinct was to paid dividends and that hunch, together with the chance meeting with Captain George Gordon Lennox, was probably one of the most crucial decisions in the whole intricate web that made up the BEF evacuation. Promoted to lieutenant general, Lumsden was killed by a Japanese *kamikaze* aircraft while on the bridge of the USS *New Mexico* in January 1945.

Fortune was evidently smiling on the British that morning and 4 Troop, 12/Lancers, under Second Lieutenant Edward Miller-Mundy, arrived at 9.30am to find the town in flames and under aerial attack. By 11.00am, Miller-Mundy had completed his reconnaissance of the area and taken up position about 300 yards from the bridge over the Ijzer, just in time to spot the advanced patrol of German motorcyclists arrive from

The 12th Lancers, probably on exercise in England prior to moving to France.

the direction of Westende. An intense fire fight erupted, with casualties on both sides, before the surviving Germans escaped through the crowd of refugees. Taking up a defensive position on the canal bank, the arrival of Second Lieutenant Henderson's troop released Miller-Mundy to find the French officer with responsibility for blowing the bridge. Failing to locate him, pressure from the reinforced German troops compelled him to withdraw over the wide main road bridge [Langbrug] to the west side of the canal, where he found the remaining two troops of B Squadron.

13/Field Survey Regiment

Apart from the 12/Lancers, the officers and men of 13/Field Survey Company were possibly the first troops to arrive in Nieuport, at 1.30am on 28 May. Commanded by Lieutenant Colonel Fryer, the regiment consisted of some sixty five officers and men armed with one Bren gun and a Boys anti-tank rifle. Establishing his headquarters at the Brickworks, he then proceeded to order the bridges surrounding Nieuport destroyed. Fryer writes that he had been sent up to Nieuport by Lawson and thinks it was at about 4.00pm on 28 May that he met Lieutenant Colonel Brazier:

> *He told me he had been up in Nieuport earlier in the day and he had placed an officer and some men forward on the canal bank at Nieuport and that armoured cars and light tanks were operating on my left. He also told me he had seen the bridges being blown in his rear. In view of this information, modifications were made to my dispositions, especially on the right, where the RASC were moved up to the canal.*

As senior to Fryer, Brazier took over command and Fryer became second in command. On Brazier's instructions, he reported to Brigadier Clifton at Wulpen to inform him of the arrangement and the rather precarious nature of the defences, particularly as the main road bridge into Nieuport from the east remained intact. Clifton wrote that on his arrival he found a very mixed bag of personnel defending the canal:

> *About 200 dismounted Royal Artillery personnel armed with rifles, about 50 mixed RE, RASC and four 18-pounders were in the process of taking up a position between Nieuport and the sea under the command of Lieutenant Colonel Brazier RA* [referred to in some accounts as Brazier Force] ... *One squadron of 12/Lancers were carrying out a reconnaissance in the area with one troop in Nieuport. This troop reported the main bridge over*

the canal in Nieuport had not been blown and that enemy motor-cyclists, motorised infantry and a few large tanks were immediately north of the bridge and it was not possible to cross the bridge or blow it. The Bridge had been prepared for demolition by the Belgians [sic] *but the leads were on the wrong side of the river.*

Lieutenant Colonel Edward Brazier, 53/Medium Regiment, had disabled his guns and brought his men to Hoogstade, south of Furnes, when he was ordered to move immediately to Nieuport and command the infantry defence of the town, arriving soon after the 12/Lancers had disposed of the motorcycle patrol. Clifton's description of Brazier's deployment highlights the almost laughable defence of the perimeter at Nieuport:

Apart from the twenty five officers and 200 men of his [Brazier's] *own regiment, his largest contingent was 147 officers and men of the II Corps Ammunition Field Park, and these he placed on the right of the line, where the canal bends round the town. Next to them were 13/ Field Survey Company RE from I Corps, his own 53/Regiment, 127 troops from 1/Heavy Anti-Aircraft Regiment and a small contingent from 2/Medium Regiment, RA. He also had twenty Grenadier guardsmen, rushed over from Furnes, and two light tanks provided by myself.*

Like Clifton, Brazier's biggest problem was the failure of the 4th Division Engineers to blow the main road bridge when they had the opportunity. Now, after Miller-Mundy's troop had been forced back over the bridge to the west side, the German 256th Division were well placed to sweep the bridge with mortar and machine gun fire. It was not until 8.00pm that evening that 7/Field Company RE, who the previous day had led the counter attack on the banks of the Ypres-Comines Canal, arrived at Nieuport. Their infantry duties were interrupted by an unsuccessful attempt to blow the bridge, a foray which cost them dearly. Lieutenant Beasley, a gunner officer serving with 210/Battery, 53/Medium Regiment, recalled watching a young sapper officer volunteering to take a small party to blow the main bridge, his unsuccessful attempt resulting in a 'scuffle with a German patrol on the bridge' and several casualties.

As with the rest of the officers and men of Brazier's Force, Lieutenant Beasley found himself fighting on the front line as an infantryman:

This was our first taste of real war and the casualties in our mixed force were pretty heavy. The regiment was pretty lucky on the

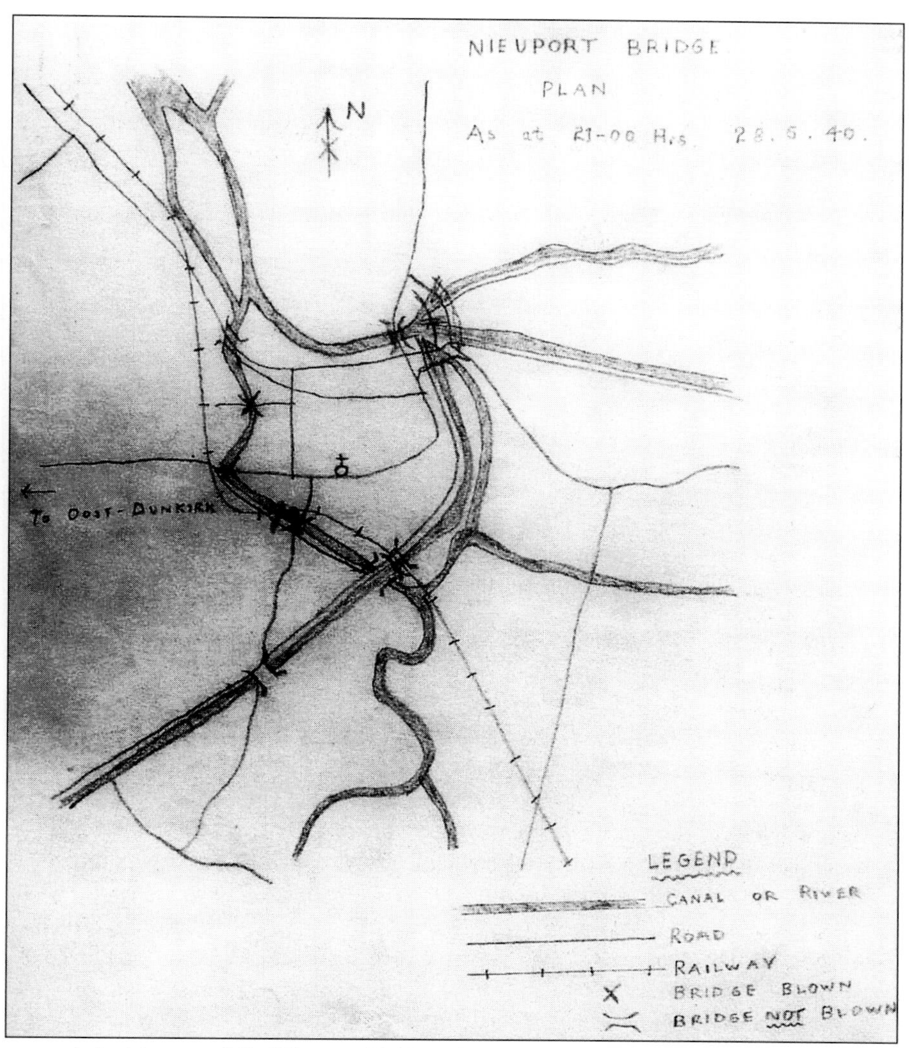

A sketch map of the Nieuport Bridges from the war diary of 13/Field Survey Unit.

whole but lost a lot of young boys and we were all stunned to hear that Lieutenant Bruce Thornton had been killed trying to rescue a Bren from an impossibly exposed position … On the second day this cosmopolitan force was relieved by the 2nd Battalion Royal Fusiliers. We felt pretty embarrassed at handing over a forlorn task to infantry who had been marching and fighting for five days without sleep [sic], *well knowing they had come so we, amongst others, could get away – a rotten mission to give anyone.*

22/Field Regiment, Royal Artillery

At daylight on 29 May, the first gunners from 22/Field Regiment, RA, arrived with a full complement of 25-pounders, which added considerable weight to the British fire power. Clifton had by this time moved his headquarters west of Oost-Dunkerke and Lieutenant Colonel Young, commanding 22/Field Regiment, deployed his guns northwest of the village to commence firing on enemy forces in Nieuport at 5.00am that morning. While there appeared to be little pressure from the enemy during 29 May, over the following two days the battery positions came under severe shelling and bombing, forcing one troop and both command posts to move:

> *During the day the enemy made several unsuccessful attempts to cross the unblown bridge in Nieuport, in an area christened Piccadilly Circus* [the Ganzepoot]. *Many opportunity targets in this area were fired on by batteries, which also fired on enemy columns approaching Nieuport along the coast. During the late afternoon one gun per troop was destroyed ... on 31 May the Regimental Aid Post* [RAP] *was heavily shelled during the morning, Lieutenant* [Guy] *Reid being killed as he was going in for attention.*

At 12.00 Midday on 31 May, a German aircraft bombed Regimental Headquarters, killing four men and wounding Lieutenant Colonel Young and Captain Hudson. Further casualties included Lieutenants Coleman and Greenwood, but by this time orders had been received to destroy all equipment and withdraw to La Panne, leaving only one troop remaining in action to cover the infantry until the small hours of 1 June.

The 4th Division

The division was under the command of 56-year-old Major General Dudley Johnson, who, as a lieutenant colonel commanding the 2nd Battalion Royal Sussex Regiment, was awarded the Victoria Cross in November 1918 on the Sambre Canal. He was appointed to the 4th Division in 1938. As can be imagined, Clifton was somewhat relieved to meet Brigadier John Hawkesworth, commanding 12 Brigade, on the morning of 29 May, a meeting which heralded the arrival of the 4th Division and the relief of Brazier's men. 47-year-old Hawkesworth and 12 Brigade only left the Lys at 8.00pm on 28 May and had been on the road continually for ten hours in order to reach Nieuport. Hawksworth was appointed to command X Corps with the rank of lieutenant general in 1944 but was destined not to see the shores of England again; he died after a heart attack on his way home in June 1945.

Brigadier John Hawksworth pictured with Rear Admiral Richard Connolly in 1943 after his promotion to major general.

At about 11.00am on 29 May one company of the 2/Royal Fusiliers, under the command of 42-year-old Lieutenant Colonel Geoffrey Allen, finally got through to Nieuport. Allen's initial assessment highlighted the seriousness of the situation, particularly as the Germans had brought up reinforcements and Brazier's forces on the right flank were beginning to crumble under an increasing crescendo of fire. Despite the approaches to the town being swept by a hail of fire, Allen committed one company of his Fusiliers and these, supported by the carrier troop, threw the enemy back and held them until the arrival of the main body of the battalion. Following close behind was A and B Companies of the 1/South Lancashires and between them these two battalions secured the town and canal banks, allowing Brazier's men to withdraw. But as Clifton wrote, it was not an easy task:

As the evening wore on advantage was taken of any lull in the firing at different places throughout my sector to carry out the relief of my party. In certain cases, however, reliefs did not take place until the early hours of the following morning. This was due, I understand, to the difficulty of finding the parties concerned in the dark as they had not been accurately located by the relieving troops during daylight. In some instances the movement of the

Daniel Beak being awarded the Victoria Cross by George V in 1919.

relieving troops caused heavy fire to be reopened and troops were caught in exposed positions, and some gallant acts were performed in getting away casualties which then occurred.

The two companies of the South Lancs took up positions west of Nieuport and, as the left flank battalion of 12 Brigade, was responsible for the crossings over the canal from the sea to the bridge at Nieuport itself. Under the command of 49-year-old Lieutenant Colonel Daniel Beak, an officer who had been awarded the Victoria Cross in 1918, the battalion dug in under shellfire amidst indications of growing enemy activity on the far side of the canal. Late on 29 May the 6/Black Watch took over from B Company, allowing Daniel Beak to extend the battalion's positions to the right.

The 2/Royal Fusiliers established their headquarters in a former blockhouse in a strip of woodland that runs west of the town on the N396, probably near the area now called the Leopold II Park. It was in this woodland, on 30 May, that Lieutenant Colonel Allen, the brother of 'Gubby' Allen, the England cricketer, was wounded by a sniper's bullet and later died of his wounds, giving some credibility to the claim made by 7/Field Company that German snipers had already established themselves in the town itself.

Soon after the arrival of the main party of Royal Fusiliers, Lieutenant Colonel Charles Armstrong arrived from Oost-Dunkerke with the 1/6 East Surreys. They were quickly deployed to the east of the town and west of the main Nieuport-Furnes road. Armstrong had been in command of the battalion since April 1940, when promotion saw him posted to it from the 1st Battalion. He deployed the 1/6 East Surreys with an amalgamated C and D Company on the left, A Company behind the canal and B Company around the Brickworks, to the east of the Nieuport Memorial.

Lieutenant Colonel Charles Armstrong, 1/6th Battalion East Surrey Regiment.

At daybreak on 31 May, a heavy enemy bombardment under the cover of smoke announced a determined German effort to force the British positions. By 8.00am B Company, 1/South Lancs, had reported fourteen casualties, including Lieutenant Hargreaves and Second Lieutenant Warren. By 10.00am German troops were pushing forward between the South Lancs positions and the 2/Royal Fusiliers, gaining ground on either side of the town and threatening to envelope the Fusiliers. Both battalions held on and a counter attack by the South Lancashires, led by Captain 'Tubby' Butler, put an end to the left hand penetration.

Despite this, the company of 1/6 East Surreys, holding the Brickworks, was coming under increasing pressure from German infantry who had crossed the canal.

Ist Battalion East Surrey Regiment

During the night of 30 May, the 1/East Surreys, who were in Brigade reserve near Oost-Dunkerke, received orders to embark for England and march to the pre-arranged lying-up area at Coxyde Bains, a journey they completed by 6.00am the next morning. Their breakfast was disturbed by fresh orders to proceed immediately to Nieuport and mount a counter attack in support of 1/6 East Surreys at the Brickworks. It was a tall order for already tired troops; but the two battalions had fought side by side on the Escaut and many of the 1/6 were well known to the officers and men of the 1st Battalion.

Fortunately, the battalion had retained its transport, which followed behind their commanding officer, 44-year-old Lieutenant Colonel Reginald Boxshall, who had motored ahead to liaise with Brigadier Barker. The situation in Nieuport was deteriorating by the hour, German troops were in the town, with the Royal Fusiliers reporting that at 4.00am

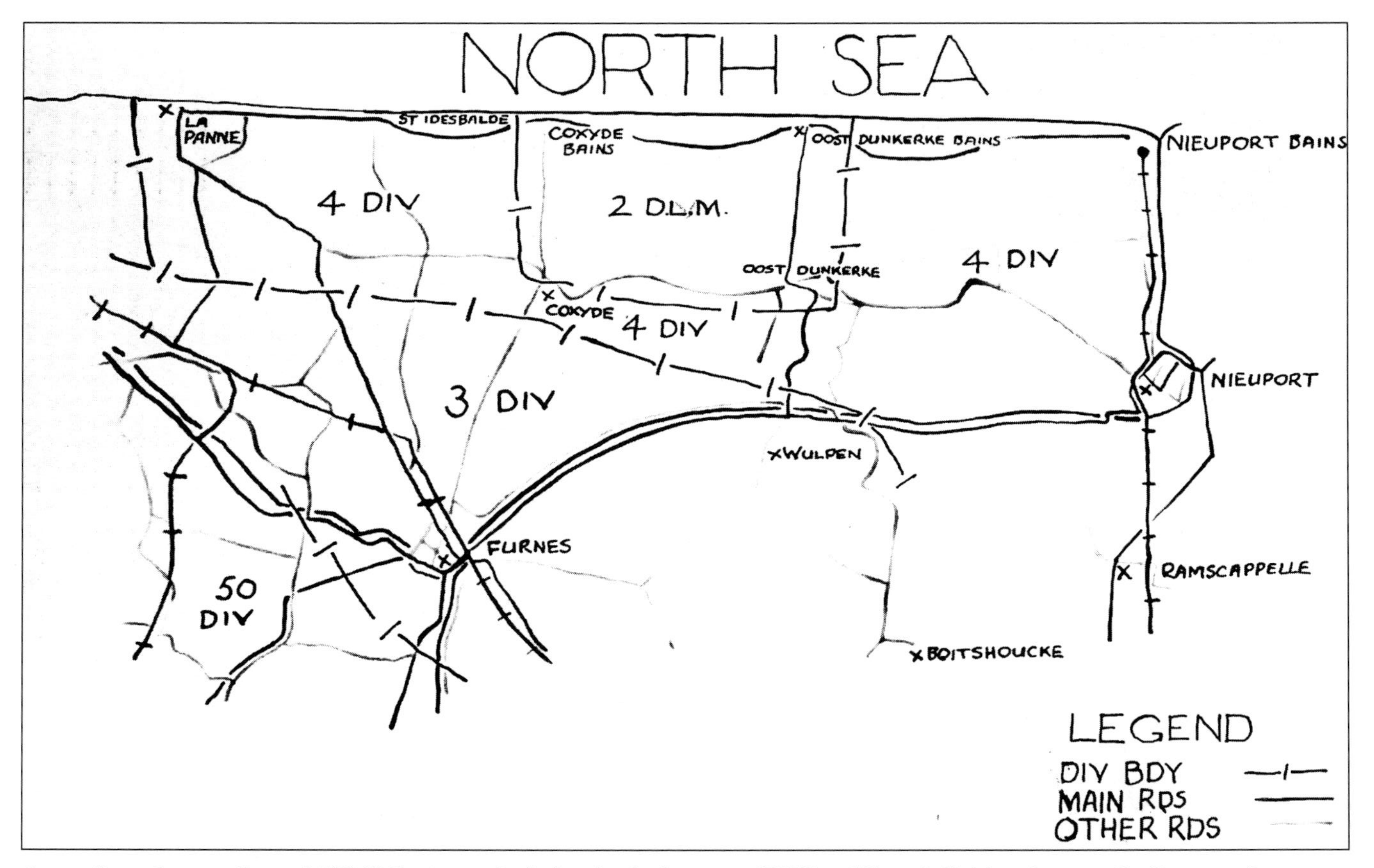

A map from the war diary of 7/Field Regiment depicting the deployment of BEF and French divisions between La Panne and Nieuport.

some 800 shells fell forward of Battalion Headquarters in the space of seventeen minutes. The Germans had forced a gap towards the main Nieuport bridge on the left flank of the 1/6 East Surreys and B Company were desperately holding part of the Brickworks. The arrival of the 1/East Surreys could not have happened a moment too soon. Private Robert Lloyd was part of the counter attack:

Lieutenant Colonel Reginald Boxshall, 1st Battalion East Surrey Regiment.

> *A message came that the Battalion was to move at once to Nieuport where the 10th Infantry Brigade were holding the perimeter. The battalion was moved in its own transport which we had refused to jettison. The 1/6th Surreys were under attack and desperately holding part of the Brickworks. A counter attack was launched with B and D Companies and A and C in support.*

Boxshall's account of the counter attack is quite short and does not properly communicate the seriousness of the situation facing the Surreys, but he does record that his Intelligence Officer was hit in the bottom by shrapnel during his initial reconnaissance with Brigadier Barker:

> *We were ordered to counter attack and fill the gap. This we did on a narrow frontage without any opposition but on reaching our objective we found a small detachment of the 1/6 Surreys holding some brickworks. Lieutenant Colonel 'Wix' Armstrong, commander of the 1/6, and I then went forward to sort things out, and I agreed to relieve his men. Whilst there, we spotted some Boche, so he and I borrowed a LMG* [Bren gun] *and had a private strafe. We then decided we had better go back to our own headquarters and leave the company to carry on.*

The small detachment of the 1/6 East Surreys referred to by Boxshall was all that remained of B Company! Nonetheless, the counter attack brought some stability to the situation but, as the defenders at the Brickworks soon realised, it was not quite over. In the late afternoon the Germans were seen massing on the far side of the canal for yet another attack on the East Surreys.

The Air Attack on Nieuport bridge

What exactly happened next is unclear, but we are told the German

The Bristol Blenheim is said have been one of the aircraft that attacked the Nieuport Bridges.

assault was halted by British aircraft attacking their positions. Whether these aircraft were Bristol Blenheims or aircraft from the Fleet Air Arm is, again, not clear, but it was one of the rare occasions that British aircraft were seen by the troops defending the perimeter to be supporting them. Several contemporary accounts report seeing Blenheims, and there certainly was a sortie carried out by 2 Group on enemy positions in the Dunkerque area on 31 May, but RAF records do not specify where and at what time. Second Lieutenant Robin Medley, serving with 2/Bedfordshire and Hertfordshire Regiment at Oost-Dunkerke, reported seeing forty Blenheims flying across his front towards German occupied territory on 31 May, but this was just before dusk, and he may have confused the Blenheim with a twin engine German aircraft. Lieutenant David Tyacke, serving with the 2/Duke of Cornwall's Light Infantry (DCLI), also saw a squadron of Blenheims flying at low level in the afternoon of 31 May who, he says were on their way to bomb Nieuport. But there is no record of this taking place and a growing weight of evidence suggests the attack at Nieuport was carried out by the Fleet Air Arm.

In May 1940 units of the Fleet Air Arm were assigned to RAF Coastal Command to provide support for Operation Dynamo and, according to some sources, on 31 May ten Albacores and nine Skuas bombed German positions on the Nieuport Canal. Returning home the Skuas were engaged by twelve Messerschmitt Bf 109s of I/JG20 and two Skuas of 801 Squadron were shot down. The battle was not all one sided; the Skuas claimed one Bf109 shot down and another damaged. Nevertheless,

The Langebrug at Nieuport was constructed after the First World War and made entirely of wood. The photograph shows German engineers inspecting the bridge for demolition charges.

whether it was the RAF or Fleet Air Arm, the result brought smiles of delight to the tired troops below, who stood cheering and waving as the enemy was thrown into confusion.

Nieuport Abandoned

Boxshall's men were ordered back to the beaches near La Panne to await embarkation; however, at dawn on 1 June they received orders to march to Dunkerque as La Panne was being heavily shelled. Boxshall's car was hit during this move and 49-year-old Major Hambleton Bousfield and Private Dennis, the driver, were injured but luckily Boxshall and his adjutant, Captain Peter Hill, escaped unscathed. Sadly, Bousfield was killed shortly afterwards when the ambulance he was travelling in was hit by a shell.

The Royal Fusiliers war diary tells us it was at 10.00pm on 31 May before they finally withdrew and were held up at a crossroads - probably at Oost-Dunkerke – for some eighty minutes due to heavy German shelling. The 1/South Lancs began thinning out at approximately the same time, covered by Second Lieutenant Humphrey Kemball's remaining carriers, which finally left their positions at 2.15am on 1 June.

2/Bedfordshire and Hertfordshire Regiment

The 2/Bedfordshire and Hertfordshire Regiment (2/Beds and Herts) began arriving in the perimeter on 29 May. Second Lieutenant Robin Medley was in command of 13 Platoon, C Company:

> *We arrived at Oost-Dunkerke at about 7.00pm and went to an assembly area near the church and waited for orders. The company was fed and Captain Johnson told us the battalion was to deploy with all companies on the line of the canal, with C Company on the right. He told us that we were to hold defensive positions and that the BEF was withdrawing to England ... We marched forward after dark. 13 Platoon was on the right of the company and battalion and deployed.* [We] *dug in close to the canal astride the road, with its bridge blown, at Wulpen.*

Lieutenant Colonel James Birch established his headquarters at the crossroads near the church and deployed the battalion along a frontage of 2,700 yards along the Nieuport-Furnes Canal. He writes of his dislike of crossroads, a dislike that began on the Escaut and was confirmed at Oost-Dunkerque:

> *Just as the battalion* [Medley does not mention this] *arrived the Boche started shelling the crossroads and square very heavily. For a minute or two things were a bit disorganised but commanders soon got control. The town hall had been a civil aid post and had already been used for military casualties. The first salvo or two wrecked it and with it a carrier, which had just arrived.*

Medley was relieved to find the bridge had been demolished but his platoon was under small arms fire almost continually. On more than one occasion they were victim to machine gun fire from Wulpen:

> *After stand-down, I was dozing in my trench when Sergeant Chandler shouted out he had shot a German across the canal and was very excited about it. Not long after, two Germans rushed out of a front door of a house close to where their wounded comrade lay, grabbed him and carried him to safety. Later I was making my rounds of the sections, which meant I had to cross a road, to find myself being chased by a burst of fire from a machine gun. It was obvious this weapon had been sited to cover the road. At about midnight I heard a vehicle drive up along the road, it was the A Company pick-up driven by Private Carlton. Curiously the Germans had not fired as yet. I shouted to him to turn and drive off quickly, which he did, to be followed by a burst of fire. I was*

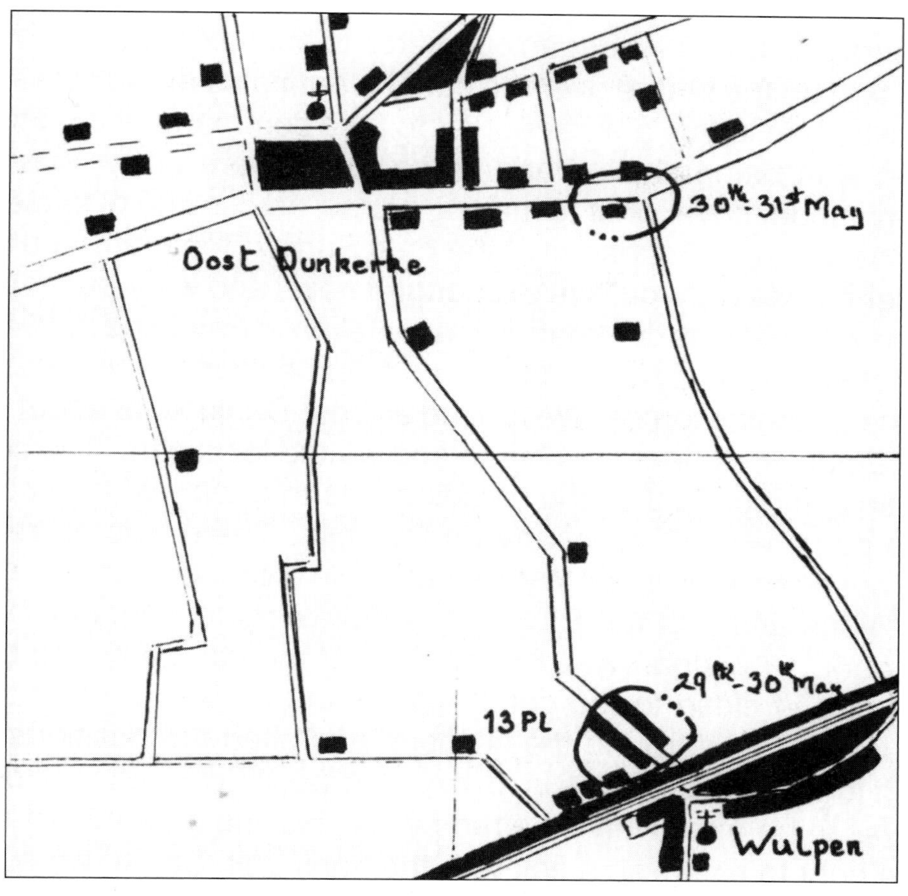

A map drawn by Second Lieutenant Robin Medley, illustrating the two positions occupied by his platoon at Oost-Dunkerque.

> *told later that this went through the left side of the vehicle, missing the mess cook sitting in the back but breaking five out of six bottles of the A Company officers' whisky.*

Just after dusk a message was received ordering C Company to hand over to B Company and move back to Oost-Dunkirke, a handover which Robin Medley says was completed by 3.00am on 30 May. It was nearly daylight by the time C Company arrived back at Oost-Dunkerke but there was to be little rest, as by 6.00am a heavy German bombardment commenced, destroying the majority of a section of carriers in the process:

Activity was building up and there was continuous enemy artillery fire. The response from the British side was minimal as the shortage of ammunition meant the guns [presumably from 22/Field Regiment, who were close by] *could only fire one round every 30 minutes.*

Enemy shellfire was assisted by the presence of observation balloons, all of which made life extremely uncomfortable for all concerned, and who had little choice but to burrow deeper into the ground. Second Lieutenant Thomas McMillen was commanding the battalion's Anti-Tank Platoon:

We had not fired a shot in anger during the retreat to Dunkerque until we took up defensive positions near Bray Dunes. Up until that time we had been plagued by German observation balloons, flown from behind their lines, which saw every move we made and brought down artillery fire, even if two people walked along a road together. My platoon of three 25mm Hotchkiss anti-tank guns, which fired solid shot, had dug into a position in a hedgerow on the left flank where we were overlooked by two of these insolent observation balloons. I thought that we ought to do something about them so decided to have a go myself. I cleared the crew of one of the guns away to safety and with Sergeant Percival as loader and with maximum range on the telescopic sights, fired at the nearest balloon. The third round must have scored a hit as the nose cone deflated rapidly and the balloon was hauled down even more rapidly.

The answering shellfire did little to reduce the elation felt by the gunners and Brigadier Evelyn 'Bubbles' Barker, commanding 10 Brigade, turned the whole Brigade Anti-Tank Company of nine guns to counter the balloon fire. The result was another five balloons being destroyed and the enemy balloon detachment was withdrawn. However, the resulting enemy shellfire had provided enough cover for small groups of enemy infantry to cross the canal near the B Company positions. Under constant harassing sniper fire, the company repulsed an attack and reoccupied the canal bank, supported by the last six rounds of a 3-inch mortar.

Brigadier Evyelyn 'Bubbles' Barker.

On 31 May the whole brigade was ordered to abandon their forward positions and to be clear of the crossroads at Oost-Dunkerke by 1.30am on 1 June. Lieutenant Colonel Birch's orders detailed C Company and the carriers to hold onto Oost-Dunkerke until 2.30am, when their withdrawal would be covered by the carriers. Robin Medley recalled his part in the withdrawal:

> *A and B Companies passed through our positions at the appointed time. German shellfire continued and houses alongside our path of withdrawal had been set ablaze. These houses received a salvo of four shells at about two minute intervals. We sat in our trenches waiting to see if the Germans would follow up A and B Companies. Lance Corporal Dilley's section was covering the track leading up from the canal, so I waited with him. The burning houses were run past between the arrival of incoming salvoes. At the RV we met the Adjutant, Captain Bob Senior, who saw us onto the transport and sent us on the way to La Panne.*

2/Duke of Cornwall's Light Infantry

Arriving on the canal on 29 May, the battalion, under the command of Lieutenant Colonel Eric Rushton, began to move into positions on the right flank of 1/6 East Surreys at dusk.

Lieutenant David Tyacke, serving with C Company, noted with some disquiet that the ground on his side of the canal was flat meadowland, intersected by deep, water filled, irrigation ditches:

David Tyacke, photographed after the war, when he was GOC Singapore District.

> *There wasn't a stitch of cover except in the water filled ditches or in isolated groups of farm buildings, and, being a salient the whole area was swept by enemy fire. The chances of getting into position on the canal itself did not therefore appear very bright, as this involved crossing at least six hundred yards of this very unpromising country. As soon as it was dark, therefore, C Company set off across this waterlogged billiard table ... we got past the isolated farm buildings without incident, but then came under un-aimed but, nonetheless, disquieting, machine gun fire from the Germans and from our own side.*

The 30 May was enlivened by spasmodic shell fire and after dark Tyacke's company were relieved by C Company, 1/6 East Surreys to go into battalion reserve. It was to be a short 'rest' as the next day C Company were ordered to Nieuport to support the 2/Royal Fusiliers:

Here were scenes of considerable confusion. A number of wounded were making their way to the rear, and no one had any precise idea of where the enemy were. We reached the start line and were in the act of forming up ready to advance when the Brigade commander arrived on foot and informed us a complete battalion – 1/East Surreys - would now take on the task.

This episode was, of course, the prelude to the counter attack by the 1/East Surreys to relieve B Company of the 1/6 East Surreys at the Brickworks. Although he does not say as much, I imagine Tyacke and C Company were more than happy to withdraw and leave the counter attack to Boxshall's battalion. Marching back to their former positions at the rear of D Company, they learnt the battalion, now under the command of Major Hugh Joslen, had been ordered to withdraw to La Panne at 1.00am on 1 June. [Rushton had been detailed for duty on the beaches on 31 May and was never seen again, presumably meeting his end later that day in the HMS *Skipjack* bombing when nearly 300 men were killed. The CWGC records his death on 1 June 1940.] Under the cover of a rearguard consisting of C Company and the Carrier Platoon, it was only later that they heard D Company had not been so lucky and 27-year-old Lieutenant Andrew Le Grice had been mortally wounded as the company vacated its positions.

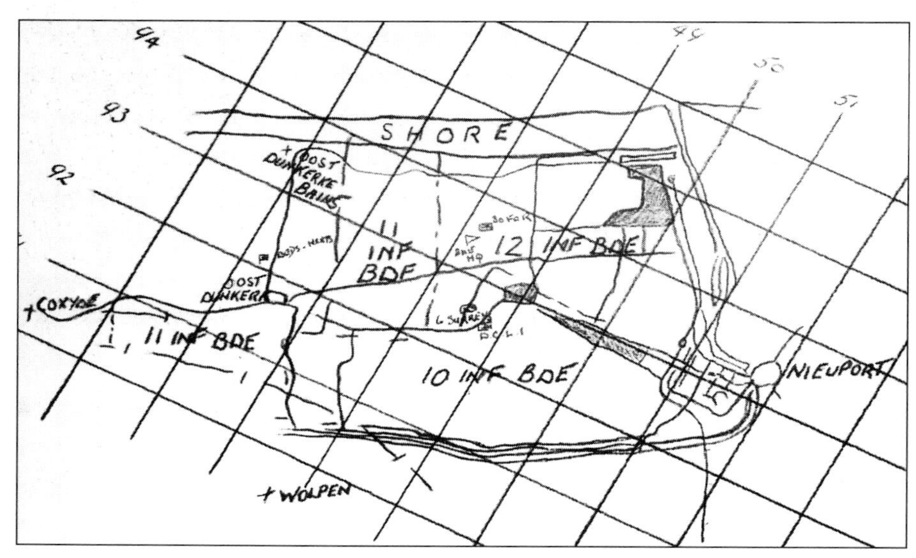

A map from the DCLI war diary showing the positions of the three infantry brigades of the 4th Division.

2/Lancashire Fusiliers

According to the account written by Major Lawrence Manley, who had been in command of the battalion since the death of Lieutenant Colonel Leslie Rougier on the Escaut, they too had been placed on immediate standby to assist the 1/6 East Surreys. Arriving on 29 May, they were deployed in reserve with the 5/Northamptons behind 10 and 11 Brigade. The following day they received orders to march to La Panne, orders that were rescinded at 11.45am with the news they were to move to new positions east of Oost-Dunkerque. The battalion marched to La Panne, where seventeen officers and 478 other ranks were eventually evacuated.

The 3rd Division

Known as the 'Iron Division' and commanded by Major General Bernard Montgomery, Divisional Headquarters moved on 29 May from Oost-Vleteren, some twenty minutes south of Furnes, to the dunes south of La Panne, in preparation for embarkation. Disaster had already struck the divisional staff in the early hours of 29 May when Montgomery's principal staff officer, 46-year-old Colonel 'Marino' Vincent Brown, Royal Marines, was shot and killed, probably by an overzealous French sentry, on his way to Corps Headquarters. A day later, on 30 May, Montgomery took over command of II Corps in place of Lieutenant General Alan Brooke.

While Second Lieutenant Robin Medley was dug in opposite Wulpen on 29 May, he managed to get in contact with a section of machine guns from the Middlesex Regiment who were holding the line of the canal on his right flank and supporting 8 Brigade. This would probably have been a section from D Company, 2/Middlesex, a machine gun battalion whose companies were allotted to the three infantry brigades of the 3rd Division. A Company were in support of 9 Brigade opposite Bulskamp, B Company in and to the south west of Furnes, C Company were supporting 7 Guards Brigade and in support of 8 Brigade were D Company. The battalion was under the command of Lieutenant Colonel Brian Horrocks, who arrived from England on 13 May and who achieved fame after Montgomery identified him as one of his most able officers, appointing him to corps commands in both North Africa and Europe. He is chiefly remembered as the commander of XXX Corps in Operation Market Garden.

Lieutenant Colonel Brian Horrocks, taken after his promotion to lieutenant general in 1942.

Command of the Middlesex devolved to Major Reid on 30 May, a day that began quietly enough until the enemy began its attacks on the line around noon. D Company was particularly unfortunate with the amount of shell and mortar fire that was directed at them: 32-year-old Captain Robert Parsler, D Company commander, was killed, as was 24-year-old Second Lieutenant Patrick Lyon, who had taken over command from him.

2/East Yorkshire Regiment

8 Brigade was supported by the machine guns of D Company, 2/Middlesex, and one section was positioned with the 2/East Yorkshires along the line of the canal. The battalion was commanded by 46-year-old Lieutenant Colonel Thomas Given, an officer who was commissioned into the Royal Irish Fusiliers in 1915. The East Yorkshires' war diary provides a glimpse of the carnage caused by German shelling:

> *We were in contact with the enemy almost immediately and suffered a considerable number of casualties from his mortar fire. The chief reason for this was that we had by now lost all our picks and shovels, the transport having being abandoned, and we were relying on local farm implements, of which there were not many, for digging in ... All day on the 31 May the whole of our position was under constant shell, mortar and machine gun fire and communication was very difficult, especially with B Company. Signallers made brave attempts to maintain and lay lines, those that existed were being broken constantly. Casualties from B Company had to be cleared in carriers.*

Earlier in the day the Germans had managed to cross the canal on the battalion's right flank and, although a local counter attack deterred the Germans from advancing further, they were now established – albeit tenuously – on the northern bank of the canal. Late in the evening of 31 May the battalion was ordered to withdraw to La Panne at 2.30am on 1 June - orders which could not have come sooner. Thinning out was undertaken company by company, leaving a rear party consisting of Lieutenant Baker and his A Company platoon and the battalion carriers. Baker and his party did not reach the dunes until after daylight on 1 June.

4/Royal Berkshire Regiment

Until a few days before the battalion had been under the command of Lieutenant Colonel Geoffrey Bull, a rather stiff, archetypical, former Grenadier Guardsman, who had been seriously wounded during the battalion's last rearguard action. Evacuated to England, Bull died of

A German mortar team in action.

German troops waiting for the order to advance.

wounds on 20 July 1940. Now under the command of Major Roper, the battalion should never have been placed in the front line, particularly after the heavy casualties received at Steenstraat, where they lost three company commanders as well as the commanding officer. The battalion – eighty officers and men - took up its position on the canal on 30 May, with 7 Guards Brigade on its right flank and the 1/Suffolks on the left, and was reinforced by 17/Field Company [commanded by Captain John Donaldson] and later by eight Bren guns from 20/Anti-Tank Regiment. The Germans opened fire with their artillery at about 11.00am, which, together with the fire from enemy snipers, made it almost impossible to move without being shot at from all sides.

The Berkshires' Withdrawal

The war diary records the battalion positions being further reinforced by Number 1 Company, 1/Coldstream Guards, at dusk on 30 May, but makes no mention of the precarious state of the officers and men or the fact they they 'withdrew' under German mortar fire. Further evidence as to the state of the Berkshire defence came from the adjutant, 27-year-old Captain Francis Waldron:

> *The sappers to our left had broken back, and our men, after the heavy mortar fire, had also broken back. This meant we had nobody on the canal bank. If the enemy should choose to attack, there was nothing to stop him ... I was thankful it was getting dark, for if the Hun had seen our precarious position we were in for the next few hours, nothing would have stopped him from getting more men across.*

In fact, it looks very much as if the Berkshires withdrew just as the Coldstream Guards were preparing to take over part of their positions, a withdrawal that did allow the German engineers to erect pontoon bridges across the canal and gain a bridgehead on the British side. The subsequent counter attack led by Major John Campbell was extremely costly in terms of casualties, but it does appear that the Coldstream eventually took over most of the Berkshires frontage.

1/Suffolk Regiment

The Suffolks were in a similar precarious state but being regular troops were perhaps more disciplined under fire. The battalion was now under the command of Major Frank Milnes; the former commanding officer, 46-year-old Lieutenant Colonel Eric Fraser, having been seriously wounded on 20 May whilst on the Escaut. Evacuated to England, Fraser died on 23 May. The regimental historian writes the battalion took up their positions along the canal at 4.00am on 30 May, along with 253 and 246/Field Companies, Royal Engineers, and a battery from an anti-tank regiment [possibly from 20/Anti-Tank Regiment, which was also in support of the Berkshires]. Major Mark Henniker and his Sappers had been drafted in to support the Suffolks' and attended the rather hurried conference held by Major Milnes at the Suffolk's Headquarters on 30 May:

> *On their* [Suffolks] *right was a Guard's battalion* [Henniker's account was written in England and it is assumed the Coldstream Guards had already taken over some of the Berkshire's positions], *and we, that is 253/Field Company, were to take up our positions near the right boundary of the Suffolks. Our role was to launch a counter attack against any penetration by the Germans across the canal on our front ... I buttonholed the adjutant, a tall dark haired captain called 'Tiny' Heal. He told me the danger point was, in his opinion, a brick factory that I would see as soon as it became light. It was at the junction of the Suffolk and Guards battalion and was easily recognisable by its tall chimney.*

Dawn on 31 May opened with heavy German shelling along the whole battalion front and the Suffolks' war diary states that 246/Field Company [commanded by Major Harold Drayson] then withdrew in the face of mortar fire and were collected by Major Baker and led back to their positions. No mention is made in the Suffolks' war diary of the part played by the 2/Grenadier Guards in stabilising the situation, and Mark Henniker makes no mention of this withdrawal at all, writing that Baker arrived at 253/Field Company Headquarters with the news that the Germans had crossed the canal in strength near the battalion's left flank, and his Sappers were to drive them back. This was clearly a reference to the withdrawal of 246/Field Company. For a company of engineers not trained in infantry tactics it was a tall order indeed and an indication of the fragile nature of the British defence in this sector:

Major Mark Henniker was commanding officer of 253/Field Company.

> *It will be remembered we were at the other end of the Suffolks' front, so to counter attack the left flank meant a considerable diagonal move across open fields. We had made some plans for*

mortar and even artillery fire in case we wanted to counter attack against the Brickworks, but this operation that we were being asked to attempt was totally different.

Desmond Harrison, the 3rd Division Chief Royal Engineer (CRE), wrote afterwards that the Suffolks were only about 250 strong and the Royal Berkshires had virtually ceased to be an effective unit and he appears, although he does not actually say so, to acknowledge the fact that the Royal Berkshires and 243/Field Company had 'bolted' in the face of a heavy German shell and mortar attack:

The next day was worse [31 May] *because 17 and 243 got a hammering with mortar and long range shelling (very accurate), and the Berks packed up at one stage for a bit, leaving a hole, which 17 and the Guards had to stretch to fill.*

What he, or for that matter anyone else except the 2/Grenadier Guards, fails to mention is that at least one man was shot by Second Lieutenant Jack Jones, 2/Grenadier Guards, and the remainder were turned around at bayonet point and led back to their positions.

This places the counter attack led by Henniker into context, an attack that went quite well to begin with, as there was little retaliatory fire coming from the enemy positions, until the Sappers had advanced 'about half the length of a football pitch', at which point a German machine gun opened fire on the advancing men. Henniker takes up the story:

I found I was the only man still standing. I shouted to the others to get up and come on and I walked across to the nearest man to see what the hell had happened. He was dead! The next one I came to was badly wounded, lying in some standing corn. ... We fired at a cluster of farm buildings where we believed the enemy to be and watched the broken tiles fall from the roof. Suddenly we saw about twenty Germans break and run from the building towards the canal to disappear from sight.

Much to the surprise of Henniker's Sappers, the counter attack had been successful, leaving him to wish he had known more about infantry tactics. After this the fighting died down as the front was again temporarily stabilised, leaving Desmond Harrison to proclaim that 'morale was beginning to drop a bit, but Henniker and 253 sat like a rock and did a lot of saving the day'.

At 7.00pm on 31 May orders were received by the Suffolks to

German machine gunners in action.

withdraw, which commenced at 9.30pm that night, the war diary noting that enemy shellfire also began about that time but that no attack was attempted. The rear party, which included two sections of Henniker's Sappers, were to take over the whole position after dark to allow the remaining officers and men to get away. Henniker wrote afterwards that he was much relieved that all his men were evacuated without further casualties being inflicted.

Furnes

There are two days during the Dunkerque evacuation that can be regarded as critical. The first of these was 29 May, a day on which Adam realised that if the Dunkerque perimeter was not adequately defended against the advancing German divisions then the initial estimate of only 45,000 men being evacuated might well become fact. Thus it was with some relief that Adam wrote that by the 'evening of the 29 May, 4th, 3rd, 50th and 1st Divisions were manning the perimeter, and the situation appeared to be in hand'.

The second crisis point came two days later, on 31 May, when German forces finally got their act together and began a concentrated effort under von Küchler and the German 18th Army to mount the final assault on the perimeter, which was still intact, although there had been no orders for II

Corps to withdraw to the beaches. Dawn brought with it a renewed vigour in German shelling all along the line of the canal and the cloud cover, that hung protectively over the beaches, showed signs of breaking up. For the battle weary and very much depleted battalions, prospects looked decidedly bleak and the 31st would be a day, to use the words of Robert Jackson, 'on which the evacuation would float or flounder'.

The touch and go situation of 29 May was no better illustrated by the arrival of 7 Guards Brigade at Furnes. Signalman George Jones, who was marching with the 1/Grenadier Guards, remembered a column of Germans approaching the town from the east:

> *At one stage, on the same march, Harry came up alongside and with a backward jerk of his head drew my attention over to our right rear. About a mile away, and out of range as far as we were concerned, a party of Germans could be seen marching and wheeling bicycles at about the same speed as our column. Friend and foe arrived in Furnes at about the same time. We took up positions on one side of the canal and most of the Germans the other.*

The defence of Furnes had been allocated to 7 Guards Brigade and, being in divisional reserve, they began their march, with C Company, 2/Middlesex, from Oostvleteren at 3.00pm on 29 May, a distance of some ten miles or so from Furnes. The route north was plagued with refugees and military traffic and was made much worse by the French 2/DLM, who were meant to be providing a protective flank to the Guards, clogging up the already congested roads. The regimental historian wrote with some disgust that the Guards' march discipline was also disrupted by intermittent shelling from German artillery!

2/Grenadier Guards

Approaching the outskirts of Furnes in the early evening, the 2/Grenadiers were greeted by Captain J Harrison, commanding Number 3 Company, who reported that the enemy had broken through, had already reached the line of the canal and that three of the reconnaissance party, led by the commanding officer, were lying in an exposed position on the canal bank. The commanding officer, Lieutenant Colonel John Lloyd, was killed instantly and two of the company commanders, Major Hercules Pakenham [HQ Company] and Captain Christopher Jeffreys [Number 4 Company], were seriously wounded. Major Rupert Colvin, the second in command, immediately drove a carrier to the scene, to find that Second Lieutenant Jack Jones, commanding the Carrier Platoon, had pulled the bodies into the cover of a nearby house. It had not been an easy task as the house was under such heavy fire that it was quite impossible for stretcher bearers to approach it. Eventually Jones, assisted by Major Robert Bushman [Number 2 Company] and the Battalion IO, Captain William Kingsmill, managed to retrieve the bodies by entering the house via a back entrance. Lloyd and Jeffreys were later buried in the close of Sint-Walburga's church and Pakenham was evacuated home, where he died of his wounds on 2 June. It had been a sharp reminder of the high cost of warfare for a battalion that had already suffered at Louvain and on the Escaut.

Furnes suffered considerable damage during the Second World War. The photograph, taken between the wars, depicts part the Grote Markt and the church of St Niklaas.

The reconnaissance of the 2/Grenadiers' positions was continued by Major Colvin, who now assumed command of the battalion and allocated his companies on the left of the town. With 8 Brigade to the north of the town and 9 Brigade to the south, the 2/Grenadiers held the central part of the town while the1/Grenadiers held the southern outskirts. The1/Coldstream were placed in reserve on the Coxyde road, having first disposed of their transport. Colvin established Battalion Headquarters in a house in the Grote-Markt and under considerable difficulties the Grenadiers occupied the houses overlooking the canal, many of which were already burning fiercely. German snipers were creeping forward amongst the ruins and the artillery bombardment seemed to be never ending and, as Signalman George Jones was later to remark, 'we saw the town of Furnes tumble about us'.

7/Field Regiment, Royal Artillery

On 29 May 7/Field Regiment arrived at its new position in the dunes near Coxyde, close to a battery of 30/Field Regiment, who were supporting the 10 Brigade battalions with harassing fire. On 30 May Lieutenant Robin Dunn was ordered to proceed to Furnes, where the 2/Grenadier Guards were asking for artillery support in dealing with German snipers on the far bank. In an article published in the *Journal of the Royal Artillery*, he wrote that Furnes was a town bisected by a canal with houses down to a road's breadth of each bank:

> *We held one bank, the Germans the other, so observation was somewhat limited. In addition we had to shoot off our maps, and the Michelin road maps, with which we had provided ourselves before the campaign, were the only ones available.*

Handicapped by the Michelin maps and adding 500 yards to his estimated range for luck, he was able to correct the aim from the first shot and then had the satisfaction of watching the house containing the snipers destroyed. Dunn had established his observation post (OP) in a private house that contained 'some passable hock and some good cigars', which, he says, 'provided some much needed fortitude'.

> *In the afternoon the Germans started shelling the town with heavier guns than we had yet the misfortune to meet. One of these demolished our house, by then we were sensibly in the cellar, but left a grandfather clock still standing, ticking obstinately in the debris. At 6pm the bombardment became very heavy, and a smoke screen was put down by the Huns on our left. We fired once again, and then again, and then reports began to filter in to Company HQ, near the OP. The company to our left had been intensively shelled, the Germans had tried to launch boats, but we had restrained them.*

The company in question was probably Number 4 Company, under the command of Captain Gerald Potter. At about 10.00pm a message was received that the Germans were attempting to bridge the canal between the Grenadiers and the Berkshires. Dunn again brought down defensive fire, but we know that the vastly under strength Berkshires withdrew the next day in the face of heavy mortar fire.

The 2/Grenadiers' war diary reports that at about 10.30am on 31 May, one section of the Carrier Platoon was sent out to fill a gap between the Suffolks and the Royal Berkshires. Second Lieutenant Jack Jones returned at 2.00pm with a sapper, who provided information that the line on the 8 Brigade front had been broken and the Germans were crossing the canal. Jones was sent to investigate:

> *When he arrived he found the Royal Berkshires and Royal* [sic] *Suffolk Regiments, accompanied by men of 246/Field Company who had been put in the line, were about to withdraw without orders. An effort was made by one of their officers to rally them but they broke under heavy enemy shellfire before they could be organised. Mr Jones found it necessary to shoot some of the men and his NCOs turned others at the point of the bayonet. However, he succeeded in restoring order and himself led the remains of both battalions and the Royal Engineers back to the line of the canal.*

There is much in this account that contradicts the versions contained in other war diaries and contemporary descriptions of the day, but seven sappers from 246/Field Company were killed on 31 May – including 23-year-old Second Lieutenant Douglas Evans. Whether these men were amongst those shot by Jones, or killed by enemy fire, is not recorded.

1/Grenadier Guards

Lieutenant Colonel John Prescott established Battalion Headquarters in Sint-Walburgapark, north of the Grote-Markt, the war diary noting that both the headquarters of the 1st and 2nd Battalions came under a heavy

The men of King's Company, 1st Grenadier Guards taken earlier in 1940.

bombardment almost immediately and it was only later the next day that an abandoned OP was found in the tower of Sint-Walburga's church. The 44-year-old Prescott was wounded slightly on 30 May returning from a Brigade conference at a farm on the Furnes-La Panne road but, with assistance from Major Charles Venables-Llewelyn, continued to command the battalion. Like their sister battalion, the 1/Grenadiers suffered heavily from enemy shelling and sniping but both Grenadier battalions were clear of Furnes by 2.30am on 1 June.

1/Coldstream Guards

Commanded by 42-year-old Lieutenant Colonel Arnold de Lèrisson Cazenove, the battalion took up its positions in reserve on the outskirts of Furnes. It was not until the afternoon of 31 May that they were called upon to take over the defences of part of the canal on their right flank. As darkness fell, Number 1 Company moved to relieve the Royal Berkshires; but before they could establish themselves the Berkshires withdrew and the Germans crossed the canal and established themselves on the canal bank. The subsequent counter attack to dislodge the enemy resulted in Major John Campbell being killed. According to the regimental historians, things now became very confused and Number 3 Company were called upon to assist in retaking the line of the canal:

> *Captain* [Cecil] *Preston made his way along the canal with Lieutenant* [Peter] *Allix to reconnoitre the position for his company; but before they had got very far both of them were shot down by enemy on the near bank, and when the commanding officer arrived with the mortar detachment he found nearly all the officers had become casualties ... He* [the commanding officer] *then put the Adjutant (Captain Walter Burns)in command of the remnants of 1 Company, and the Transport Officer (Lieutenant Graham-Clarke) in command of Number 3, and these officers succeeded in reorganizing the position.*

The casualty count was not quite over, enemy sniper and machine gun fire was still being directed at the Coldstream and 24-year-old Graham-Clarke was killed by a shot from the far bank while attacking one of the pontoon bridges. It had been a costly night for the Coldstream.

92/Field Regiment, Royal Artillery

The regiment came into action west of Bulskamp on 29 May with its two batteries of 25-pounders under the command of Lieutenant Colonel Charles Wood. Captain Richard Austin was battery captain with

The St Charles Windmill was probably 92nd Field Regiment's observation post.

368/Battery, whose guns were in position on one side of the regimental observation post - a white windmill - a feature that Austin admits was 'startlingly conspicuous'. Bombardier Ralph Wild, who worked in the regimental orderly room, remembered the farm and the white windmill:

25-pounder guns in action.

> *In the centre of the sector allotted to the regiment there was a white windmill, on each side of which the batteries were deployed ... opposite this position and a little to the right, at a distance of 4,000 yards, was the parish church of Bulskamp. Its tower was the only elevated observation post for the Germans.*

The officer sent to dispose of the church steeple was Captain Austin:

> *Just as the white windmill was our only possible OP, so the grey church of Bulskamp was the Germans. Windmill and church stood facing one another over that stretch of flat land, like a couple of sharp exclamation marks. One British and the other German ... I wasted no more time. As soon as I had measured the switch, range and angle of sight to the church I sent them down to the guns, and gave the order to fire ... up went my glasses and I saw the shells go tearing through the roof of the church. I sent down a correction ... This time I had the satisfaction of seeing two of the four shells crash into the windows at the top of the belfry. Great lumps of masonry began falling.*

The battery continued firing on Bulskamp whenever any new target appeared while 365/Battery provided supporting fire for 9 Brigade and the 50th Division by firing in support of the counter attack by the 9/Durham Light Infantry (DLI) and 1/King's Own Scottish Borderers (KOSB). On 31 May the regiment was ordered to move to a new position, in support of 151 Brigade near Leffrinckoucke, in the north eastern sector of the perimeter. On their left was 18/Field Regiment and on the right

27/Field Regiment. Ralph Wild had vivid memories of the regiment's last position:

> *Here we occupied a brickfield, which consisted of long stacks of bricks about eight feet high and eight feet wide. The vehicles were parked between the rows of bricks because there were no buildings, our office was established in a similar position.*

Today an equestrian centre has been built on the site of the brickfields, which lie to the left of the D79 on the banks of the Dunkerque-Furnes Canal. At 11.30pm on 1 June the regiment marched to Dunkerque and was evacuated the next day.

9 Brigade

On the right flank of the Guards were the three battalions of 9 Brigade or as Montgomery called them, his 'International Brigade'. Early on 30 May Major Lawe took over command of the 2/Lincolnshire Regiment from Lieutenant Colonel Newbury, who was evacuated from La Panne on 1 June. Congestion on the roads, together with the companies being dispersed over a wide area, saw the Lincolnshires being placed initially in reserve, east of Adinkerke, and the 6/DLI from the 50th Division taking over their positions along the canal until they could reorganise. Thus, the 2/Royal Ulster Rifles took over the left flank, with the 1/ KOSB on the right flank.

Officers and men of the 2nd Battalion Royal Irish Rifles being embarked from a lorry pier at Bray-Dunes. *From front to rear*: Captain Garnett, Rifleman Weir, Lieutenant St Maur Shiel, Lieutenant Sturgeon, Lieutenant Colonel Knox and Lieutenant Carberry .

On 30 May a strong enemy thrust came from Bulskamp and succeeded in forcing a wedge between the KOSB and the 9th DLI, who were on their right flank. It looked very much as the inevitable British counter attack would draw in the two battalions on either flank. Lieutenant Colonel Fergus Knox, commanding the Royal Ulster Rifles, certainly thought so, prompting him to scrawl a hasty note to Captain Ted Wilson and B Company, whose flank nestled up against the KOSB:

The KOSB have taken a kick in the pants, the Boche is across the canal on your right. Be prepared to counter attack, and Christ help you!

The KOSB war diary gives no space to the attack whatsoever and it was left to the 9/DLI war diary to provide us with an account of what took place:

D Company on the left withdrew to the line of the railway to conform with the KOSB who had been forced out of their positions by enemy infiltration. Second Lieutenant Milnes and a PSM of the KOSB remained in the Bulskamp position and engaged the enemy with a 25mm anti-tank gun, which had been abandoned. The 92nd Field Regiment brought artillery fire down on Bulskamp bridge and the farm to the southwest. A Company, less one platoon, advanced with D Company and regained the canal bank at the same time as the KOSB advanced and occupied the bank on the left of the battalions.

The 50th Division

Only two brigades of the division were deployed along the perimeter, Brigadier John Churchill's 151 Brigade, consisting of three DLI battalions, and Brigadier Cecil Haydon's 150 Brigade, made up of three Yorkshire battalions. Of these two men, Haydon was killed in action in Libya in June 1942 and Churchill distinguished himself in the newly raised commandos, surviving the war.

As we have seen, 30 May saw the 9/DLI, under the command of Lieutenant Colonel 'Jos' Percy, subjected to almost continual fire and resulted in two of Percy's companies counter attacking with the 1/KOSB to regain lost ground. On 31 May about 100 reinforcements arrived from what was left of 70 Brigade [23rd Division], which included a large contingent from 11/DLI under Captain Alan Shipley. It was a timely arrival, as that afternoon the 6th and 9th Battalions were driven back onto the 8/DLI defensive positions by the ferocity of the German attack. Just before dusk two machine gun battalions, the 4/Gordons and 2/Royal Northumberland Fusiliers, moved up and provided support across the brigade front, giving Brigadier Churchill the opportunity to reorganise his command:

He put the right of the brigade front, by now a jumble of several units of the brigade, under the command of Lieutenant Colonel Percy of the 9th DLI, the left sector under the command of Major McLaren.

It was also providential that the guns of 92/Field Regiment were close by as, from his OP near Moëres, Austin could see the enemy advancing across the flat countryside. Moments later, he writes, the phone rang requesting both batteries to begin firing on the enemy. Austin made his calculations and gave the order to fire:

Soon I had ranged and got a shell in the area. It was an impressive sight when those twenty-four guns commenced rapid fire on the fields. The shells hailed down on them, the entire ground sprouted with red-orange flashes. Of the German flanking movement I saw nothing more.

News of the successful counter attack must have come as a welcome respite to the 3/Grenadier Guards, who had been placed on immediate standby to regain the lost ground if required. Major Allan Adair, commanding the Grenadiers, had even been forward with his company commanders to reconnoitre the ground, which, he discovered, was flat and intersected by dykes:

All that night and the following morning they waited in suspense but when the order came, it was not to counter attack but to fill a gap that had opened between 151 Brigade and the 9th DLI. The battalion were rushed forward in some lorries which had escaped the almost universal destruction of transport, and were in their position – at last – by dusk. They sent out their patrols in the dark, but the enemy did not attack.

151 Brigade

Major Ross McLaren had been in command of the 8/DLI since 21 May, when Lieutenant Colonel Tim Beart was wounded at Warlus, near Arras. He, along with Lieutenant Colonel Harry Miller, commanding the 6/DLI, and Jos Percy, commanding the 9th, established their headquarters at the Château Sint-Flora on Kasteellaan, two miles north east of Houthem, which by now was suffering under an enemy artillery bombardment:

Casualties came in fast and the familiar cry of 'stretcher bearers' became frequent. Lieutenant Wilkinson, the 8/DLI Medical Officer and Captain Rutherford, the Medical Officer of the 9/DLI, established a joint Regimental Aid Post in the cellars of the château, which was soon blazing above their heads. Assisted by the redoubtable Padre Duggan they did some excellent work. Throughout the afternoon the figures of the Padre and Corporal

The Château Sint-Flora was the temporary headquarters of the 8th and 9th DLI .

> *Fletcher could be seen wherever the shelling and casualties were heaviest. Journey after journey was made by the two men to carry in the wounded to the cellars of the château, where the Padre's cheerful humour was like a tonic to the long lines of men who lay on the floor waiting to be evacuated.*

At 2.30am on 1 June the 'Durham Brigade' was ordered to break contact with the Germans on the Ringsloot Canal and, covered by the carrier platoon of the 8/DLI, withdrew north. McLaren reported that he temporarily lost his way and fell into a ditch, getting soaked in the process!

150 Brigade

The 4/Green Howards received their orders to withdraw from Poperinghe at 9.00pm on 29 May. Apart from losing contact with the Medical Officer's convoy and about 100 other ranks, the remainder of the battalion moved forward to fill a gap between the 1/Duke of Wellington's and the 5/Green Howards. The battalion's right flank lay exactly on the border between Belgium and France, with the left flank on Canal Bridge at Houthem, a distance of some two miles, which, with only fifteen officers and 292 men, gave Lieutenant Colonel Charles Littleboy some anxious moments.

The 5/Green Howards, under the command of Lieutenant Colonel William Bush, were positioned on the left of their sister battalion with seventeen officers and 516 men. Bush established Battalion Headquarters in a large white château:

> *... in front of which strutted a peacock, whose raucous cries grated on the already tangled nerves of the defenders – so much so, in fact, that Captain Allen, RAMC, shot it with an airgun.*

Two attempts were made on the evening of 30 May to break through the battalion's positions, both were repulsed. The next day the Germans attacked on both sides of the 4/Green Howards, which again was repulsed with few casualties. Second Lieutenant Peter Kirby, the Battalion Intelligence Officer, described the attack as well coordinated:

> *The forward companies came in for some shelling and mortaring but because they were well dug in they were able to take their toll of the attacking enemy with well aimed rifle fire. It was B Echelon which got the worst of the shellfire. The Motor Transport Officer continually moved the transport but they were frequently shelled out of their new positions. Fortunately no transport was lost.*

Not content with these attacks, the next onslaught fell on the 4th Battalion Headquarters in the form of heavy shellfire and, as casualties mounted, a German spotter plane flew across the British lines, relaying information back to Houthem church spire. Fortunately, both battalions were out of the line soon after midnight on 31 May and withdrew to a bivouac area astride the Adinkerke-Dunkerque road.

The 4/East Yorkshires left Ypres at 3.00am on 29 May, arriving at Houthem at 10.00pm that evening, where they dug in along the canal. The 30 May saw their positions continually mortared and, apart from one attack mentioned in the regimental history, they appear to have been withdrawn to Bray-Dunes on the night of 1 June. At 11.30pm on 2 June the battalion marched to Dunkerque, from where they were evacuated.

The remaining units of the 50th Division were placed under the orders of the 1st Division on 31 May and deployed to a new position behind the French 12th Division near Bray-Dunes. They were eventually embarked on 1/2 June.

Chapter 5

Defending the Perimeter – III Corps

On 9 April 1940 III Corps came into being with the arrival in France of the 42nd Division, under 48-year-old Major General William Holmes, and the 44th Division, under Major General Edmund Osborne. Overall command was the preserve of 55-year-old Lieutenant General Sir Robert Adam. On 26 May, Adam was instructed to hand over command of III Corps to Major General Sidney Wason, who until that point had been the Major General Royal Artillery on Gort's staff. The choice of Wason raised some concerns and one would have thought Major General Thomas Eastwood, who was senior to Wason, would have been a better choice, particularly as he already had experience of command under fire. Although Wason had an excellent record for bravery in the First World War, he had no experience of commanding such a large formation and certainly had little knowledge of what was occurring on the III Corps front. For example, Wason's handling of the 2nd Division in the latter stages of the campaign has been criticised, raising the question why the 2nd Division did not withdraw north of the Lys Canal earlier than 27 May. See the Battleground Europe title: *The Canal Line 1940*.

Many historians feel the answer lies in the two days spent by Wason attempting to coordinate his plans for the withdrawal into the Dunkerque Perimeter. Certainly Wason did not manage any contact with his divisional commanders until shortly before they were evacuated but, more to the point, Irwin, recently promoted from command of 6 Brigade, without a corps commander to confer with, may possibly have felt he was exceeding his authority to order a withdrawal. Had he done so then the 2nd Division would perhaps not have been needlessly sacrificed and been in a better position to defend the perimeter.

The sector of the perimeter allocated to III Corps ran along the Canal de Bergues from Dunkerque to a line running south-north from Warham to the coast. Wason established III Corps Headquarters on 28 May, first at Téteghem, and then at a large farm some 300 yards south of the village. As the III Corps battalions withdrew north, it became apparent there was some considerable disarray, particularly amongst the 2nd and 44th Divisions, and it was left to the French to defend the III Corps perimeter until such a time as Wason's divisions could take it over. In the event, the

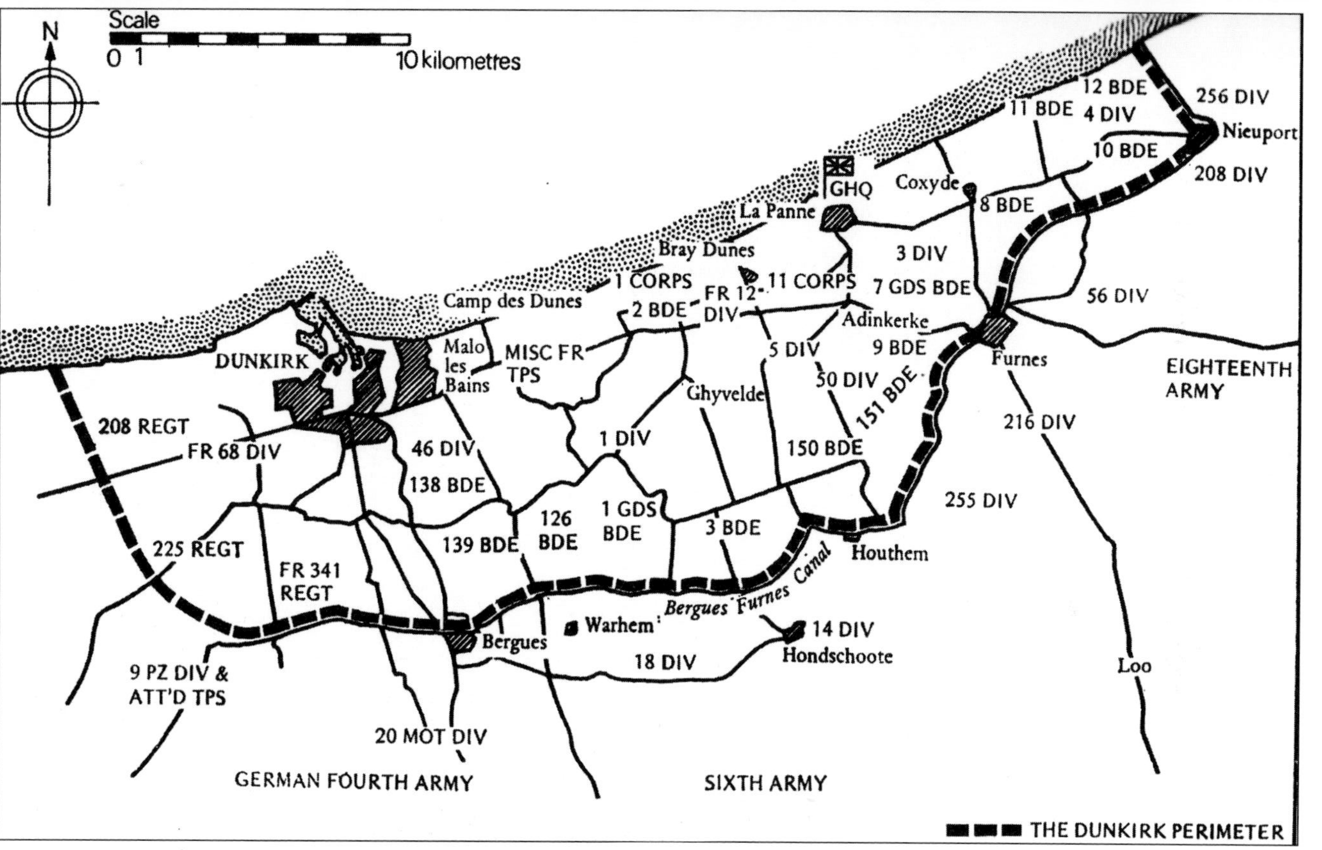

The Dunkerque perimeter on 30 May, depicting the British, French and German forces.

only troops Wason could put into his sector of the perimeter were two very under strength battalions of the 46th Division, one platoon of the Cameron Highlanders under Lieutenant Laurie and a remnant of the 2/Dorsets from the 2nd Division. Opportunely, at midday on 30 May, III Corps were ordered to withdraw and I Corps took over the perimeter from their left to the Belgian frontier.

The 2nd Division

Major General Noel Irwin's 2nd Division came under III Corps command on 26 May. The division was a shadow of its former self and struggled to muster enough officers and men to man its allocated sector on the perimeter. During their stand along some twenty miles of the La Bassée Canal, it is difficult to decide which of the three brigades suffered the most, but of the ninety officers and 2,480 other ranks of 4 Brigade, that had advanced into Belgium on 10 May, only twenty-five officers and 697 other ranks mustered on 15 June to reform the brigade. A single stark sentence in the brigade war diary recorded that, 'no commanding officer, 2nd in command, adjutant, nor any forward company commander of the three battalions, appeared from amongst the stragglers'. It was also from 4 Brigade that ninety-seven men of the 2/Royal Norfolks were murdered on 27 May at Louis Creton's farm, an atrocity that would remain largely unknown until after the war. What was left of the Norfolks were evacuated from Dunkerque on 29 May, along with 134 officers and men of the 1/Royal Scots. Of the 7/Worcesters in 5 Brigade, only about 400 officers and men made it to Dunkerque. The Worcesters' war diary gives us some impression of the confusion that reigned:

Major General Noel Irwin was promoted to command the 2nd Division on 20 May 1940.

> *Unsuccessful efforts were made to contact Headquarters, 2 Division, and instead advice from 1 Division was forthcoming which amounted to 'keep going.' The message from Brigade, scribbled hastily across three pages of a small note-book, made no mention of Dunkirk. On reaching the rendezvous, 1 Division H.Q. were able to direct the party on to Dunkirk. On reaching the suburbs of Dunkirk on the evening of 30th May, the Area Commandant was anxious to get the small party away as soon as possible owing to the food shortage; and the final stage was an*

anti-climax in which the remnants of 7th Worcestershire on 31st May walked along the sea wall and waited for the first boat to come in. Then with simple formality they stepped aboard and were soon away from the coast of France.

The 1/Cameron Highlanders, who had fought alongside the Worcesters, suffered very badly and only about a hundred officers and men made it to Dunkerque, where they were evacuated on 30 May. The 2/Dorsets, who marched out of Festubert under the noses of the surrounding Germans, after a short spell on the perimeter were also evacuated on 30 May.

Even less of the 2/Durham Light Infantry and the 1/Royal Welch Fusiliers in 6 Brigade were able to escape from their heroic stand at St-Venant. Barely five officers and 240 other ranks of the Welch Fusiliers assembled on the beaches with the Durham Light Infantry, both battalions without their commanding officers:

All that remained of the Durhams - the survivors of D Company, the transport carriers and the men of B Echelon, together with odd stragglers – came together in due course under the Quartermaster, on the Hazebrouck side of the canal running behind St-Venant. They were joined by what was left of 6 Brigade to continue the retreat and embark from Dunkirk some two days later.

25 Brigade

The three battalions of 25 Brigade were under the command of 52-year-old Brigadier William Ramsden. The brigade was an independent brigade; between arriving on the La Bassée Canal and the Dunkerque evacuation, it was variously assigned to a succession of infantry divisions, causing some irritation amongst battalion commanders who were, at times, unsure of the division to which they were attached. On 23 May the brigade became part of Polforce and was given the task of holding Béthune and the six miles of canal linking Béthune with La Bassée. Three days later, as the 1/7 Queen's historian noted, on the morning of 26 May 25 Brigade was definitely placed under the orders of the 2nd Division, but for a short time there 'seemed to be some doubt as to what formation actually commanded the 25th Brigade'. Accordingly, on 29 May the 1/Royal Irish Fusiliers, under the command of Lieutenant Colonel Guy Gough, arrived at Bergues under the III Corps flag, where they were told to proceed to Dunkerque and embark. Gough's account reveals the extent to which Brigadier Ramsden went to have his brigade usefully employed:

The 1st Battalion Royal Irish Fusiliers.

> *However, the brigade commander was not satisfied that we could not be of use and might not be required for temporary local defence. Therefore, he told the CO* [Gough] *to go off to try to find Corps HQ, while he himself endeavoured to find HQ 2nd Division to get further instructions.*

One cannot help but ask why the three battalions of 25 Brigade were not more usefully placed in defending the perimeter, and it is tempting to lay blame at the feet of Wason. However, in mitigation, the confusion and fog of war that existed at the time probably has much to do with the apparent misdirection of 25 Brigade. After being passed from pillar to post, Gough and his battalion gave up their attempts to be redeployed and were embarked for England on 30 May. The 1/7 Queen's were told to proceed to Dunkerque independently by companies; Lieutenant Colonel Gerald Pilleau only managed to collect about 150 officers and men on 30 May, the remainder of the battalion being embarked over the next few days. The battalion had been fortunate in that their casualties only amounted to six officers and men killed, forty wounded and forty-seven missing, which was slightly more than the 2/Essex, who left their

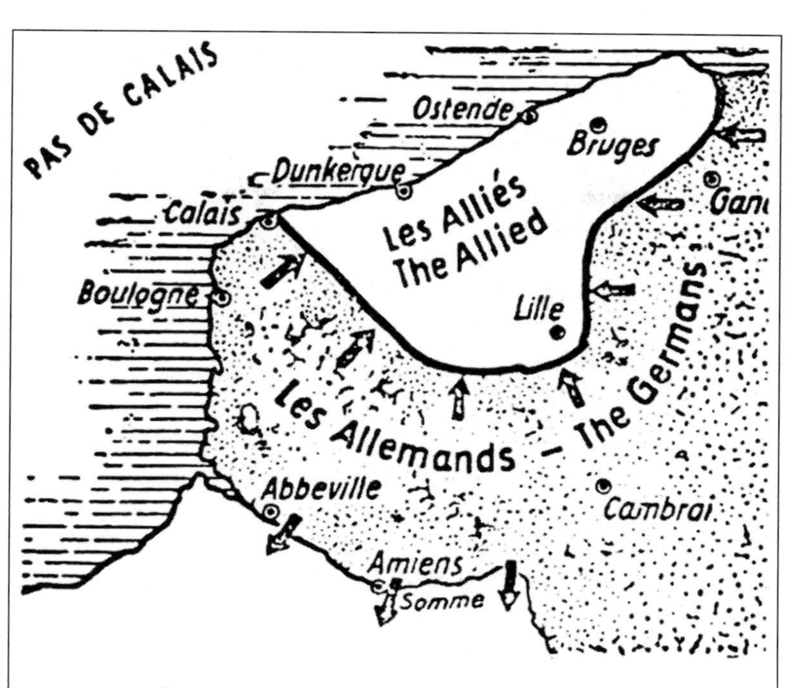

Camarades!

Telle est la situation!
En tout cas, la guerre est finie pour vous!
Vos chefs vont s'enfuir par avion.
A bas les armes!

British Soldiers!

Look at this map: it gives your true situation!
Your troops are entirely surrounded —
stop fighting!
Put down your arms!

A copy of the leaflet that was dropped by the Germans calling for the British to surrender.

positions along the Deûle Canal on 25 May. The battalion reported two officers and men killed, nineteen wounded and fifty-three men missing and embarked for Dover aboard HMS *Whitehall* on 30 May.

The 23rd Division

Major General William Herbert's 23rd Division also came under III Corps command after being released from its duties with Thomas Eastwood's 'Rustyforce'. This was an untrained Territorial division of only two brigades, which had been employed on airfield construction duties. On 20 May 70 Brigade had been all but annihilated at Arras by the 8th Panzer Division.

69 Brigade had been ordered to move north to Gravelines and deploy along the right bank of the River Aa at Gravelines. However, reports of German panzers in or near Hazebrouck and enemy air activity along the road leading north, resulted in the convoy being turned back at Estaires after a frantic search by divisional staff officers. In the event, only 6/Green Howards made it to Gravelines on 23 May, along with Advanced Divisional Headquarters. Their sister battalion, 7/Green Howards, returned to Gondecourt and then moved north towards Furnes:

> *They had only proceeded about three miles, however, when it was ordered to destroy all its transport. The remainder of the journey was completed on foot, and the night was spent close to the road and rail junction just north of Bulskamp. The next morning the troops breakfasted off tinned rations and chocolate obtained from abandoned French transport, and in the afternoon moved to Les Moëres, where they got into contact with the 5/Green Howards* [50th Division, who were in position along the canal]. *Their role was to relieve the 5/Green Howards of all manual labour.*

It was a task they never began, as during the night of 30 May they were ordered to Bray-Dunes, embarking eventually from Dunkerque at 7.00pm on 31 May. The 6th Battalion began their march back to Bray-Dunes at 9.00pm on 29 May and embarked on the *Lady of Man* on 31 May. It was a similar story with the 5/East Yorkshires, another 69 Brigade battalion, who had also been largely employed on airfield construction duties. Their move north from Thélus via Poperinghe culminated at Adinkerke, from where orders were received at 2.00am on 31 May to march to Bray-Dunes.

The 44th Division

Wason's absence certainly had a detrimental effect on Major General Osborne's 44th Division, where a guiding hand would have been much

Units of the German army were continually pushing forward after the retreating BEF.

appreciated. Having suffered almost continual contact with the enemy since their withdrawal from the Escaut, the remnants of the division arrived at Mont des Cats. With 65/Field Regiment – without their guns – 57/Anti Tank Regiment and a battery of 5/Royal Horse Artillery, together with Queen's Own Royal West Kents and 4 and 5/Royal Sussex, the monastery and its enclosure was crammed with men and transport. Quite why Osborne intended that the division would make a stand on Mont des Cats is beyond belief but, fortunately, the heavy artillery fire and airborne assault that greeted the division on 29 May was enough to convince everyone that the position had to be abandoned. The experience of 57/Anti Tank Regiment was one that was shared by every officer and man on the hill:

> *As soon as it became daylight the position revealed itself as a high isolated hill visible for miles and thick with troops. The Germans started at once to attack with artillery and mortars, followed later by intensive dive bombing, which clearly heralded a ground attack ... Shortly before 10.00am the troops started to move out in two columns, shelled but not molested by the enemy, and with orders to make their way, via Poperinghe, to the beaches.*

The BEF were constantly harassed by flights of Stukas, highlighting the cooperation between German ground forces and the *Luftwaffe.*

Luck was very definitely on Osborne's side as, incredibly, the 6th Panzer Division, situated between the division and Dunkerque, failed in its bid to cut off his men on their march to the beaches. The German division had been reportedly on the frontier by 28 May but appear to have been thwarted by French troops at Steenvoorde and by Prioux's Cavalry Corps covering the retreat of the French III Corps. Whether Wason was fully aware of the difficulties surrounding the 44th Division is not clear, but by his absence he effectively transferred all decision making to Osborne, who by this time was under the most enormous stress. Nevertheless, Wason's account does provide some explanation as to the circumstances of his absence, and any failings on his behalf can perhaps be attributed to his inability promptly to grasp the strategic situation facing III Corps. The final communication from GHQ arrived on 29 May:

> *They were to the effect that III Corps were to hand over their sector to I Corps at noon on 30 May, that 2 and 46 Divisions were to proceed for embarkation, that 44 Division would embark in the next phase and that III Corps HQ was to embark on the afternoon or evening of 30 May .... Owing, however, to the late arrival and great disorganisation of 44 Division, I decided to change 44 and 46 Divisions around and to send 44 Division back first and 46 Division last.*

What Wason fails to mention is that the 46th Division was retained at Dunkerque and came under the orders of I Corps on 30 May, but by that time he was probably on his way across the channel.

Amongst the first units of the 44th Division to arrive at Dunkerque early in the evening of 29 May were the men of 1/West Kents under Major Lovell. Organised control had become all but impossible from the moment the brigade left Mont des Cats and the brigade split into smaller parties as they joined the stream heading for the coast. On the beaches the officers of 132 Brigade gathered together what men could be found and large numbers were evacuated from Malo-lés-Bains on 29 May. The 2/Royal Sussex had been placed under the command of 132 Brigade on 27 May and were also evacuated on 29 May. The battalion, which had been hit hard near Hazebrouck, arrived at Dunkerque with just three officers and a hundred other ranks. Embarkation began again at dawn the next morning under the cover of a slight mist: about 150 officers and men were taken off from the Mole, while others were evacuated from the beaches. It was not until 31 May that the whole brigade had finally left France. The number of casualties sustained by 132 Brigade during the

The look of relief on the faces of these soldiers is plain to see as they disembark in England.

HMS *Malcolm* made eight trips between Dunkerque and England, rescuing over 3,000 troops, including elements of the 1/6 Queens Royal Regiment.

last thirteen days of the campaign was approximately half of the 2,400 officers and men who had first gone into action. Hardest hit were the 4/West Kents, who embarked on the SS *Dorien Rose* on 30 May with their commanding officer, Lieutenant Colonel Arthur Chitty. At a roll call on 19 June the battalion could only muster 381 officers and men.

The first parties of 131 Brigade to turn up were the 1/6 Queen's Royal Regiment, who arrived at 4.00pm on 29 May and were embarked the next morning aboard HMS *Malcolm*. The 1/5 Queen's Royal Regiment spent 30 May at Malo-lés-Bains and left aboard HMS *Excellent* the next evening at 10.00pm. The 2/Buffs arrived in small groups late on 29 May - without their commanding officer - who had been taken prisoner earlier that day. The 50-year-old Lieutenant Colonel George Hamilton had been wounded twice in the previous war and was captured as the battalion withdrew from Mont des Cats. The battalion war diary gives little away regarding their march to the beaches, merely noting that some men spent as much as two days before getting aboard a ship.

Of the two remaining Royal Sussex battalions in 133 Brigade, The 5/Royal Sussex managed to leave in two parties, the first at 4.30 pm on 30 May and the second three hours later at 7.30pm. It was a sad fact that between the two groups they could only muster a total of sixteen officers and 150 other ranks.

Chapter 6

Defending the Perimeter – I Corps

As previously mentioned, I Corps arrived in France in 1939 under the command of 58-year-old Lieutenant General Sir John Dill who, after being ordered home on 21 April 1940 to become Vice CIGS, was replaced in France by the newly promoted 55-year-old Lieutenant General Michael Barker. The news of his appointment was one that prompted Montgomery to remark that only a madman would give a corps to Barker. Unfortunately, it was a prediction that proved to be largely true, as Barker was already exhibiting signs of the strain of command during the early part of the campaign. His downfall came on 30 May, largely at the hands of Montgomery.

The I Corps sector of the Perimeter ran initially from Warhem to the Franco-Belgian border. After the withdrawal of III Corps to the beaches, which was largely completed by midday on 30 May, the defence of the Perimeter was split between I Corps and II Corps. As II Corps evacuated the area east of the Franco–Belgian border, the remaining Perimeter became the preserve of I Corps. It was a plan that worked well on paper and worked remarkably well in practice. Consequently, at approximately 12.00 midday on 30 May I Corps took over the defence of the Perimeter from Bergues to the Franco-Belgian frontier and the next day Alexander moved I Corps Headquarters to Rosendael. It should be remembered that, although I Corps had taken over the Perimeter defences, there were still men from II Corps – and indeed from III Corps - waiting on the beaches for ships to take them to England, a process we will examine further in Chapter 7.

All that remained of the BEF defending the Perimeter by the evening of 1 June were seven brigades of infantry along with one medium and six field regiments of artillery, under the overall command of Major General Alexander. We know from Chapter 3 the circumstances surrounding Alexander's appointment as commander of I Corps, an appointment that was to open a Pandora's Box of difficulties for the man who was to command the BEF rearguard. The seven brigades of infantry available to Alexander comprised:

- 139 Brigade, 46th Division (2/5 Leicesters, 2/5 and 9/Sherwood Foresters)

Sir John Dill (seated) with Major General Horace Alexander on the left, Major General Charles Lloyd and Major General Andrew Thorne.

- 138 Brigade, 46th Division (6/Lincolns and 6/York and Lancaster)
- The 1/Loyals from 2 Brigade, 1st Division
- C Company, 2/Royal Warwicks, from 144 Brigade, 48th Division
- 126 Brigade, 42nd Division (1/East Lancashire, 5/King's Own and 5/Border Regiment)
- The 1/Guards Brigade, 1st Division (2/Coldstream and 2/Hampshire)
- 3 Brigade, 1st Division (1/Duke of Wellingtons, 2/Sherwood Foresters and 1/King's Own Shropshire Light Infantry)
- 150 Brigade (4 and 5/Green Howards) and 151 Brigade (6, 8 and 9/Durham Light Infantry), from 50th Division
- The French 12th Division

The 46th Division came under I Corps command on 30 May and were joined a day later by the 5th and 50th Divisions, delaying the 50th Division's embarkation and moving them to hold a sector of the eastern edge of the Perimeter behind the French 12th Division. However, by 1 June the 5th Division, which had been reduced to little more than a brigade, had been withdrawn for evacuation. Armoured support was provided by a composite regiment of the 4/7 Dragoon Guards and two squadrons of the 5/Inniskilling Dragoon Guards.

1/ Duke of Wellington's Regiment

Lieutenant Colonel Edmund Beard, seen here as a major general.

The 1st Battalion Duke of Wellingtons' (1/Dukes), under the command of Lieutenant Colonel Edmund Beard, had fought with 3 Brigade, 1st Division, from the Dyle to their arrival at Les Moëres on 27 May. Early the next morning the companies were deployed along a 5,000 yard frontage: A and B Companies were amalgamated and placed under the command of Captain Terence Carroll, taking up positions on the north side of the canal; C Company - Captain Waller - occupied the area surrounding the bridge at Pont aux Cerfs, while D Company was held in reserve at the crossroads immediately east of Les Moëres. Battalion Headquarters was established at a farm on the narrow Chemin Vicinal

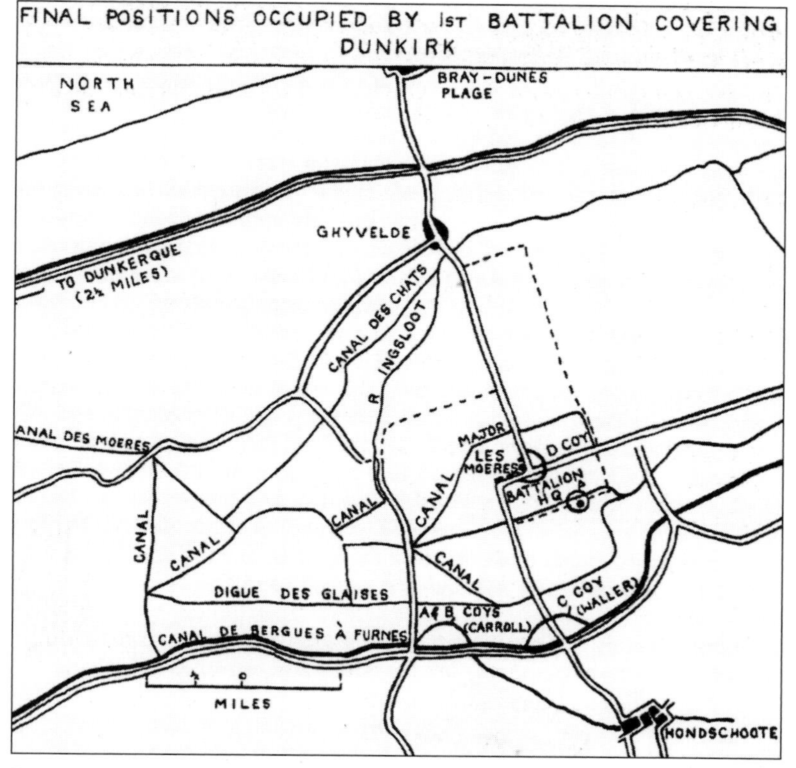

The positions occupied by the 1st Battalion Duke of Wellington's Regiment in late May 1940.

N1 dit de l'Octogne, and quickly named 'The Piggery' after the large number of pigs that ran in all directions whenever anyone moved. Needless to say the battalion cooks produced a number of fine meals!

On the battalion's left flank were the 4/Green Howards, while on the right were the 1 Guards Brigade. All three battalions suffered from poor fields of fire caused by the abandoned vehicles on a road running along the far side of the canal. Despite several of these vehicles and some buildings that butted onto the canal being demolished, the field of fire remained inadequate. As the whole front exploded with enemy shellfire, German infantry began to cross the canal under the cover of the bombardment, but it was to no avail. The disciplined Dukes were well dug in and, armed with an abnormally large number of Bren guns, which they had picked up en-route, ensured any Germans that reached the British side of the canal did not live to tell the tale.

It was about this time during the afternoon of the 30 May that it was observed the level of the surrounding dykes was rising rapidly and the troops were soon lying in water with the enemy on the dry higher land. At dawn on 31 May C Company were withdrawn and a flank guard formed under Major Norman Temple of the 2/Sherwood Foresters. Expecting trouble, the bridge at Pont aux Cerfs was blown at 11.00am on 30 May, with the anticipated attack coming three hours later, just when Lieutenant Colonel Beard and the battalion Intelligence Officer were visiting C Company, Foresters. His unit comprised about seven platoons from the 1/King's Own, the 2/Foresters and the 5/Cheshires and, for the short time it was active, became known as Temple Force. Temple died of wounds after being shot by a German sniper on 1 June and command was assumed by Major Wathen.

The almost continual enemy bombardment was having a detrimental effect on the Dukes and wounded in large numbers began arriving at the Regimental Aid Post, where the battalion medical officer, Captain Cullen, was crawling about amidst the shellfire, dressing wounds and administering morphine. Back on the Furnes-Dunkerque Canal, rising water and enemy incursions forced a withdrawal at dusk on 31 May to the line of the Ringsloot Canal, in the hope that the inundations would slow any enemy advance. But, despite this move, the situation on the left flank was now causing considerable anxiety, especially as Major Wathen reported a continuous stream of German infantry moving northwest along the railway line. Just as all ranks had resigned themselves to a last stand amidst the flooded fields, orders arrived at 7.00pm on 1 June for a dusk withdrawal to Bray-Dunes, a move they accomplished under cover of an artillery bombardment, courtesy of 19/Field Regiment.

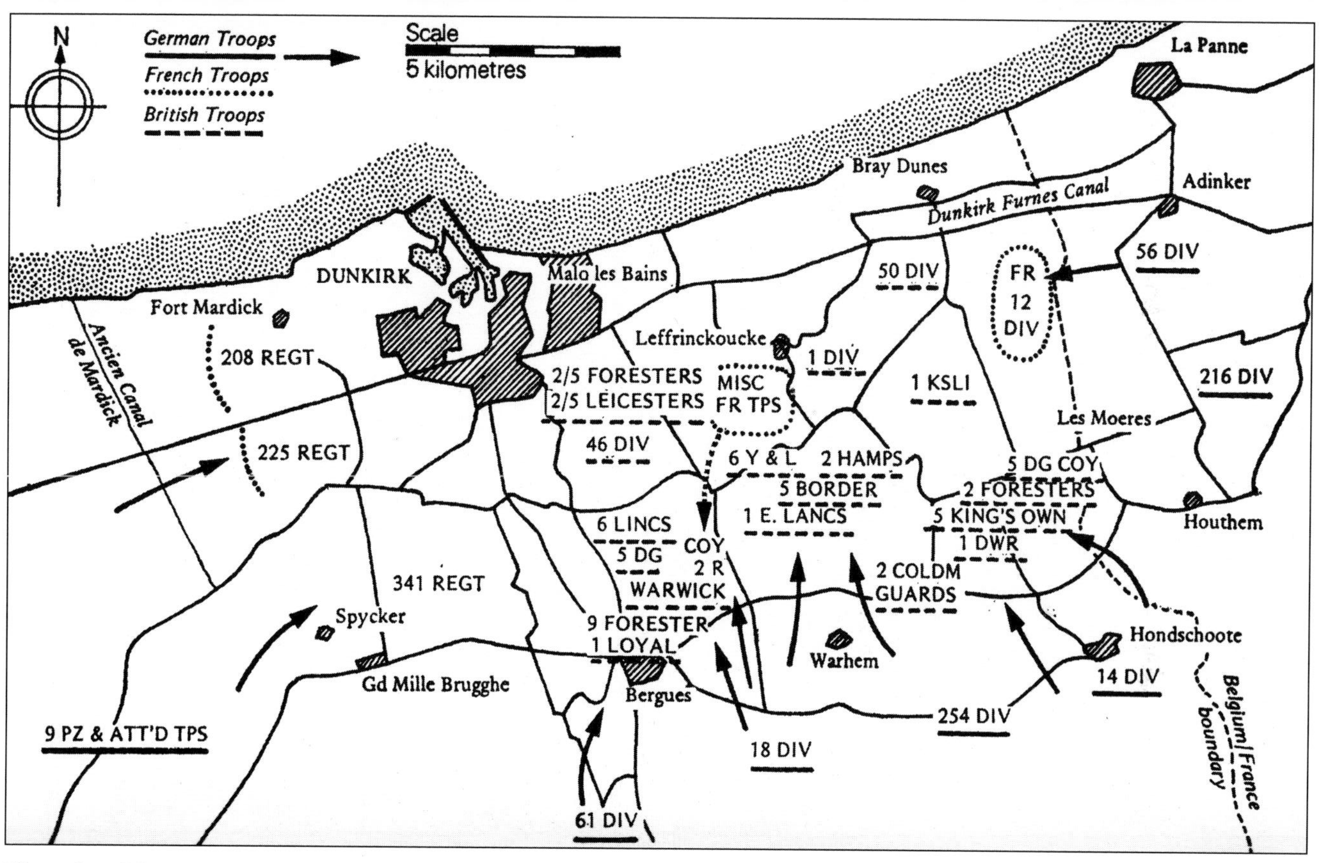

The reduced Dunkerkqe Perimeter after the II Corps sector had been abandoned.

19/Field Regiment, Royal Artillery

The Regiment holds the honour of being the first unit of artillery to open fire on the enemy while deployed on the Maginot Line on 6 May 1940. 29/Battery, commanded by 33-year-old Major Charles Crawford, had supported the 1/Dukes since the BEF first went into action on the Dyle. Crawford was at the Dukes' Headquarters during the enemy bombardment of 1 June:

> *Their HQ was by now a shambles – some 200 hopelessly wounded officers and men, many of whom were lying in the garden of the château* [sic]. *The Boche were within 200 yards and their mortars never ceased shooting at us. The Colonel, the Doctor and the Adjutant stand out in my mind for their heroism ... The Dukes had been selected by their brigadier to stay until 8.30pm and if necessary fight to the last man. The other battalions were to leave sooner. I promised the Colonel to stay until 10.pm and shoot like hell from 8.10pm. I then left to tell my own colonel of the contract. He at once agreed and told me to meet him at the Blériot Memorial* [sic] *on the Dunkerque promenade when I had embarked the battery.*

Crawford writes that his battery remained at their post until 10.15pm, 'firing for all they were worth', at which point they destroyed their guns and set off for the beach in lorries. It appears from his account that he failed to meet his Colonel at the Blériot Memorial [it was in fact the memorial to the First World War flying ace, Georges Guynemer] but did manage to see 29/Battery embarked from the beach at Bray-Dunes. We shall hear more from Crawford in Chapter 8.

2/Coldstream Guards

There is a story told by Lieutenant Jimmy Langley [Number 3 Company] in which he mentions a visit by Brigadier Beckwith-Smith. The battalion was resting north of Poperinghe and had already been informed that the evacuation was taking place when Beckwith-Smith arrived in his staff car:

> *'Marvellous news Jimmy' he shouted. 'The best ever!' Short of the German army deciding to call it a day, which seemed improbable, I could think of no news deserving the qualifications of 'marvellous and the 'best ever!'.*
>
> *'It is splendid, absolutely splendid. We have been given the supreme honour of being the rearguard at Dunkirk. Tell your platoon, Jimmy – come on, tell them the good news.'*

German soldiers at the Guynemer Memorial at Malo-lés-Bains. Major Crawford and others incorrectly refer to it as the Blériot Memorial, which was dismantled in 1941 from its site on the promenade.

Langley's reply was to suggest to his 50-year-old brigade commander that they would undoubtedly appreciate hearing the news from the Brigadier himself. Whether this news was greeted with enthusiasm by all the assembled men remains unknown, but at least the Guards knew they would be amongst the last to leave, if indeed they were able to leave at all! The ever enthusiastic Beckwith-Smith went on to command the 18th Division and died in November 1942 of diptheria at Karenco PoW Camp in Taiwan.

Brigadier Merton Beckwith-Smith.

The 2/Coldstream was commanded by 44-year-old Lieutenant Colonel Lionel Bootle-Wilbraham who, apart from a short spell with the Hampshire Regiment, served with the Coldstream Guards almost continuously from 1915 until he retired in 1949. They arrived on the canal on 29 May, Bootle-Wilbraham recording the deployment in his diary:

> *On our right was a North-Country regiment, recently arrived from England and on our left was the 3rd Infantry Brigade. The Grenadiers had left the 1st Guards Brigade and had been transferred to the 5th Division ... We had a front of 2,200 yards to cover with two important approaches and bridges over the canal. No. 1 Company was on the right, No.3 Company right centre, No.2 Company left centre and No. 4 Company on the left. Battalion Headquarters were badly placed in a little farmhouse to the south of the windmill at Krommelhouck.*

The 2,200 yards that the Coldstream had to cover represented the whole of the frontage allocated to the 1 Guards Brigade. It will be remembered from Chapter 4 that the 3/Grenadier Guards had been diverted to fill a gap in the 50th Divisional line while the Hampshires were placed in reserve near Uxem. Until Captain Raoul Robin, the Battalion Intelligence Officer, returned on 30 May from defending a bridge near Houthem with Headquarters Company and most of the Signal Platoon, the battalion had little more than 200 officers and men to cover their frontage. It was with some relief that Bootle-Wilbraham recorded the return of his men, together with two officers and 120 men of the Lancashire Fusiliers as reinforcement, but his comments regarding the retreating British forces are typical of a Guards' officer:

> *All day long British and French troops straggled over the bridges into the perimeter. Two platoons of the Welsh Guards were the only units who marched across in formation, looking like Guardsmen and remarkably clean and well turned out in comparison with the rabble which was shuffling along the roads ... The men were cheerful, if weary. It did us good to see them.*

That evening both bridges over the canal were blown, which added an explosive content to the burning vehicles on the far bank of the canal.

It was when the Hampshires were withdrawn to a rear position on the afternoon of 30 May, that the Coldstream finally resigned themselves to fighting it out until the bitter end, a prospect that became all the more real when Captain Evan Gibbs reported the arrival of German infantry opposite Number 1 Company. Fortunately, the encounter did little more than give the enemy positions away, but it was a prelude of what was to come. The next day, as the inundations became more apparent, the water rose into an almost continuous sheet on either side of the road, German shelling forced Battalion Headquarters to move from the windmill and the order came through that all specialist and non-combat personnel were to report to the beaches. It was a bombardment that became 'troublesome' on the morning of 31 May, with several men killed and wounded. The day was also marked by the news that Bootle-Wilbraham was to take over command of the Brigade on the temporary promotion of Beckwith-Smith to divisional commander. Command of the Coldstream was devolved to Major 'Bunty' Stewart-Brown.

A cartoon drawn by Guardsman Kingshott in 1939 of Jimmy Langley and Angus McCorquodale.

Significant action did not really begin until 1 June when the Coldstream position was severely compromised by the unit on its right flank withdrawing, thus exposing Number 1 Company's right flank to the enemy. This flank was protected by the 5/Border Regiment, a territorial unit that was having a bad time under German shelling. The incident was recorded by Jimmy Langley, whose company commander was Major Angus McCorquodale:

> *Our gossip was interrupted by a visitor who introduced himself as the captain commanding the company on Number 1 Company's right, and said he had been sent over by Evan Gibbs. He informed us that the Germans were massing for an attack on the bridgehead, that his men were exhausted and he proposed to withdraw while the going was good. Angus merely said 'I order you to stay put and fight it out.*

The conversation ended with a furious Angus McCorquodale ordering Jimmy Langley to shoot any officer or man that was seen to withdraw:

> *'Get a rifle,' Angus ordered me, picking one up that was lying nearby. When I returned with mine he said 'Sights at 250. You will shoot to kill the moment he passes that tree. Are you clear?' We had not long to wait before the captain appeared, followed by two*

men. They stood for a long time by the tree and then the captain walked on. Both our rifles went off simultaneously.

Whether anyone was killed is not said but, if they were, it was the second time that a British officer was alleged to have been shot during the campaign for failing to carry out his duty, although the CWGC Database has no officer of the 5/Border Regiment recorded as killed between 31 May and 1 June 1940.

Later in the day the enemy crossed the canal, forcing Number 1 Company back onto Langley's position; Captain Evan Gibbs was killed in the process, along with Lieutenant Charles Blackwell and Ronnie Speed. Langley's memory of the battle is rather disjointed but he does remember firing from the attic of the canal side cottage where they were based into the mass of German infantry who were advancing along the road. After setting three lorries on fire, his next memory was a 'most frightful crash and a great wave of heat, dust and debris' knocking him over. A shell had hit the roof:

There was a long silence and I heard a small voice saying 'I've been hit,' which I suddenly realized was mine. That couldn't be right; so I called out, 'Anybody been hit?' A reply from behind – 'No sir, we are alright.' 'Well,' I replied more firmly, 'I have.' No pain, just a useless left arm, which looked very silly, and blood all over my battledress.

Captain Jack Bowman, the Battalion MT Officer, managed to extract the remnants of Numbers 1 and 3 Company and the battalion withdrew under the cover of darkness. Langley was evacuated in a wheelbarrow but unfortunately was refused a passage home owing to the severity of his wounds. He later escaped, minus his left arm, which had been amputated at Zuydcoote. Details of the battle reached Lionel Bootle-Wilbraham whilst he was still at Brigade Headquarters:

The Germans had outflanked No. 1 Company, having got across the canal where our neighbours had abandoned their positions. The three officers of the company had been killed ... The warrant officers and senior NCOs had been killed, including CSM Dance and Sgt Hardwick; and the leaderless company had been forced back on to No.3 Company. The men had been rallied by the officers of No.3, which had been outflanked. Angus had been killed when his bit of trench had been enfiladed.

The 35-year-old McCorquodale, whose brother married Barbara Cartland in 1936, was killed about the same time as Langley was hit. Few of the battalion got away that night and those that did were taken aboard HMS *Sabre* on the night of 2 June, leaving behind seventy officers and men who had been killed and another thirty-six designated as missing or prisoners of war.

1/East Lancashire Regiment

Brigaded with the 5/Border Regiment and 5/King's Own in 126 Brigade, 42nd Division, the battalion was under the command of Lieutenant Colonel James Pendlebury. His son, Second Lieutenant Michael Pendlebury, was killed in April 1945, aged 19 years. On arrival at the Bergues Canal on 30 May, the battalion was ordered to jettison all transport, apart from three carrriers, and proceed to Bray-Dunes for embarkation. There must have been a profound relief felt by all the assembled men as they marched towards the beach; at least they stood a chance of being evacuated! But it was not to be. Three miles from the canal a staff officer arrived and, after a hurried conversation with Lieutenant Colonel Pendlebury, the column turned around to take their place on the canal between the 46th and 1st Divisions. It was another almost impossible order, one which resulted in the award of a Victoria Cross and which highlighted the battalion's lack of equipment.

Apart from the three carriers, the only weapons that had been retained were those carried by the men. Pendlebury must have realised they could do very little to stop a determined infantry assault. With C and D Companies deployed on the canal, A and B Companies were kept in reserve at Uxem, where Battalion Headquarters was established. The war diary confirms that the 5/Border Regiment were between them and the Coldstream Guards.

Early on 31 May the enemy attacked D Company at Benkies Mille; fortunately, the bridge had been destroyed and Corporal O'Neill and his section deterred any enemy advance with sustained rifle and Bren gun fire. During the attack the 5/Border Regiment retired and had to be put back on the canal by their brigade commander, Brigadier Eric Miles. Whether this prompted Pendlebury to relieve C Company and place B Company on the canal is not recorded, but it did set the scene for the action involving 28-year-old Captain Harold Marcus Ervine-Andrews.

Captain Harold Marcus Ervine-Andrews.

Dawn on 1 June began with the crash of an enemy bombardment and, under this cover, enemy infantry crossed the canal on both flanks of the battalion and effectively cut much of B Company off from the battalion, who found themselves unable to reach their beleaguered colleagues. Ervine-Andrews recalled that:

> *There was a tremendous barrage of artillery and mortaring throughout the first attack. It must have gone on for two to three hours ... During the course of the morning most of my four positions were pretty alright – the odd casualty here and there, but one position was in desperate straits. They were running very short of ammunition and were forced to search the dead bodies to find some more ... They now asked for urgent help, I had no reserves whatever. I picked up my rifle and some ammunition and, looking at the few soldiers with me in company headquarters, said 'I'm going up. Who's coming with me?' Every single man came forward.*

In actual fact 12 Platoon had retired and Ervine-Andrews was on his way to fill the gap in the line. Lieutenant Joe Cêtre, the company second-in-command, had just returned to Company Headquarters when he met Ervine-Andrews:

The 24-year-old Joe Cêtre was awarded the Military Cross for his actions at Dunkerque.

> *Ervine-Andrews was rushing with seven or eight men to fill a gap which had been left open by Corporal Snelson's retirement from his position. I was ordered by Captain Andrews to remain at Company Headquarters and organise it for defence. I observed, far away to our left, that the Germans were again infiltrating in that direction. They were about 200 to 300 yards away. I got hold of as many men as I could and organised rifle fire against them. This was effective as they either dropped or crouched, but no more came on.*

Fernand Octavo Cêtre, the only son of a French immigrant father from Burgundy and a German mother, was in no mood to be hounded out of his position by German infantry, and returned a vigorous fire against the grey shapes ahead of him. Unaware that the Borderers on the battalion's left had again withdrawn and the way was clear for German infantry to cross the canal unopposed, the company maintained its fire and hoped for the best. It was this attack that overwhelmed the Coldstream Number 1 Company and eventually resulted in the death of Angus McCorquodale.

For the besieged men of B Company the situation was rapidly becoming serious. A further attack later in the afternoon of 1 June resulted in the enemy being beaten off again and Ervine-Andrews and his men were forced back into the barn. Joe Cêtre was dispatched to get assistance:

> *By now the enemy had worked round both flanks and was enfilading us in the rear with both snipers and machine gun fire. An enemy attack on the house (Coy HQ) was delivered frontally and repulsed by the defenders. The Company Commander now asked me to try and gain contact with our troops and, if possible, to explain the impossibility of holding on without support.*

The survivors of B Company were now in a sticky situation and running short of ammunition. Pushed back onto Company Headquarters and giving little thought to surrender, Ervine-Andrews and his men fought on:

> *My men didn't fire much because we were too short of ammunition. They realised that it was better that I should do the firing rather than waste the few bullets we had. If you fire accurately and can hit men, the others get discouraged. Its when you fire a lot of ammunition and don't do any damage that the other chaps start being very brave and push on. When they're suffering severe casualties they are inclined to stop or, in this case, move round to the flanks.*

By 2 June Dunkerque was all but destroyed. The photograph, taken after the evacuation, shows the damage done to the town by shell fire and bombing.

Holding off the attack, Ervine-Andrews personally accounted for seventeen enemy soldiers with his rifle and several more with a Bren gun. Mercifully, Joe Cêtre returned with a fresh supply of ammunition and a handful of reinforcements, having threaded his way through crossfire and, for the moment, the real danger had abated. Under the cover of darkness the company withdrew, leaving behind five dead and taking with them the wounded on the one remaining carrier; Ervine-Andrews and eight of his men electing to march to Dunkerque on foot. The battalion was taken off at 11.00pm on 2 June, with Ervine-Andrews' party being taken off the Mole the next day on one of HMS *Shikari's* last evacuation runs. His Victoria Cross was the last to be awarded during the France and Flanders campaign and was the seventh to be awarded to a former pupil of Stonyhurst College.

1/Loyal (North Lancashire) Regiment

As with the 1/East Lancs, the officers and men of the 1/Loyals initially thought they would be evacuated on 29 May and had even marched to Bray-Dunes and taken up a defensive position in the dunes to the west of the town. Indeed, at 10.00pm that evening three officers and sixty other ranks had already been embarked at Dunkerque.

Unbeknown to the battalion, the enemy had reportedly broken through the Perimeter at Bergues at around lunchtime on 29 May and, although this was untrue, it did highlight the weak position occupied by Bergues and its importance to the defence of the Perimeter. It was a notion that had not escaped the minds of the Germans! Readers will remember that Bergues was under the overall command of Major General Andrew Thorne, who, apart from Lieutenant Colonel Usher's scratch force, had what remained of the officers and men of 139 Brigade at his disposal. The departure of Thorne left Bergues in the care of 139 Brigade's commander, the 50-year-old Brigadier Raleigh Chichester-Constable, a man who was probably better known for his cricketing career than his military prowess. His brother, Cecil, a major in the 2/Royal Warwicks, was killed at Wormhout on 27 May.

Brigadier Chichester-Constable.

The Loyals received their orders to march back to Bergues at about 1.00pm on 30 May; and although the war diary records the enthusiasm shown by all the officers and men, one cannot help but wonder if this was in fact true of all those who received the news! Reduced to 470 officers and men, the battalion marched the seven miles back to Bergues, entering the town by the Ypres Gate bridge, at which point Lieutenant Colonel John Sandie reported to Brigade that he and his battalion had arrived safely. The reply received from Brigadier Charles Hudson VC must represent one of the finest compliments received by a battalion commander:

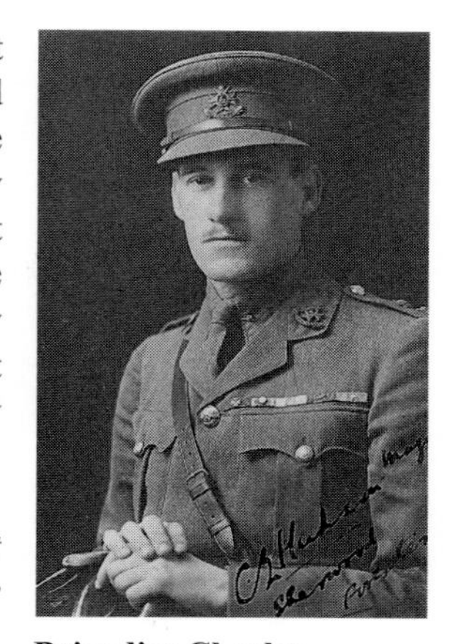

Brigadier Charles Hudson VC, pictured as an acting lieutenant colonel in 1918. His VC ribbon can be clearly seen on the left of his ribbon bar.

> *Well done John, if other blokes could do the sort of thing the Loyals have done, it wouldn't be necessary to ask the Loyals to do the things they do! Tell them all how well I think they have done.*

Hudson knew only too well the sacrifice made by the Loyals as he had been awarded the Victoria Cross himself for his actions in June 1918 near Asiago, Italy, as a 26-year-old lieutenant colonel in command of the 11/ Sherwood Foresters.

At Bergues, Sandie conferred briefly with Lieutenant Colonel Usher and his staff, who then left for Dunkerque under the orders of III Corps. Most of Usher's staff got away that night on the SS *Hythe*, Usher finally swimming out to a boat with his batman, Lance Corporal William Carle, a non-swimmer, clinging to his back. The regimental historian described the situation into which John Sandie and his men had been propelled:

> *Outside Bergues, the line of the Canal de la Colme, on the western side of the town, was held by a reliable French battalion. East of the town, the 2/5 Battalion, Sherwood Foresters took up strong platoon positions on a frontage of two miles, covering three bridges opposite Hoymille and Warhem, which were later blown. In the rear, behind Bergues, the 9th Battalion, Sherwood Foresters occupied a reserve position along the Dunkerque-Bergues Canal. The third battalion of 139 Brigade, the 2/5 Leicesters, now reduced to seventy-four of all ranks, was in brigade reserve at Nôtre Dame des Neiges, a village two miles to the north of Bergues.*

Sandie deployed his companies at the four main entrances to the town: B Company at the Dunkerque Gate, A Company at the Railway Gate, C

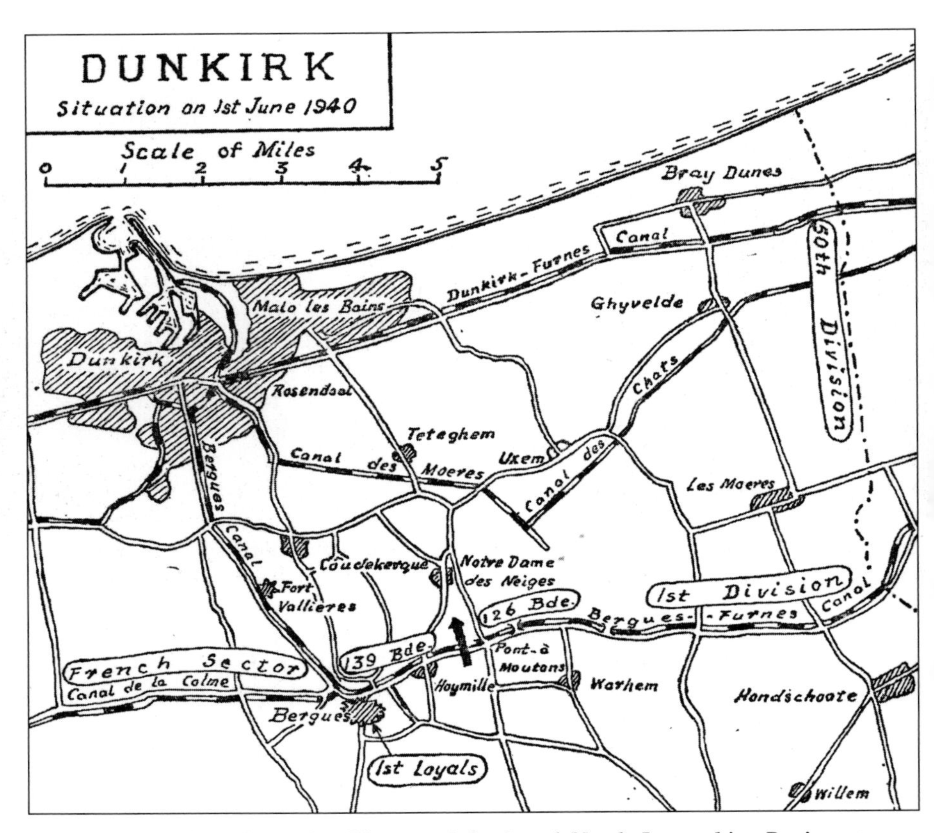

A map taken from the *History of the Loyal North Lancashire Regiment* depicting the situation on 1 June 1940.

Company at the Cassel Gate and D Company at the Ypres Gate. A reserve, consisting of C Company, 2/Royal Warwicks and a composite company of stragglers, was stationed at the old barracks near the Railway Gate. That night the 2/5 Sherwood Foresters were forced back to the line of the Canal des Moëres, all of which had a direct impact on C Company of the 2/Royal Warwicks, who were redirected from their march to the beach and ordered by Chichester-Constable to return to the canal and occupy the positions opposite Hoymille. The 2/5 Forester's war diary is slightly confusing in this respect, as it makes no mention of a fighting withdrawal and merely states that on 31 May they withdrew to billets at Téteghem.

Heavy trench mortars were brought up by the Germans after dusk and during the night of the 31st the town was shelled and mortared continually. Private Hector Morgan, who was serving with D Company near the Ypres Gate, recalled attempting to anticipate where the next shell would explode:

Bergues was badly damaged in the First World War and again in1940. Pictured here is the central square and the belfry, the remains of which were destroyed in 1944 before being rebuilt in 1961.

> *We were jumping from door to door. The German gunners were dropping shell after shell and as soon as they had dropped one, off we'd go to another doorway, when he* [the Germans] *dropped one about fifty yards from us. All of a sudden I felt this terrible bash on my back and I said to my mates, 'That's my lot, I've had it'.*

Fortunately Morgan lived to tell another tale and he had only been hit by a cobblestone thrown up by an impacting shell. But there had been many other casualties, the Battalion Medical Officer, Lieutenant Richard Doll, reporting a continual stream of wounded pouring into his aid station.

By daybreak on 1 June the fires, which had started near the church, engulfed the *Marie* and whole rows of houses. The heat was so intense that it was felt by the troops dug in along the ramparts, who found the smoke so dense that it was almost impossible to navigate around the town. Casualties were mounting steadily, one shell alone accounting for nine men killed and two officers and fifteen men wounded. Bergues was rapidly becoming untenable and at midday the garrison was ordered to leave the town and take up new positions on the canal outside the northern ramparts.

Owing to the heavy shelling, the occupants of the RAP were unable to leave until 4.00pm. Doll was determined not to leave the wounded behind and filled a 30cwt lorry with wounded and drove through the burning town:

A difficulty soon arose, for the town was so shattered that we were unable to recognise our way about. We made one false attempt to get out, being halted by a blown up bridge, when to out delight we found a soldier who was apparently still on duty; he turned out to be a Royal Engineer who was dealing with the last bridge, and he redirected us to it. Once again we lost our way, and following a dispatch rider, we came out near the crest of the hill well in sight of the enemy. We turned round at full speed and tore back over the heaps of bricks and rubble into the town; two shells must have landed very near us, for twice the vehicle was shaken as loud explosions seemed to crash above us. This time I was luckier, for I took the right turning and saw Captain Leschelles, D Company commander, and I breathed a sigh of relief.

Richard Doll in later life.

But it was not all over for Sandie's men. The battalion was in the process of leaving the burning town when orders were received from 139 Brigade to counter attack an enemy incursion. German infantry had crossed the canal at 7.30am that morning and were advancing towards Notre Dame des Neiges. Leaving D Company to oversee the withdrawal, Sandie organised two counter attacks, both of which floundered in the knee deep water of the inundations. At 4.50pm Major Gornall, commanding C Company, suggested a third attack should take place by advancing along the canal bank and, although costly in terms of casualties, was far more successful, in that it prevented enemy reinforcements from crossing the canal and allowed 139 Brigade to withdraw. By 8.20pm the whole of the brigade, except the 1/Loyals and the 9/Foresters, had withdrawn behind the Canal des Moëres. The last to leave, D Company, 1/Loyals, left Bergues at 10.00pm and arrived at Malo-lés-Bains with the aid of the 9/Foresters' lorries and embarked with Doll's party that evening on the SS *Maid of Kent*. The remainder got away on 3 June, having spent the whole of Sunday on the beach.

Chapter 7

Evacuation – The Logistics

Although Operation Dynamo officially began on 26 May, there was an incident involving the French destroyer *L'Adroit* on 21 May that was to point towards the carnage that gripped the port and its beaches six days later. Critically damaged by German bombing, the ship was beached off Malo-lés-Bains, where she suffered another huge explosion in the forward magazine, creating a large gap between the bridge and the bow. Referred to in several personal accounts, the damaged ship lay like a harbinger of doom for all to see as they reached the beaches.

The French destroyer *L'Adroit* beached off Malo-lés-Bains.

Already an early indicator of the impending evacuation was the preparation made for the evacuation of surplus BEF Personnel on 19 May. Termed the 'useless' or 'unwanted mouths', this rather unflattering term was used to describe the specialist, non-combatant troops, together with the wounded, who 'were not central to the functioning of the British Expeditionary Force'. As to who first coined the term, guilt lies at the

Wounded troops were counted amongst the 'useless mouths' and many were evacuated before Operation Dynamo began.

door of Lieutenant Colonel Viscount Bridgeman, although day to day control was delegated to Lieutenant Colonel Gerald Whitfield, who was given the rather grand title of Assistant Adjutant General GHQ, Commander Dunkerque Area. Whitfield arrived at Dunkerque on 20 May armed with orders to 'evacuate at [his] absolute discretion as many unwanted mouths as the situation permitted'. In his account of the evacuation, he makes frequent reference to the German bombing attacks on the port, reporting the town water supply was cut off by a heavy raid on 24 May and that the main oil tanks were on fire by nightfall on 27 May. Nonetheless, what is disturbing is his reference to the behaviour of many of the officers and men who appeared at the harbour to be evacuated, many of whom were clearly not 'useless mouths':

> *The order soon became known and a somewhat alarming movement towards Dunkerque by both officers and men became apparent. At times it was not a question of men coming into the town; on many occasions both officers and men hurried into the report centre at a speed which made one suppose the enemy were only a few yards behind them. It was clearly impossible for me to check on the credentials of so many individuals ... In many cases*

both officers and men had been detached from their units for many days and, as the food and water shortage became acute in Dunkerque, I had no option but to send them home.

However, apart from the occasional acts of discipline breaking down on the beaches during Operation Dynamo, this was one of the few occasions that referred to an almost wholesale stampede to get away from the beleaguered port. By midnight on 26 May some 28,000 'useless mouths' had been landed at Dover, a figure that did not feature in the Operation Dynamo totals.

Operation Dynamo Begins

The image most often associated with the evacuation from Dunkerque is of lines of soldiers queuing patiently on the beaches, waiting their turn to board the 'little ships' to ferry them out to larger vessels lying offshore. However, the truth is that only a third of the men evacuated from Dunkerque were actually taken off the beaches and it was the East Mole, a long stone and wooden jetty at the entrance to the port, that provided the embarkation point for some 200,000 soldiers. According to Admiralty records, the first ship after the commencement of Operation Dynamo to make the round trip from the south of England to Dunkerque was the armed boarding vessel *Mona's Isle*, which left Dover at 9.16pm on 26 May. Her return trip was more eventful. Escorted by the destroyer HMS *Windsor*, she reached Dover with 1420 troops on board at noon on 27 May. Sadly, of these men, twenty were killed and a further eighty-three wounded when she was hit by the coastal batteries at Gravelines and attacked by enemy aircraft. Private Stanley Priest, one of the first troops to be evacuated from Dunkerque on board *Mona's Isle*, recalled arriving amidst an air raid:

We had a quiet time for about an hour or so until we saw some planes approaching. The boys thought that they were Spitfires but they turned out to be Dorniers who strafed the boat ... I had a premonition that they weren't British and took shelter in an alcove, the bullets were passing within an inch or two from my feet, had I been on deck I certainly would have been killed. As it was I got a bullet in the shoulder and, as I was being treated for that, we were shelled by German guns.

Priest survived, but the ship was badly damaged and towed into Dover harbour by the tugs *Lady Brassey* and *Simla*. *Mona's Isle* made a second round trip to Dunkerque, bringing out a further 1,200 troops on 2 June.

The *Mona's Isle* was, however, not the only ship to leave Dover on 26 May, as even before the official commencement of Operation Dynamo a flow of vessels had begun to evacuate troops from Dunkerque. The armed boarding vessel *King Orry* sailed at 9.30am on 26 May, to be followed by *Mona's Queen* at noon and the *Maid of Orleans* at 5.30pm. The first of these ships to arrive back at Dover was the *Mona's Queen*, which berthed at midnight on 26/27 May.

The Air War

By 24 May the *Luftwaffe* had achieved almost total air supremacy in the north, with the exception of the Channel coast, which was within range of the British fighter squadrons. The cost to the *Luftwaffe* had been high and its squadrons, like the panzers, were badly in need of respite, a rest that was, according to Hermann Goering, not required, as he insisted he could reduce the Dunkerque pocket from the air. Nonetheless, despite Dunkerque being beyond the effective range of the VIII Fliegerkorps JU 87s (Stukas) early in the evacuation, the port was attacked on 26 May by a small number of bombers from I and IV Fliegerkorps operating from airfields in Holland and the Rhine valley, but it was not until the next day that the *Luftwaffe* was in any position to launch a serious attack against the British. Consequently, at dawn on 27 May, a wave of Heinkel IIIs bombed the port and beaches, sinking the French steamer *Aden* by the East Mole, while Stukas sank the troopship *Cote d'Azure*. Shortly

The Heinkel III was one of the principle twin engine bombers used by the *Luftwaffe*.

afterwards the oil storage tanks were set on fire by another wave of Dornier 17s. By 7.15am Dunkerque was a blazing shambles.

The BEF Air Component had already lost the equivalent of six Hurricane squadrons in France and British fighter cover at Dunkerque was provided by a total of sixteen squadrons from 11 Group, which rotated with the squadrons of 12 and 13 Groups. On 27 May Air Vice Marshal Keith Park's squadrons flew twenty-three patrols over Dunkerque, clashing with the twelve major attacks on the port flown by the *Luftwaffe*. The next day was overcast, and as the weather grew steadily worse, very few German bomber formations got through to Dunkerque. The low cloud ceiling that dominated the morning of 29 May forced many of the enemy aircraft low enough for anti-aircraft batteries of 51/Light Anti-Aircraft Regiment to claim successes. But it was not to continue. The dispersing cloud cover in the afternoon enabled all three *Stukageschwader* of Wolfram von Richthoven's Fliegerkorps VIII to bomb Dunkerque and the beaches indiscriminately, a task made much easier by the absence of 2 Anti-Aircraft Brigade's heavy guns! Later in the afternoon the bombers of Luftflotte II, commanded by 55-year-old Albert Kesselring, caught several vessels in the process of embarkation and sank a number of ships; by the end of the day twenty-two ships had been sunk by bombing or other means and twelve others damaged. The aerial score at the close of the day ended with sixteen British fighters shot down against fourteen German.

Albert Kesselring commanded Luftflotte II at Dunkerque.

Visibility on the morning of 30 May was poor, with the fog persisting through the day to the morning of 1 June. Clearing towards midday, the *Luftwaffe* launched an attack with forty Stukas from Fliegerkorps VIII attacking shipping at Dunkerque, sinking four destroyers and damaging others in the process. German air activity was not so apparent on 2 June and apart from one early morning raid by 120 aircraft at 8.00am, the demands of Operation Paula – an attack on the airfields around Paris – drew many of the available aircraft away from Dunkerque, to the extent that on 3 June the Stukas of Fliegerkorps VIII were the only German formation operating over Dunkerque.

During the nine days of the evacuation the RAF carried out 171 reconnaissance, 651 bombing and 2,793 fighter sorties, losing 177 aircraft, including 106 fighters. Fighter Command claimed the destruction

610 Squadron Spitfires from Biggin Hill on patrol over the English coast.

of 377 German aircraft – later reduced to 262 – and the Royal Naval gunners claimed another thirty-five. It was frequently a one sided battle and, despite the often bitter criticism offered by British troops at Dunkerque, the RAF emerged with credit. It is easy to forget that the daily RAF losses over Dunkerque were generally higher than those sustained during the Battle of Britain.

Naval Personnel at Dunkerque

Vice Admiral Bertram Ramsey was answerable directly to the Admiralty Board and was responsible for the co-ordination of the evacuation of the BEF. Based at Dover Castle, Ramsey first went to sea as a 16-year-old midshipman in 1899 and concluded the First World War as commander of HMS *Broke*. On 26 May the Admiralty informed Ramsay that it was 'imperative for Dynamo to be implemented with the greatest vigour with a view to lifting up to 45,000 of the BEF within two days, at the end of which it was probable that evacuation would be terminated by enemy action'. Ramsay's work in evacuating the BEF was greatly improved by the presence of 50-year-old Captain William 'Bill' Tennant, chief staff officer to the First Sea Lord. Tennant disembarked at Dunkerque at 6.00pm on 26 May and, like Private Stanley Priest, arrived in the middle of an air raid. His orders were to assume the duties of the senior naval officer (SNO) on shore and take control of the naval shore embarkation parties. Crossing in HMS *Sabre,* he took with him a dozen communications officers and 160 petty officers and ratings, to find one of Europe's most modern ports in ruins and the town in flames. One of these officers was Lieutenant Gavin Goodhart RN, who remembered being issued with a revolver and a tin hat and told to 'do what you can to help the army get away by boat and ship, but preferably do not get taken prisoner yourselves'. As Goodhart wrote later, 'it was the beginning of a long week'.

Tennant's energy was apparent to all. Lieutenant Harry Lennard, one of six Royal Artillery Embarkation Staff Officers from 5/Field Training Unit, sent across from Dover on 28 May, noted that they had some initial difficulty finding Tennant amongst the chaos that greeted them:

Vice Admiral 'Bill' Tennant.

> *He was perched clean in the open, on top of a shed in the sands, with details of parties, and thousands of men extending westerly under his direction. He continually rallied them, issued instructions, sought Medical Officers and arranged casualty stations. Although he had nearly lost his voice, he still managed to shout in a thoroughly Naval way.*

Tennant's first assessment of the situation at Dunkerque was not a good one. One of the earliest signals he sent to Dover on 26 May was a request for all available craft to be sent to the beaches east of Dunkerque to speed up the lifting of men from the beaches. The ships already there were spread along the coast and used their lifeboats to ferry troops out to the larger ships that were handicapped by the gently shelving shore line. It proved to be a slow business as only 7,669 men reached England on 27 May.

Evacuation Routes from Dunkerque

Ramsey was justifiably concerned by the disruption to evacuation shipping by the German shore batteries situated between Gravelines and Les Hemmes. At 6.23am on 27 May *Biarritz* and *Archangel* were shelled off Calais while en-route for Dunkerque, ten minutes later *Sequacity* and *Yewdale* were also shelled from Calais, with *Sequacity* sinking shortly after her crew had been transferred to *Yewdale.* At 7.50am *Mona's Isle* fell victim to the guns off Gravelines. Ramsey reported to the Admiralty that the normal – or southern route – known as Route Z (thirty-nine sea miles) was all but impossible to navigate safely in daylight. The more northerly Route Y (eighty-seven sea miles), which used the Kwinte Whistle Bouy as its most easterly point, was adopted as an alternative.

The route substantially increased the round trip, necessitating a third, shorter route – Route X – which had the advantage of shortening the voyage (fifty-five sea miles) and was used by the majority of British shipping after 4.00pm on 29 May.

The East Mole

In an effort to increase the numbers of troops being evacuated, Tennant made the decision to try and use the East Mole at Dunkerque, a narrow structure consisting of concrete piles with a wooden walkway. On 27 May he called in the Thames excursion vessel, *Queen of the Channel*, to tie up beside the Mole. There was bated breath as it came alongside without mishap. It was a gamble that worked and from that moment the embarkation of troops gathered momentum. Larger vessels were given priority at Dunkerque while others were ordered to operate off the beaches.

With the greatest number of men now being evacuated from the East Mole, it was the introduction of 'ticketing' arrangements that were issued to the waiting troops that controlled the passage of men into the waiting ships. Once on the narrow pier, the troops were chivvied along by Commander Guy Maund and other naval officers, who used a loud

The East Mole at Dunkerque. Soldiers are using ladders and planks to board the waiting ship.

speaker system to address the troops, encouraging them to remember their pals and get aboard the waiting ships quickly. Maund later wrote that:

This worked like a miracle, the thousands of troops, tired, depressed and without food or water for days, broke into a double and kept it up for the whole length of the Eastern Arm.

This was also the day that the so called 'little boats' began moving down the south coast in preparation for crossing the channel.

Tuesday 28 May saw 5,930 men evacuated from the beaches and almost 12,000 taken from Dunkerque and its harbour, figures that temporarily allowed Tennant to feel the evacuation was proceeding reasonably satisfactorily. However, the 29 May brought with it severe losses amongst the naval and personnel ships and the news that the Admiralty was withdrawing the most modern H, I and J Class destroyers. With three destroyers sunk - *Wakeful*, *Grafton* and *Grenade* - and seven more badly damaged, Ramsey was left with fifteen of the older craft. In addition, the *King Orry*, the ship that had led the German Fleet to surrender in Scapa Flow at the end of the First World War, *Crested Eagle*, *Waverley*, *Gracie Fields* were lost, along with *Normania*, *Lorina*, *Fenella* and *Mona's Queen*. Nevertheless, despite the formidable list of ships sunk and damaged, 47,310 troops were landed in England.

Rear Admiral Frederic Wake-Walker.

On 29 May Rear Admiral Frederic Wake-Walker was appointed SNO with responsibility for all embarkation arrangements off shore and arrived at Dunkerque on HMS *Esk*. Wake-Walker writes that at the time of his appointment it was thought the embarkation of the BEF could only go on for a day or two and each day was expected to be the last. At the time he had very little idea of what was going to be possible or how to set about it.

The Little Boats

By this time small craft, under the command of the Royal Navy, were arriving off the beaches from a variety of south coast ports. Wake-Walker's first sight of this armada of small boats, the story of which was

The Gorleston lifeboat, *Louise Stephens,* was amongst the little ships that went to Dunkerque.

A number of the little ships broke down and had to be taken in tow by larger vessels. The photograph shows a single screw motor yacht, possibly the *Glitter*, being towed by an unidentified Drifter.

to become famous, came when he saw from the deck of HMS *Keith* a strange procession of craft of all kinds. Some forty-one additional craft reached the beaches on 30 May, while many others arrived during the next day; all were directed to the beaches by Lieutenant Commander Cecil Wynne-Edwards:

> *Small craft were hastening from Portsmouth, Newhaven and Sheerness; six tugs were plodding along from Tilbury (towing 23 motor and 46 rowing lifeboats), and five others had left Gravesend towing barges. Yachts, drifters and trawlers; launches, lighters and steam hopper barges, car ferries, coasters and cockle boats; train ferries, speed boats and picket boats; seaplane tenders, fishing and pleasure craft and a Thames fire boat – a host of vessels – were heading in ever increasing numbers for Dover or Dunkirk direct.*

Arthur David Devine was one of those who crossed the Channel as captain of a small boat shuttling men from the beaches:

> *The picture will always remain sharp-etched in my memory - the lines of men wearily and sleepily staggering across the beach from the dunes to the shallows, falling into little boats, great columns of men thrust out into the water among bomb and shell splashes. The foremost ranks were shoulder deep, moving forward under the command of young subalterns, themselves with their heads just above the little waves that rode in to the sand. As the front ranks were dragged aboard the boats, the rear ranks moved up, from ankle deep to knee deep, from knee deep to waist deep, until they, too, came to shoulder depth and their turn. The little boats that ferried from the beach to the big ships in deep water listed drunkenly with the weight of men. The big ships slowly took on lists of their own with the enormous numbers crowded aboard. And always down the dunes and across the beach came new hordes of men, new columns, new lines.*

Divine crossed the Channel three times and during the last of these he received a stomach wound. For his efforts he was awarded the Distinguished Service Medal (DSM). The following year he published a novel based on his experience at Dunkirk, *The Sun Shall Greet Them: A novel based on the Author's experience of the English evacuation at Dunkirk, WW II*. He would go on to write the screenplay for the 1958 feature film *Dunkirk*.

The tug *Fossa* beached off Bray-Dunes. The sails of the Thames Lighter *Aidie* can be seen behind.

HMS *Vanquisher* at the East Mole.

Thursday 30 May saw the greatest number of troops evacuated from the beaches, with 29,512 men being lifted, as opposed to 24,311 men from Dunkerque harbour. But, with the German advance closing in and warnings that the II Corps sector of the perimeter was at the point of collapse, a huge effort was made to take off as many troops as possible from La Panne on 31 May and by midnight 29,512 men had been evacuated from the beaches together with 24,311 from Dunkerque. Further losses were suffered on 1 June, with three destroyers – *Basilisk*, *Havant* and *Keith* – sunk in the space of a few hours and four more badly damaged. The French destroyer *Foudroyant* was also sunk, along with the *Brighton Queen*, *Skipjack* and *Scotia*. Almost forty other vessels were sunk or damaged through collision, mines, shellfire and air attack, forcing the Admiralty to take the sensible decision to abandon daylight evacuation. Ramsay reluctantly agreed that the risk to shipping operating in daylight was out of all proportion to the numbers of troops being lifted. But, although the losses of ships was at its highest on 1 June, it was also the day on which the second largest number of troops were lifted to safety, with 64,429 men being landed in England.

The survival of the BEF owed little to the cooperation – or lack of it – between themselves and the French high command. Once Alexander had presented himself at Bastion 32 as the commander of the Dunkerque rearguard, Abrial reminded him that he and the remaining British units

Général Weygand at the entrance to Bastion 32 on 21 May.

were now under Fagalde's command and went on to detail how Alexander's men were to be deployed. The resulting discussion was said to have become heated after Alexander replied that his job was to evacuate the remainder of the BEF and not defend the Perimeter! This was, however, not something the French had invented to keep the BEF from leaving France. Earlier, Fagalde had been given the distinct impression by Gort that the three divisions of I Corps were his to use at his discretion and Fagalde had planned to integrate them with his own men until they were forced to surrender.

Alexander's reply was to the effect that he would like to help but his orders were to evacuate the BEF rearguard. He left Bastion 32 with the words of Abrial's chief of staff ringing in his ears, namely that he had abandoned his honour. Clearly, there had been some misunderstanding between what Gort intended and what the French understood, but it would appear that there was a great deal of mind changing and uncoordinated guarantees taking place behind the scenes, influenced perhaps by Gort's account to the British War Cabinet of French performance during the campaign and the seemingly maverick behaviour of Winston Churchill, which was still influenced by a desire to respond to French demands.

As the Perimeter contracted further, only Malo-lés-Bains and Dunkerque itself remained in British hands on 2 June. The reduction of the Perimeter also meant that Dunkerque was now within range of the German medium guns, but fortunately they had yet to realise that the best targets lay on the approaches to the East Mole. Indeed, there was plenty of room at the Mole and during the night Wake-Walker diverted some of the redundant ships from Malo-lés-Bains, which were led into position by Commander Maund in a small motor launch. Amongst a number of ships that crept into Dunkerque that night was HMS *Sutton,* embarking 725 troops in one and a half hours and the *Duchess of Fife,* which embarked 550 troops. The first pair of destroyers to berth alongside the Mole were HMS *Codrington* and HMS *Sabre*, who took off a combined total of over 1,600 troops, adding to an impressive total of 26,256 men who were landed in England on 2 June, 19,561 of which embarked from the East Mole.

During the afternoon of 2 June some doubt was expressed at Dover as to exactly how many men of the BEF remained to be evacuated; Tennant estimated some 5,000 British and 30,000 French, but Dover felt the number was higher. Apart from the BEF, Ramsey was sure there some 50,000 French troops waiting to be evacuated, a figure that Abrial says was more like 60,000. A meeting was hastily convened at Dover from where a programme was devised to allow ships to come in at intervals of half an hour, thereby ensuring three or four ships could berth alongside

British troops on the outskirts of Dunkerkque.

the Mole continuously. Thirteen destroyers were ordered to arrive at Dunkerque at intervals of half an hour from 9.00pm on 2 June, along with groups of minesweepers sailing from Margate, Sheerness, Dover and Harwich. The first destroyers to reach Dunkerque were the *Sabre* and *Shikari*, followed by *Venomous*, which evacuated, amongst other, Alexander and his staff. Almost 25,000 men were lifted from the Mole, the remainder – apart from the seriously wounded who were left behind - were taken off the beach and out to waiting ships. The last battalion to be taken off the Mole was probably the 1/King's Shropshire Light Infantry, a battalion that suffered the first casualty incurred by the BEF in December 1939, with the death of Corporal Thomas Priday near Metz. Led by their formidable commanding officer, Lieutenant Colonel Richard Bryans, they edged slowly along the Mole, wondering no doubt where the next shells would fall. At 11.30pm on 3 June Tennant signalled Dover: 'BEF Evacuated'.

The Final Night

After the last ship left Dunkerque at daylight on 3 June there were still some 30,000 French troops awaiting evacuation. Tennant agreed on a final embarkation window that would run from 10.30pm on 3 June and

French troops arriving at Dover.

2.30am on 4 June, after which time the ships would leave Dunkerque for England. Owing to the confusion that existed, it is impossible to determine which ships berthed where; but during this time both the East and West Moles were in use and a number of British ships, including the Schoots *Lena* and *Bornrif*, evacuated troops using the West Mole. It proved to be a highly successful conclusion to Operation Dynamo; 26,175 troops were landed in England, of which British ships evacuated 21,600. The British pier party was lifted by HMS *Express* at 3.30am and last British ship to leave was HMS *Shikari*, which sailed with Général Barthélemy on board; as the ageing destroyer pulled away from the Mole the Germans were reported to be only three miles from the port. Amongst those senior French officers who also left Dunkerque behind them that night was Fagalde – who you will remember regarded the evacuation as indefensible - and Abrail, who left aboard a French MTB, which broke down near the Goodwin Light Vessel and had to be towed into Dover by HMS *Malcolm*.

The Cost

Dunkerque had been an unmitigated disaster for the BEF and although over 338,000 officers and men had been successfully evacuated under the noses of the Germans, the cost was horrendous. Out of 693 British ships engaged in transferring and transporting men from the beaches and the harbour, 226 were sunk – with a similar number damaged - including six destroyers and five minesweepers. In addition, nineteen destroyers were damaged. The most significant French losses were the destroyers *L'Adroit*, sunk by air attack and *Bourrasque,* which struck a mine on 30 May. *Sirocco* was sunk by the *S-Boote S-23* and *S-26* on 31 May, and *Foudroyant* was sunk by air attack off the beaches on 1 June. The RAF lost 177 aircraft against a reported German loss of 240, which pale into insignificance when one considers that 2,472 guns, 63,879 vehicles and 20,548 motorcycles were left behind, figures that do not include personal and battalion weaponry that was abandoned on the beaches. The total number of casualties at Dunkerque is estimated to have been around 3,500 out of a figure of 68,111 killed, wounded or taken prisoner for the entire campaign.

Chapter 8

Evacuation – The Reality

To aid embarkation from the beaches at night and enable ships to identify which beach they were assigned to, an identification signal of two lights was established at La Panne and one at Bray-Dunes. Quite how effective this was remains unknown. The naval officer who was responsible for the system was Sub Lieutenant Edmund Croswell, an officer who spent much of the war in submarines and retired in 1958. Other Naval personnel at La Panne included Commodore Stephenson, Lieutenant Commander McClelland and Lieutenants Gavin Goodheart and Stanley Nettle, were each appointed to a sector of the beach with instructions to organize the embarkation. In his account, Goodheart writes of groups of soldiers arriving for embarkation, mostly in good order, under the command of NCOs or officers. His task was to collect suitable numbers for the wide variety of small craft, and make sure they were not overloaded and, hopefully, find soldiers capable of rowing out to the larger vessels off shore.

The *Oriole*

As the need for embarkation points on the beaches increased, over two thousand troops passed over the decks of the paddle-minesweeper *Oriole,* which had beached herself at La Panne on 29 May in an effort to provide a temporary pier head for the smaller boats to moor against. On board was Sub Lieutenant John Rutherford-Crosby, who took some of the most poignant photographs of the evacuation and wrote a graphic personal account of his time at Dunkerque:

> *The* [captain] *had run the ship aground and she was in ten feet of water or so. Many pongos tried to swim out, but hadn't the sense to ditch their equipment. It's a wonder many of them did not drown ... Shortly the troops could wade out up to their necks holding onto the line. They came aboard and we acted as a pier head for several ships anchored off shore. They sent in whalers and pinnaces and loaded from our sponsons ... What a scene of desolation on the beach as the tide receded, leaving rifles, haversacks, coats, pouches all lying on the wet sand. Most of the haversacks were*

Sub Lieutenant John Rutherford-Crosby was serving aboard the *Oriole* and was responsible for a number of photographs of the evacuation. The *Oriole* can be seen in the background.

> *burst open and scattered about were photos of wives, mothers and kiddies, toothbrushes, socks and even a baby cine camera. It was all rather tragic.*

The ship refloated at 6.30pm and survived the evacuation, but Rutherford-Crosby was drowned when the minesweeper HMS *Horatio* was sunk in 1943.

One of the most poignant photographs taken by Rutherford-Crosby, showing the deck of the beached *Oriole* and a line of British troops making their way out from the beach at La Panne.

The *Devonia*

The ship had previously seen service as a minesweeper during the First World War and was ordered to the Dunkerque beaches on 30 May. Lying off La Panne, she was badly damaged by bombing and deliberately beached after serious leaks in the hull compromised her seaworthiness. Signalman Leslie Rashleigh joined the ship's crew on New Year's Day 1940:

> *Before long the bombing and shelling came too close for comfort and then we reeled from a stick of bombs immediately astern. This opened up the* Devonia's *stern and before long the Naval commodore* [Commander Stephenson] *appeared to see the captain. Because of the severity of the damage, we were instructed to beach as far in as possible in the hope that the ship would act as a jetty for the troops.*

The ship was beached at 12.30pm on 31 May and, although there is no record of any troops using the ship as a temporary jetty, it is unlikely that she remained merely abandoned. Fortunately there were no casualties amongst the crew and they were taken off and transferred to HMS *Scimitar*.

The badly damaged *Devonia* beached near La Panne.

The Lorry Piers

There is still some debate as to who first thought of the idea of driving lorries into the sea at low tide to form a pier. The resulting structure allowed troops to clamber into the small boats that were now able to come alongside. It was a brilliant idea and is said to have originated from a suggestion made by Edmund Croswell on 29 May, who had been landed from HMS *Harvester* at La Panne. However, another naval officer, Lieutenant Pollard, serving on HMS *Codrington*, writes that after he was landed at La Panne he asked for lorries to be pushed down the beach into the water at low tide to form a makeshift pier:

This had started when I was recalled, as the ship was full and we returned to Dover. We turned round as quickly as possible and went back to La Panne, I was ashore again but loading this time was reduced to about six hours - the lorry pier was very useful.

While it seems probable that the idea originated from the Royal Navy, Lieutenant Harold Dibbens, serving with 102 Provost Unit, may well have had the same idea:

I suddenly hit on the idea of building a jetty by taking into use the many three ton lorries abandoned on the beach or on the roads nearby. I realized that the lorries would have to be anchored and that planks would be needed to construct a walk-way over the lorry roofs ... I quickly found a Royal Engineers captain commanding 250/Field Company and told him what I had in mind ... To anchor the jetty, all lorry tyres were punctured, mostly by firing through them and, when settled on the rims of their wheels, the backs of the lorries were filled with sand and lashed to each other ... The walkway was made up of panels taken from other lorries and the gaps between the roofs on the three tonners were covered by planks borrowed from a timber yard.

There were three lorry piers at La Panne and at least two others at Bray-Dunes and, from the evidence provided by unit war diaries, others were constructed elsewhere along the beaches. The piers were worked upon by a number of RE units, including 7/Field Company, 59/Field Company, 38/Field Company, 225/Field Company, 246/Field Company and 250/Field Company. Lieutenant Colonel Desmond Harrison, CRE 3rd Division, wrote of the high cost in casualties in building the piers at La Panne:

We built a grand pier of lorries using everything from decking to bathing boxes as a floor, and salvaged enough boats to get a lot of men off. Our own companies started coming in about 8.00pm, the last of them not until well after daylight, by which time our beach was a total shambles and nearly all the boats sunk. John Le Sueur, who was CRE 5th Division, was killed alongside me, and

A lorry pier at La Panne; note the wooden walkway over the tops of the vehicles.

> *in the same bombing attack we lost Paul Hodgson* (wounded), *Galloway and Barrow, plus eighteen sappers killed* [Captain Angus Galloway, 59/Field Company, Second Lieutenant John Barrow, 38/Field Company.]

Captain Paul Hodgson later died of his wounds. Casualties aside, the effectiveness of these piers was highlighted by Lieutenant Ludlow-Hewitt, a gunner officer with the 3/Medium Regiment, who watched the little boats drawing into an improvised pier at La Panne, 'consisting of open lorries lined up end to end into the water and over which the troops clambered to be taken off'.

Attached to the 2/Royal Scots Fusiliers from the RAOC, was Sergeant Bradshaw, an NCO who had lost touch with the battalion during the retreat and arrived at La Panne on 29 May, where he managed to join a line of men waiting to be taken off from a lorry pier:

> *It was later in the day* [30 May] *that I was ordered along the beach to where a line of lorries had been run into the sea to form a jetty along which we went and clambered into canvas bridging pontoons towed by a ship's motor boat to – I think – a*

minesweeper. Then we had to climb up cargo nets hung over the side. It was the hardest climb of my life.

Another Royal Scot was Second Lieutenant Gordon Wilmot, who had been wounded on the Ypres-Comines Canal and evacuated with a wound in the thigh. Taken to a casualty clearing station and from there to La Panne, he was deposited on a chair on the beach and slept for twenty-four hours until he was woken and directed towards one of the lorry piers. Told that if he could manage to make it along the pier he could be evacuated, he struggled along the pier and dragged himself aboard a Royal Navy minesweeper. He only discovered when in England that he was one of the few survivors of the battalion's action on the canal.

Sergeant Parsons, serving with 53/Medium Regiment, Royal Artillery, avoided the lorry piers and was taken off the beach by a ship's lifeboat, but his impressions remained with him for years afterwards:

At dawn [30 May] *the beach at La Panne was reached and we saw for the first time a sight that can never be forgotten – desolation and destruction – and, standing out amongst it all, parties of orderly troops waiting their turn to get a boat home. The weather was cold but by the grace of God the sea was calm. All types of craft were lying off the beach: some had been hit, others were waiting to take the troops home. Eventually our turn came. It had seemed like years waiting those few hours, and it seemed too much to hope that one would really get away to safety and England. We cheerfully waded out to sea and heaved ourselves into Naval Lifeboats and were soon clambering up the side of HMS* Esk.

RSM Hill remembers the scene that greeted the 1/DCLI at La Panne on 31 May; the town was on fire, the jetties unusable and enemy shellfire rained down almost continuously:

As dawn broke the beaches presented an unforgettable picture. Wrecked MT, small arms and equipment strewn all over the place, columns of troops stretched out into the sea waiting for some small boat to ferry them to a larger one. Ships being bombed, some were burning or sinking, dive bombers were strafing all and sundry, troops were taking cover in the dunes, some wounded, others digging cover. First Aid posts everywhere and a pretty grim picture all round.

It was much the same for Lieutenant Robin Medley, serving with 2/Beds and Herts, who arrived at La Panne under heavy shellfire and recalls running the gauntlet with his platoon along a street with three and four-storey houses ablaze on either side:

The road ahead, our only route to the beaches, had been accurately ranged upon by the enemy, and a salvo came down every minute ... I led 13 Platoon through at the double and we charged down to the sands. It was about 3.00am on 1 June ... The shellfire on the high water mark seemed continuous, and this noise was increased by the thunder of guns from the RN ships off shore. As eyesight became more adjusted after the light of the fires from La Panne, the vast numbers of soldiers spread over the beaches became apparent. It was also evident that the rate of evacuation to the boats was desperately slow.

Medley's experience of air attack was one that was shared by the thousands of the men waiting at La Panne:

It was only just light when thirteen ME 109 fighters appeared in the sky overhead and, peeling off in line astern, dived down. With guns blazing, they came strafing along the beach at about twelve feet. It was a pretty terrifying spectacle as we had no cover, but they levelled off before firing and no-one near us was hit.

The remnants of the 1/Suffoks was another battalion that found the road to La Panne being systematically shelled and the town full of abandoned vehicles and burning buildings. On arrival at the beach on 31 May, the regimental historian tells us that they had little difficulty in finding an embarkation point, but the arrival of enemy aircraft scattered the men across the beach:

Soon after it was light, enemy planes appeared and began to machine gun the beach and water's edge. They were met by a terrific small arms fire from some 5,000 rifles. One of them was brought down into the sea, whether by rifle fire or from the ships is difficult to say. Then several flights of dive bombers came over and, although met by very heavy fire from the shore and ship's guns, succeeded in sinking or damaging a number of naval and merchant ships.

It was, however, obvious that only a fraction of the waiting men could be got off before daylight and Lieutenant Colonel Milnes, commanding

British troops arriving at Dover, probably on board HMS *Vanquisher*.

the Suffolks, had been warned – presumably by a naval beachmaster - that the beach would close down at first light on 1 June and any remaining troops would have to make their way towards Dunkerque. Although the respective war diaries make no mention, the Suffolks and the Beds and Herts must have been at La Panne at roughly the same time and Robin

Medley's description of the march down to Bray-Dunes would have been similar for countless men, including the Suffolks:

> *It was an exhausting slog... The effects of lack of sleep over the whole period and more especially over the last three days, short rations and the repeated need to take cover from German bombers, which seemed to be constantly overhead, all reduced our speed of response. Bombs from the aircraft overhead were falling all around us* [while] *the Stuka attacks on shipping continued.*

La Panne Abandoned

After Gort handed over command of the BEF to Major General Alexander, the La Panne Headquarters was closed at 6.00pm on 31 May. The evacuation of Gort and his staff took place initially via HMS *Hebe*, an exercise that caused Wake-Walker to temporarily lose the commander-in-chief – and indeed his own composure – until Gort's party eventually resurfaced and embarked on HMS *Keith* to be transported to England.

By 10.00pm on 31 May the situation at La Panne had become serious for the 6,000 officers and men still waiting to be embarked. To add to the tribulations of thep naval beachmasters, the military withdrawal of II Corps would place La Panne outside the perimeter by the next day, a state of affairs exacerbated by the German guns at Nieuport that were firing almost continually and causing casualties with almost every shell that landed on the beaches.

These factors resulted in a rather hurried discussion taking place, with Major General Johnson, GOC 4th Division, and McClelland closing down the telephone link with England after informing Dover of his subsequent instructions to the troops still at La Panne to march towards Dunkerque via Bray-Dunes. At 2.00am on 1 June, La Panne was finally abandoned as a place of embarkation. Lieutenant Ralf Clarke, a Royal Engineers officer attached to the 4th Division, was one of the last men to leave La Panne. He kept copious notes in his diary from the time he landed in France in 1939 and records walking along the beach over the border with Belgium towards Bray-Dunes, keeping as close to the water as possible to avoid the light of the fires.

Lieutenant Ralf Lionel Clarke.

> *Another group joins us led by an officer with a flashlight. Some way along there is a ship lying close in and somebody suggests*

The hospital building at Zuydcoote before the war.

signalling for help. It works. There is an answering signal from the deck and within a few minutes a boat appears in the surf. This time we hold it well out and make people wade waist deep. A rough queue is formed and the whole party is embarked in three trips.

Zuydcoote

Some two miles along the beach, west of La Panne, was the sanatorium at Zuydcoote, which had been a hospital for tubercular children from Paris before the war, but was taken over by the French First Army after Belgium was invaded and used as a base hospital. During the evacuation, the hospital was clearly marked with the Red Cross but was repeatedly shelled and bombed, killing and wounding many of the allied casualties, who were accommodated in tents within the grounds. Driver John Browne, serving with No.3 Troop Carrying Company, RASC, found himself near the hospital on the beach at Zuydcoote on 29 May, arriving just as the *Luftwaffe* launched another of its raids on coastal shipping:

A French destroyer was hit and set on fire and sent all her torpedoes to the shore – in case they detonated, I suppose – and they ran up the sand with the propellers still turning and sending up spray. I saw a ship called Gracie Fields, *which I heard was carrying several hundred German prisoners, was set on fire and many lives were lost. Another cargo ship was set on fire at the stern and abandoned, and towards Dunkirk a hospital ship lay half in and half out of the water. She had been bombed before we arrived there. Other sunken ships were visible above the water, resting on the sand. During the bombing we made small trenches for ourselves to keep away from the machine gun bullets.*

What Browne had seen was the French torpedo boat *Bourrasque* hit by enemy aircraft. Several other ships, including the *Crested Eagle*, which was run aground near the Zuydcoote hospital, were also hit in this raid. The hospital carrier seen by Browne may have been the *Isle of Guernsey*, which was damaged en-route to Dunkerque but managed to return to Dover with 450 wounded on board. It was only on 31 May that Browne and his company managed to get taken out to a Dutch Schuit called the *Doggerbank*. Forty of these flat bottomed boats operated off the beaches at Dunkerque, of which only two survive today.

Signalman Terry Nolan, from 63/Telegraph Operating Section, was one of the hundreds of men aboard the *Crested Eagle* when she was hit opposite Malo-lés-Bains. His story is quite remarkable. After failing to find a boat at Zuydcoote and walking down to the East Mole at Dunkerque, he was ushered aboard the *Crested Eagle*. Surviving the air attack, he jumped overboard and found himself swimming for shore, only to realise that he was back where he had started from at Zuydcoote:

The burning paddle steamer [Crested Eagle] *had by now been beached and I think the sight of it must have stuck in the minds of all those on the beach at the time. Although there were other groups of soldiers on the beach I felt alone and hadn't a clue as to what to do ... In a hospital corridor I settled down for the night, but before long was called upon to be a stretcher bearer carrying injured to a huge casualty ward ... The next morning the beached*

The French torpedo boat *Bourrasque* listing heavily to port.

paddle steamer had burnt itself out and many bodies had been washed up to the shore – not a nice sight!

Sergeant Ron Jones, 143 Brigade, was another survivor of the *Crested Eagle*; he was wounded at Comines and put on board at Dunkerque and succeeded in jumping to safety as the ship was beached. He eventually got home via a 'freighter' that was lying alongside the Mole on 30 May. The number of casualties sustained by the bombing of the *Crested Eagle* will probably never be known but it may well have been the largest single loss of life incurred by any ship during the evacuation. Men on the sheet metal deck were reportedly transformed into human torches as it became white hot from the fire below decks.

Another survivor of a shipwreck was Major Rupert Colvin, who with his party of 2/Grenadier Guards arrived at Zuydcoote early on 1 June. After some waiting about, the party were ordered to march towards Dunkerque:

It was an amazing sight to see these thousands of men trekking across the sands, more or less in a solid mass five miles in length and about one hundred yards broad. Squadrons of Messerschmitts periodically attacked, and there were many unpleasant sights of wounded men left on the sands to die or be drowned by the flood tide.

Faced with a long march down to the port, Colvin and his party decided to wait until high water returned in the hope they could be taken off the beach. They were probably at, or near to, Bray-Dunes when they were picked up and taken out to a waiting ship. Having got underway the ship was hit:

The ship then heeled right over and everything came crashing down. Everyone made a rush for the side, and I remember a horrid feeling of going down into a bottomless pit. I took a deep breath, said a short prayer, and thought this was the one end I least desired ... The next thing that I realised was my head was above water and I was some fifty yards away from a lot of wreckage and struggling people. This probably saved my life, as most of the soldiers drowned each other through panic, though a lot must have been killed by the bomb.

Colvin does not mention the name of the ship in his account but it may have been the *Scotia*. He eventually managed to board a beached ship

The cross Chanel Ferry *Scotia*, seen here between the wars. This may well have been the ship described by Major Rupert Colvin.

with some difficulty and there found some dry clothes and blankets. He and the small group of survivors eventually managed to hail a passing Thames lighter, who took them off and landed them at Margate.

Major Allan Adair and 3/Grenadier Guards arrived at Zuydcoote sometime on 1 June, where they were ordered to leave their transport in a field and proceed to the dunes. Adair describes the sinking of the French destroyer *Foudroyant*, which 'went up in a great mushroom of flame shooting hundreds of feet into the air':

> *About midday I was sent for by 151 Brigade Headquarters, and had a most unpleasant journey there; shells falling pretty near, and the casualties on the outskirts of Zuydcoote had been very heavy. I got the cheering news we were to move along the beach at 2.00pm to the Mole at Dunkerque.*

At Dunkerque Adair writes that he was told by Major General Alexander that he was very doubtful the French could hold the Germans back for another day and there was no question of embarking during daylight hours and they would have to wait until dusk:

At last dusk came and the battalion were ordered to move along the Mole. This was a slow and nerve wracking business. There were several yawning gaps covered by loose boards where bombs had fallen. At length we reached the end of the pier.

Here they boarded the cross Channel ferry *Newhaven,* which took off 716 troops and, apart from a few parting shots from German shore batteries, the crossing was uneventful, arriving at Dover in 'brilliant early morning sunshine'.

Bray-Dunes

The scene at Bray-Dunes was similar to that of La Panne and Zuydcoote. When Lieutenant Peter Hadley of the 4/Royal Sussex arrived with his platoon, he admits being taken aback by the scale of the evacuation:

The beach was an extraordinary sight. As far as the eye could see it stretched away into the distance, the firm sand of the shore merging father back into the dunes. Covering this vast expanse, like some mighty ant heap upturned by a giant's foot, were the remnants of the British Expeditionary Force. Some were standing in black clusters at the water's edge, waiting for the boats that were to take them to the two or three ships lying off shore, while others, whose turn had not come, or were too exhausted to care whether it was their turn or not, lay huddled together in a disorderly and exhausted multitude.

It was a similar story for the men of 68/Field Regiment, Royal Artillery. Gunner Noel James and the men of 269/Battery reached the beach at 4.00am on 31 May:

What a surprise when we finally breasted the top of the dunes and saw the beach for the first time. It was like Blackpool on a bank holiday, with thousands of troops in every direction, some sitting in thick patches, and other standing up and forming long columns running down to the sea. On our right was a jetty formed by lorries which had been driven out into the sea, with a plank walk over the top of them ... Out to sea lay all types of craft in great profusion, destroyers, gun boats, coastal cargo ships, private motor boats and launches, while here and there a mast from a sunken ship showed above the water.

With so many troops waiting to be evacuated, some arrivals were drafted

An iconic photograph, probably taken at Bray-Dunes, showing lines of troops waiting to be evacuated from the beach.

in to man the beach defences. Sergeant 'Harry' Rew was a detachment commander in 12/Searchlight Battery, who arrived at Bray-Dunes with his troop at dusk on 29 May. Their job was to man the Lewis guns on the anti-aircraft emplacements, in an attempt to put the marauding Me 109s off their aim as they strafed the beach:

> *We loaded a high proportion of tracer, more for morale than anything else I think. We did four hour spells on the beach and then returned to our hollow in the dunes for four hours ... On Friday evening, 31 May, we were told we would be going off that night. Just as it was getting dark we filed down to one of the lorry piers into a ship's boat and out to the paddle streamer* Princess Elizabeth.

Lance Corporal George Turner, 4/Ox and Bucks, was injured at Cassel and arrived at Bray-Dunes on 27 May. As walking wounded, he was taken down to the beach where large parties of troops and a number of civilians were assembling on the beach or the road above:

> *After a long wait, our particular party had orders to move down to the water's edge. Here, those of us who could walk had to wade*

out to sea quite a long way until the water came halfway up our bodies. Those on stretchers were hoisted above water and were placed in the first motor boat that arrived. Then came my turn, and the problem of getting into a boat that was bobbing up and down in a rather choppy sea, was acute. A large hand suddenly shot out of the darkness and in a short time I found myself in the bottom of a motor boat. Presently we went alongside the destroyer HMS Scimitar.

After the casualty clearing station at La Panne was closed down, Private Sydney Whiteside, 14/Field Ambulance, was one of thousands of men who marched along the beach to Bray-Dunes, where Sydney's party were able to take their place in the long line waiting to embark from a lorry pier. He recalls walking over the tops of the lorries along planks and old doors, to get to the end where the sea came almost to the tops of the lorries, and climbed into a ship's lifeboat, remarking afterwards that he had not even got his feet wet! .

Driver Andrews, serving with 524/Company, RASC, reached the beach on 31 May, where he and his mates helped the Royal Engineers push some lorries into the sea to make a pier. He appears to have been picked up fairly soon after arrival:

A vehicle pier at Bray-Dunes.

Of the sixty or so men who had set off for the beach the previous morning, our party was down to about ten, the others having wandered off to try their luck elsewhere. We noticed the Navy had set up a shuttle service of a motor launch towing three or four whalers. I also noticed a senior officer acting as a beachmaster and controlling embarkation ... after a time he waved us into the water and the Navy came in and picked us up.

This photograph of Second Lieutenant John Carpenter was taken many years later, when he was a major general.

Another RASC soldier, Second Lieutenant John Carpenter of 522/Company, was only 18-years-old when he and his platoon crammed themselves into a ship's lifeboat in the early hours of 31 May and rowed out to a Dutch coaster manned by the RNVR. Two years later, with the rank of acting major, he took part in the invasion of Sicily as adjutant of the Divisional RASC. On D-Day, in Normandy, he commanded 508/Company RASC and, subsequently, 522/Company RASC. He retired in 1971 in the rank of major general and became chairman of the Dunkirk Veterans Association. He never forgot those desperate hours he spent at Bray-Dunes.

Carpenter spent less time on the beach than Lance Corporal Kinnel, serving with No. 3 Troop Carrying Company, RASC, who spent two days and nights waiting to be evacuated. He wrote of his fear of the *Luftwaffe's* attempts to kill him as they strafed the beach at regular intervals, a feeling that eventually gave way to weariness. His memory of wading out to sea to be taken off by a small motor boat, where the skipper gave them fresh bread and butter, before leaving them into the care of HMS *Anthony,* contrasted with his arrival at Dover and the tranquillity of the English countryside.

Private Raymond Greenwood was called up and conscripted into 5/Royal Sussex in May 1939. When he arrived at Bray-Dunes he found himself on his own and isolated. 'Sand, sand, sand everywhere', he wrote:

Then, round a couple of corners of short roads, at last I was on a beach. This should have given me the greatest relief and pleasure, but I was dead beat. The tide was out, and a large ship, the 6,700 ton Clan Macallister, *holed and burnt out, lay tilted in the sand in front of me. I carried on walking across the sand into the water, where I discovered it was not possible to walk on water!*

DAILY MIRROR, Wednesday, June 5, 1940

Daily Mirror

JUNE 5

No. 11,385 ONE PENNY
Registered at the G.P.O. as a Newspaper.

WE NEVER SURRENDER

"EVEN if large tracts of Europe fall into the grip of the Gestapo and all the odious apparatus of Nazi rule, we shall not flag or fail. We will go on to the end, and will fight in France, on the oceans and in the air. We will defend our island, whatever the cost, and will fight on the beaches and landing grounds, in the fields and streets and we shall never surrender.

"Even if this island or a large part of it were subjugated, our Empire abroad, armed and guarded by the British Fleet, would carry on the struggle until, in God's good time, the new world, with all its force and men, set forth to the liberation and rescue of the old world."

That proclamation of the unbreakable Allied will to fight on for freedom was made by Mr. Winston Churchill in his speech to the House of Commons yesterday—the greatest speech ever made by a Prime Minister of Britain.

Standing as the staunch embodiment of that will to fight, he declared:—

"I have myself full confidence that if all do their duty, and if nothing is neglected, and the best arrangements made—as they are being made—we shall prove ourselves once again able to defend our island home.

"We shall ride out the storms of war and outlive the menace of tyranny, if necessary for years."

A roar of cheers answered his superb, stark confidence.

"That is the resolve of the Government—every man of it—and that is the will of Parliament, and the nation," said Mr. Churchill.

"The British Empire and the French Republic, linked together in their cause and in their need, will defend to the death their native soil, aiding each other like good comrades to the utmost of their strength."

THESE were other vital points in the Prime Minister's speech (the full report of which begins on page 3):

Thankfulness at the escape of the B.E.F. must not blind us to the fact that what happened in North France and Belgium was a colossal military disaster.

✦ ✦ ✦

We must expect another blow almost immediately.

✦ ✦ ✦

We have more military forces in this country now than ever before. This will not continue. We shall not be content with a defensive war. We shall build up the B.E.F. once again under its gallant Commander-in-Chief, Lord Gort.

✦ ✦ ✦

Meantime we must bring Britain's defences to the height of efficiency.

DUNKIRK —LAST MEN GO

THE French Admiralty announced yesterday that the last land and naval forces defending Dunkirk were embarked during the night.

The port had previously been made useless to the Germans.

The French Navy, it was added, had lost in the Dunkirk operations seven destroyers—Jaguar, Chacal, Adroit, Bourrasque, Foudroyante, Ouragan and Sirocco—and the supply ship Niger.

Confirming the completion of the evacuation, a British communique said: "Our losses, though considerable, are small in comparison to those which a few days ago seemed inevitable."

The French communique states:

"Three hundred French warships and merchant vessels of various sizes, with 200 smaller boats, as well as numerous formations of the Naval Air Arm, took part in this operation.

"Most of the crews of our lost naval vessels were saved.

3 Admirals Land

"Other ships were damaged, but some have already put to sea again.

In addition to making Dunkirk unusable as a port, the Allied forces destroyed war material which could not be removed.

"When the Germans enter they will find almost nothing," French reports stated.

Three admirals of the French Navy and three French generals arrived at a south-east coast port yesterday with French troops evacuated from Dunkirk. They travelled to London to visit the Admiralty and War Office.

254 KILLED IN PARIS AIR RAID

Death-roll in Monday's Paris air raid was 254, of whom 195 were civilians and fifty-nine soldiers, says the Paris War Ministry. It adds: 652 were wounded—545 civilians, 107 soldiers.

MILITARY objectives in Munich, Frankfort-on-Main and the Ruhr were bombed by Allied warplanes as a reprisal for Monday's raid on Paris, the official Havas Agency announced last night.

It has now been established that twenty-five of the German bombers taking part in yesterday's raid were brought down.

A Berlin report yesterday stated that a "suburb of Munich" was bombed by an Allied plane, and eight people were killed. One bomb, it was stated, hit a factory, causing much damage.

R.A.F. fighters maintained offensive patrols throughout Monday and early yesterday in the Dunkirk area.

In Germany refineries, oil tanks, supply depots and marshalling yards in the Ruhr Valley, Rhenish Prussia and in the neighbourhood of Frankfort were among the important military objectives attacked.

IRONSIDES FOR HOME DEFENCE

SMALL bodies of highly mobile and strongly-armed troops—to be called "Ironsides"—are being organised for home defence by General Sir Edmund Ironside, Commander-in-Chief, Home Forces. There will be many hundreds of these formed from the Regular Army.

The War Office, announcing this last night, says that Sir Edmund has sent to each "Ironside" a copy of the following saying of Oliver Cromwell:—

"Your danger is as you have seen: and truly I am sorry it is so great. But I wish it to cause no despondency, as truly I think it will not: for we are British. . . . It's no longer disputing, but out instantly all you can."

The name Ironside, first given to Cromwell himself by Prince Rupert after the battle of Marston Moor in 1644, was later given to the troopers of his cavalry — those "God-fearing men," raised and trained by him in an iron discipline.

It traditionally implies great bravery, strength or endurance.

400,000 Local Defence Volunteers

Lord Croft, Under-Secretary for War, stated in the House of Lords last night that 400,000 had volunteered for the L.D.V.

He protested against suggestions that officers who had come forward were too old.

"It is no mere outlet of patriotic emotion that we are endeavouring to recruit," he said, "but a fighting force which may be at grips with the enemy next week or even tomorrow.

Lord Strabolgi said that besides making open spaces unusable for the landing of invading planes we should do the same with large spaces of water.

Lord Breadalbane suggested that each local area should have a lorry armoured against spitfires and bullets and armed with a couple of guns

RUMOUR-MONGER TO BE CHARGED

A CHARGE of being responsible for a rumour that he had heard from a German broadcast by Lord Haw-Haw that the Nazis were going to attack a Mansfield school is being brought today against a man at Mansfield.

This was stated today by Mr. J. L. Nicol, Regional Information Officer, at the inaugural meeting at Nottingham of the North Midland Regional Advisory Committee, which will function under the jurisdiction of the Ministry of Information.

Mr. Nicol added: "A Ministry official will attend."

This will be the first case of its kind under the new regulations.

LIVESTOCK LEAVES COAST

As a precautionary measure, the numbers of livestock in certain areas in South-East England are being reduced, says the Ministry of Agriculture. Some store animals, particularly ewes and lambs, are being transferred to other counties.

Stock fit for immediate slaughter is being bought by the Ministry of Food. The dispersal is not in any way extensive, and will not have any effect upon supplies of home-killed meat in those areas.

The Noble Story of Calais

Given an hour to surrender, 4,000 British and French troops, ordered to hold Calais to the end, spurned the demand to give in and kept the German hordes at bay for four days.

Then silence fell on the port.

Thirty unwounded survivors were taken off by the Navy.

This noble story of the heroic defence of Calais is told on page 3.

Pictures of the Evacuation: Pages 8 & 9

The front page of the Daily Mirror on 5 June 1940.

He soon discovered why there was an absence of troops near the ship. Every time the *Luftwaffe* bombed the port any remaining bombs and ammunition was directed at the *Clan Macallister*, which the Germans obviously thought was still afloat! Moving down the beach to put some space between him and the ship, Greenwood was finally picked up by a ship's boat belonging to the Steam Hopper *W24*:

> *The iron sides of the hopper were at least 12 feet high. With 400 men on board, the engines started up and we began to move forward. I think the entire crew consisted of 5 men, one on the wheel, 2 on the upper deck and 2 in the engine room wearing blue seaman's pullovers ... for the first four hours, the old rust bucket jumped and lurched ahead, we were doing at least 5 knots and it was a real test for the engines.*

Greenwood arrived at Ramsgate at 6.00am on 31 May after a fraught crossing during which they were bombed and machine gunned.

Malo-lés-Bains

The order of evacuation directed the III Corps units directly to the beach at Malo-lés-Bains. Amongst these men was Captain Phillip Hampton, commanding 228 Anti-Tank Battery, 57/Anti-Tank Regiment, who surveyed the scene that unfolded in front of him with some astonishment. The huge plumes of black smoke erupting from the bombed oil storage tanks at Dunkerque did little to detract his attention from the seemingly endless lines of men queuing on the beach waiting to be ferried out to the larger ships off shore:

> *Down south to the left, and beyond Dunkirk, we could see the enormous fires – flames leaping hundreds of feet into the air, with thick black oily smoke. Out to sea were bombed and wrecked ships, including a French destroyer which had received direct hits. Further out was a merchant ship blazing astern. On the beach itself, thousands of men. I was immediately put in command of 50 men by an Ordnance Colonel sitting on a shooting stick and told to keep them in the queue. Having sorted them out, I wandered off to see if any of the other men had arrived. It was well after 9.00pm now. I was glad to find quite a lot of them and they all seemed remarkably cheerful ... I spent the rest of the night alternatively trying to sleep, without success, and walking about to keep warm. It was bitterly cold and my greatcoat was not much protection. About 4.00am on 30 May, there were signs of life, so we shook ourselves and formed up in the queue again. The Germans paid us one more visit and bombed Malo-lés-Bains, causing further damage to the already ruined houses.*

Hampton and his party marched down to Dunkerque and boarded HMS *Vimy* at 8.00am, where they thanked heaven for a sea mist shielding them from any unwelcome enemy attention.

After the 2/Coldstream Guards had been withdrawn from the Perimeter on 1 June, they were directed to the beach at Malo-lés-Bains, where Lieutenant Colonel Bootle-Wilbraham, surrounded by the remnants of 1 Guards Brigade Headquarters, attempted to muster the surviving guardsmen:

Captain Phillip Hampton 57th Anti-Tank Regiment

> *The night was inky black and there were a few spots of rain. No sound of firing came from the line we had abandoned. Only the oil tanks in the docks blazed, the flames and smoke billowing high into the sky. An occasional shell moaned its way across the black bowel of the night till it burst somewhere in the direction of the Mole.*

With Bootle-Wilbraham was Captain John Nelson, a Grenadier Guards officer commanding the 1 Guards Brigade Anti-Tank Company. Nelson rose to command the 3rd Battalion during the Italian campaign and ended his career commanding the British sector in Berlin. He was no stranger to the beach at Malo-lés-Bains as he had previously reconnoitred the route, where he had seen Major General Alexander, an experience he wrote, that made him a little more confident of the future:

> *Every few seconds a twelve inch shell came whistling over to land with a muffled crump, safe in the deep and deadening sand. And there, in a deck chair in the centre of it all, as though on the Brighton sea front, reading a copy of* The Times *newspaper, sat General Alexander, completely unperturbed.*

Nelson, clearly agitated by the long wait for embarkation, discarded his clothes and swam out to a deserted Thames sailing barge, the *Iron Duke*. Here, together with Captain David Strangeways, the Duke of Wellingtons' Adjutant, whose experience of sailing placed him in command, and a party of men from 1/Duke of Wellington's, he reached Dover the next day. Another officer who decided to take matters into his own hands was Major Mark Henniker. Finding two empty rowing boats, the size of ship's lifeboats, he and his party of over thirty officers and men took the risk and embarked for England. After they had been rowing for a couple of hours they sighted a pinnace:

We rowed towards her and found she was deserted, so we tied up astern and boarded her. We were still drifting with the tide more or less in the right direction, so we started to explore her ... soon the sappers began appearing on deck rigged out in sailors clothing which they had found below. Without warning the engines suddenly started and we darted forward out of control in a huge circle. One of the Sappers, who was a mechanic by trade, had been fiddling with the engines ... I discovered that it was possible to steer by inserting an iron bar in the rudder head and we accordingly transferred all our possessions from the rowing boat and retained one as a tender.

Henniker and his men reached England and were taken in tow by HMS *Locust* to Dover.

Second Lieutenant John Dibblee was still with his troop from 30/Field Regiment when he was taken aboard HMS *Skipjack* on 1 June. There he was reunited with his friend, Second Lieutenant Ronald Temple :

We soon came under fire in a concerted aerial attack. In the ward room we could see little of what was going on, until a bomb from a Junkers 88 dropped through the wardroom roof between us straight through the floor and detonated in the hold, killing all the men of my Troop and blowing a hole in the bottom. The Skipjack *turned turtle, with Ronald and I managing to escape through the hole in the roof but without life jackets. We were hours in the water and a rough sea had got up. With unshod feet, I managed to keep afloat, but Ronald with his boots on, could not. One minute I saw him above the waves and the next minute he was gone. I was eventually picked up by a commercial vessel, in an exhausted state.*

Château Coquelle

Number 12 Casualty Clearing Station arrived at the Château Coquelle on Rue de Belfort in Rosendael during 28 May and almost immediately Major Phillip Newman established an operating theatre in the large drawing room. The next three days 'were hectic in the extreme' as the increasing number of wounded flooded into the château and Newman reported he moved his operating theatre into the cellar with one electric lamp. As the Perimeter decreased in size, so the château came under an increasing shell fire:

Major Phillip Newman RAMC.

We were awakened by a terrific crash – a shell had come into the front room. The operating theatre that was. In the very dim, early morning light, we sorted out patients and masonry and carried the patients outside, there were about a dozen of the poor chaps; one lad had a slab of concrete on his face.

One of the many tragedies, which can only be attributed to the 'fog of war', occurred here on 2 June. Many of the wounded at the château had been told that there was no opportunity available for them to be evacuated, and one doctor and ten orderlies were to remain behind with them. By the evening of 2 June the Germans had still not arrived and four lorries, loaded with wounded, were driven down to the beach and got away. Newman's diary recorded their departure:

A message came through for all walking wounded to go. I had four lorries driven up and even had one of the wounded soldiers driving one of the vehicles. It was amazing who could walk. Chaps going to England in a shirt, a blanket and bare feet, with some large running wounds in their backs and legs and hobbling along on the shoulders of others. I packed about 100 into the lorries and they really were a grand sight as we wished them good luck as they drew away.

Newman writes of another party of wounded that he took down to Dunkerque at 9.45pm. On this occasion he had been told a hospital ship was on its way and five ambulances were loaded with wounded in preparation:

We waited for an hour and no boat came. At 11.00pm I saw the last of the BEF file past. We, with some marines, rushed a few of the stretchers half a mile up the jetty and put them on a boat. Forsaken by England and only the Germans to look forward to, I can never forget that moment as long as I live. It gave me the greatest feeling of desolation I have ever had.

Newman and the remaining staff and casualties at the château were taken prisoner but Newman managed to escape on his second attempt in 1942 and returned home via Madrid and Gibraltar.

The East Mole

Up until 1 June the pier master at Dunkerque was Commander James Clouston, who returned to Dover for a meeting with Ramsey on 1 June to determine just how the final evacuation was to be accomplished. The next day, during his return to Dunkerque, his boat was strafed and bombed by eight Ju 87 Stukas, and Clouston's boat was sunk, leaving the crew clinging to the wreckage. While waiting for rescue, he and his men eventually succumbed to exhaustion and hypothermia. Only one man survived. From the night of 2/3 June Commander Lewis took over the all important duties of pier master.

Commander James Clouston.

Lieutenant Stowell, RN, was serving aboard HMS *Wolfhound* when they were ordered to Dunkerque. Having being asked by his captain as to what they might expect, Stowell replied that his opposite number in another destroyer had been there before and had a whale of a time, with champagne flowing freely. As he wrote afterwards, his captain's comments when they reached the French coast and saw everything ablaze were 'terse and to the point regarding my earlier remarks'. The nature of their task was brought home very quickly:

> *We were attacked a few times on the way over but suffered no damage. When we reached Dunkerque we entered the harbour and, as we did so, a whole flock of bombers arrived ... The captain (Commander John McCoy DSC) went ashore with Captain Tennant and we surveyed the surrounding mess. Not long after they had left more bombers came over, and after the dust had settled we saw that four trawlers moored just across the basin from us had disappeared without trace except for one mast.*

Like Private Raymond Greenwood of the 5/Royal Sussex, the 2/Dorsets moved down to the Mole from Zuydcoote on 30 May, complete with all their platoon weapons and, after marching along the Mole under fire, were ushered aboard a Thames dredger, similar to the one that had taken Greenwood home from Bray-Dunes:

> *The sight of this unwieldy craft, which, as first seen in the dark, was apparently half filled with water, had so appalled Sam Symes* [the battalion second-in-command] *that he refused to take it over. It was explained to this harassed officer that this was the normal condition of dredgers and actually the craft was quite seaworthy. Crowded as they were, this night journey across open sea provided no hazards to the exhausted battalion, who in many cases slept standing up.*

Second Lieutenant Tony Younger, a sapper officer serving with 61/Chemical Warfare Company, was guided to Dunkerque by the black smoke rising from the oil storage tanks, which could be seen for miles. After a miserable night near Malo-lés-Bains, they marched down towards the Mole where they were given a boarding number and told to wait until they were called forward:

Second Lieutenant Tony Younger, seen here as a major general.

> *We had only been at the base of the Mole for a couple of minutes when a salvo of shells arrived and burst on the concrete surface, killing an officer and a number of the members of a group that happened to be passing at the time ... Another ship arrived and with it another salvo, but luckily this dropped into the sea and nobody was the worse for it.*

With deep water on both sides, the narrow Mole was ideal for marshalling and boarding large numbers of men quickly, as Sapper Norman Wickman of 62/Chemical Warfare Company found out to his cost when boarding HMS *Worcester*:

Sapper Norman Wickman.

> *The destroyer was pulling away from its berth. I hesitated. The gap was too wide. 'Jump, you silly bugger, jump' yelled a burly sailor at the ship's rail. So I jumped. Immediately, I realized I had made a big mistake. In mid-air, I glanced down. The foaming water churned wildly where the destroyer's sharp propeller blades were waiting to chop me to pieces. Leaning far out, the muscular sailor grabbed my shredded epaulette, flapping loosely from my uniform. With a crash, I slammed against the ship's rail. Using brute strength, the sailor hauled me over, where I fell in a crumpled heap on the deck. Unbridled joy and relief overwhelmed me. I was on the destroyer, safe and on my way home. Then, all hell let loose. 'Get up against the bulkhead' shouted the sailor. Stunned and winded, I stumbled across the deck. As I pressed against the grey metal, I heard the planes. Stukas, 30-40 of them, dived on the* Worcester *time and time*

again. Bombs rained down like confetti all around the ship. The destroyer, so filled with troops it was top heavy, heeled over wildly at heart-stopping, stomach-lurching angles to evade the falling bombs. Bombs to the rear lifted the stern clear of the water. The massive propellers screamed until the ship crashed down again. Colossal columns of water washed over the ship. I closed my eyes and tried to make my body disappear into the bulkhead. By some miracle, none of the bombs made a direct hit on the ship. Shrapnel killed 46 and wounded another 180 before the attacks tapered off.

Second Lieutenant Taylor, commanding the Signals Platoon, 1/East Surreys, had a comparable experience to Wickman, both men literally jumping to freedom! Taylor had been wounded in the shoulder on the Escaut, and arriving as walking wounded at Bray-Dunes, where he was told to wait for transport to take him to Dunkerque:

Later that day we were put into trucks and driven to Dunkerque town, as we were to be embarked from the main Mole in the harbour ... it was a similar scene to Bray-Dunes, except the bomb craters were more numerous and there was more general wreckage everywhere.

Having nothing to occupy his time, Taylor organised his party by sitting them in deck chairs and watched a group of soldiers enjoying themselves in highly coloured pedal cars, which they had found in a fun fair. In the evening an RAMC officer came running up to ask who they were, explaining that he had been asked to collect up all the walking wounded he could find:

At last I received an order and had a shrapnel wound to go with it. He told me there was a hospital ship [the St Andrew] *just about to leave: it was tied up at the far end of the Mole, and with the other wounded, I must reach it before it sailed ... When I was about fifty yards from the ship I could see it was no longer moored ... I reached the place where it had been tied up only a few minutes earlier, and noticed a sailor by the ship's rail. Seeing me he shouted 'jump' and jump I did. I caught the ship's rail with my one good hand, hung for a moment, then with a heave he pulled me on board.*

This was the last trip made by the HS *St Andrew,* which disembarked 130 walking wounded officers and men at Newhaven. No more hospital

carriers brought out wounded men from Dunkerque, the space taken up by the hospital ships was too valuable and walking wounded were evacuated with the troops. Sadly, stretcher cases were often refused as they took up more space on board ship than able bodied men.
Lieutenant Colonel James Birch, commanding the 2/Beds and Herts, arrived at the East Mole with Brigadier Barker late on 31 May and was probably witness to the bombing of HMS *Hebe*:

> *It was an unforgettable sight, I think it must have been waiting to escort the last few remaining boats left alongside the Mole as it was caught almost stationary. As the attack came on the usual roar of Bofors and Pom-Poms started from both shore guns and the guns of the warship. Each salvo of bombs dropped by each diving aircraft seemed to blow the destroyer out of the water, but as the smoke and water fell away, she was to be seen still steaming.*

As part of the rearguard, Corporal 'Slim' Ingley of the 5/Royal Inniskilling Dragoon Guards, was finally ushered towards Dunkerque on 1 June. Arriving in the evening, the thick pall of black smoke that hung over the town provided a sombre backdrop to the debris strewn beach and the tarpaulins covering the dead bodies, whilst the shelling was heavy but indiscriminate. Late the next day they were called to embark:

> *Gradually we neared the Mole, it appeared to be two miles long and about twenty feet above the sea. Numerous gaps were evident but matelots* [sailors] *had strung gangplanks across gaps. We stood aside to give priority to the walking wounded. Each man was heavily bandaged around the eyes. A sighted man led the way; the unsighted followed ... The smoke was thick, stinking and black. Edging forward along the Mole, we saw ships bumping alongside. Patiently we waited our turn, overhead shells were whining, splashing and crunching into the sea. A naval officer was yelling instructions into a megaphone. It was deafening.*

Having seen the majority of 29/Battery safely embarked for England, Major Charles Crawford of 19/Field Regiment collected another seventy Royal Horse Artillery gunners and made his way down the beach towards Dunkerque. His impressions on entering the outskirts of the town were recorded later, but clearly etched on his mind:

> *The confusion was indescribable. Houses, tanks, guns machine guns – nearly all destroyed – everywhere. Most of the houses in*

The scene at Dunkirk so appalled Charles Crawford that is was etched on his mind.

> *bits, British soldiers were nearly all dug in along the beach, many with no tools to dig with except their tin hats. Their discipline was admirable, which was in contrast to the French, who were too frightened to do anything. By this time the town and beaches were again being heavily shelled, big stuff, which is more deadly than bombing. The noise of bombs and shells was incessant. It is impossible to describe what was probably the biggest killing in history – everywhere lay bits of what had been soldiers and civilians – women and children.*

Crawford was eventually evacuated from the Mole on 2 June – the same night as Corporal Ingley – but even that was not without its drama:

> *Shortly before I reached the destroyer a shell or bomb took a twenty foot chunk out of the wooden portion of the Mole. I was with the Coldstream Guards and it was, I think, the last straw that nearly broke the camel's back and we knew we were lost. The soldiers were grand. Out of the dark an obviously naval voice came – 'soldiers ahoy, catch this line'. After many futile attempts we caught a thin rope. It was followed by a thicker one and an ex-sailor made fast to a bollard. Sailors swarmed up it and others on the far side of the gap found gangways and in 10 minutes we were aboard HMS* Shikari.

A boat load of exhausted troops arrives at Ramsgate.

The Coldstream Guards referred to by Crawford may well have been some of the men of the 2nd Battalion, many of whom had been taken off from the Mole aboard HMS *Sabre*. Lieutenant-Colonel Bootle-Wilbraham wrote in his diary that the BEF rearguard formed up at 8.30pm, with the remnants of the 1 Guards Brigade heading the column:

> *I led the brigade onto the Mole and followed them on board HMS* Sabre, *where I lay down on the deck amongst the troops. Shortly after 9.00pm we weighed anchor and headed for England. Never have I been so grateful for the British Navy.*

The 4/Green Howards were amongst the last of the BEF to be taken off from Dunkerque. Second Lieutenant Peter Kirby and his men, after a long day waiting on the beach, joined the queue making their way to the Mole on 2 June:

> *About 8.15pm two destroyers and a cross channel streamer seemed to appear from nowhere and tied up at the far end of the Mole. It was a difficult journey down the long Mole and, though speed was essential, shell holes in the masonry, crossed by makeshift wooden bridges, slowed the men down. But this was*

nothing compared to the hazard of crossing the wide gaps in the shell-battered end of the Mole where the ships were moored. Only a single plank about nine inches wide spanned them.

Sergeant Richard Hall, A Company, was on his last legs as the battalion reached the end of the Mole:

We shuffled along the Mole, across broken planks. When I reached the end of the queue a couple of sailors literally picked me up and flung me into a boat. There were about one hundred Green Howards on board. I can't remember any more as I think I slept the whole journey to Dover.

The vast majority of the BEF had gone and the Germans were left, in the words of Corporal Ingley, 'with an inheritance of blackened ruins, dead men floating in the water and graveyards of smashed vehicles'.

Chapter 9

The Tours

Although there are several opportunities for the battlefield visitor to stretch their legs during the tours, there are also two walks, one of which centres on the English seaside towns and ports of Ramsgate and Dover. The second walk is around De Panne in Belgium, where we visit the site of the former BEF HQ and take in several of the venues that were used by the Germans post evacuation. There is one car tour that enables the visitor to explore much of the perimeter and many of the locations referred to in the text. The author strongly suggests obtaining street maps from the various Tourist Offices along the route to supplement your excursions and, while much of the area covered by the guide is dotted with cafés and other refreshment venues, it is always wise to have something to eat and drink with you.

Maps

The tours described in this book are best supported by the IGN Série Bleu 1:25000 maps, which can be purchased at most good tourist offices, the bigger local supermarkets and online from www.mapsworldwide.com. The whole of the perimeter up to the Franco-Belgian border is covered by two maps, IGN 2302 O Dunkerque and IGN 2402O Hondschoote. The Belgian element of the perimeter, the II Corps area, can practically all be covered by the Belgian IGN 1:50,000 map of Ostend (Oostende). This is smaller scale but serves quite well. Bear in mind that satellite navigation can be a very useful supplement in supporting general route finding, particularly when trying to locate obscure CWGC cemeteries.

Travel and Where to Stay

By far the quickest passage across the Channel is via the Tunnel at Folkstone, the thirty-six minutes travelling time comparing favourably with the longer ferry journey from Dover to Calais or Dunkerque. Whether your choice of route is over or under the Channel, early booking is always recommended if advantage is to be taken of the cheaper fares. Travelling times vary according to traffic; but as a rough guide the journey from Calais to Dunkerque is about half an hour.

The Channel coast is blessed with a multitude of accommodation options; but if you are intending to base yourself in or around Dunkerque the author can recommend the 3-Star **Hôtel Welcome**, which is located in the centre of Dunkerque. It offers 24-hour reception and en-suite accommodation with free Wi-Fi access. Alternatively, the 3-Star **All Suites Appart Hôtel** is said to be of a good standard and is situated on the water front - only a short walk from the Bastion 32 Museum. There are numerous apartments in both Dunkerque and the neighbouring towns of Malo-lés-Bains and Bray-Dunes, details of which can be found on the internet. Visitors should book early to avoid disappointment.

Across the border at De Panne there is a multitude of accommodation, ranging from hotels to apartments. The author personally recommends the 4-Star **Hotel Donny**, which is extremely comfortable and has a restaurant, fitness suite and swimming pool, as well as the usual free Wi-Fi. As in France, apartments abound and are best found on the internet.

For those who prefer the outdoor life, **Camping Municipal la Licorne** has the convenience of being near the beach at Dunkerque and, apart from having several plots for motor homes, also boasts thirty-four holiday homes. A little further south is **Camping Château du Gandspette** at Éperlecques, a campsite which is amongst the author's favourites. Situated some 35 minutes from Dunkerque, the site offers a swimming pool, a restaurant and Wi-Fi and a number of mobile homes for rent. Further information on all aspects of accommodation can be obtained from the various Tourist Offices in the main centres at Dunkerque, Malo-lés-Bains, Bray-Dunes and De Panne.

Driving

Driving abroad is not the expedition it was years ago and most battlefield visitors may well have already made the journey several times. However, if this is the first time you have ventured on French roads there are one or two common sense rules to take into consideration. Ensure your vehicle is properly insured and covered by suitable breakdown insurance; if in doubt contact your insurer, who will advise you. There are also a number of compulsory items to be carried by motorists that are required by French law. These include your driving licence and vehicle registration documents, a warning triangle, a *Conformité Européenne* (CE) approved fluorescent safety vest for each person travelling in the car, headlamp beam convertors and the visible display of a GB plate. Whereas some modern cars have built in headlamp convertors and many have a GB plate incorporated into the rear number plate, French law also requires the vehicle to be equipped with a first aid kit and a breath test kit. If you fail to have these available there are some hefty on the spot fines for these motoring offences if caught driving without them. Most, if not all, of these items can be purchased at the various outlets at the Tunnel, the Channel port at Dover and on board the ferries themselves. On a more personal note it is always advisable to ensure that your E111 Card is valid in addition to any personal accident insurance you may have; and have a supply of any medication that you may be taking at the time.

Visiting Commonwealth War Graves Commission Cemeteries

The CWGC cemeteries visited in this guide are generally to be found in communal cemeteries such as **Bray-Dunes Communal Cemetery**, although you will find British casualties from 1940 located in a number of existing First World War Cemeteries, such as **Coxyde Military Cemetery** and **Adinkerke Communal Cemetery.** Visitors should also remember that where a soldier has been recovered from the battlefield it is not always possible to identify exactly when he was killed or died. To that end, on some headstones the CWGC has provided two dates, between which, it is presumed, the individual died. When visiting the fallen from the Second World War around the perimeter, it is impossible not to be constantly reminded of casualties from the First World War, the numbers of which probably horrified the men of the BEF who fought in this area during May 1940. The visitor will also come across the graves of aircrew that were shot down over the course of the war and those men who died during the 1944 advance after the D-Day landings. The graves of men killed in the area during May and June 1940 are probably some of the least visited in the whole of Northern France, as the small numbers of men, whose headstones are sometimes lost amongst the French civilians in communal cemeteries, are all but forgotten. The CWGC was responsible for introducing the standardized headstone, which brought equality in death regardless of rank, race or

Some CWGC cemeteries are marked with the more traditional Michelin signpost. This one directs visitors to the Dunkirk Town Cemetery.

The standard CWGC sign which alerts visitors to the presence of war dead in a communal cemetery.

creed, and it is this familiar white headstone that you will see now in CWGC cemeteries all over the world. Where there is a CWGC plot within a communal or churchyard cemetery, the familiar green and white sign at the entrance with the words *Tombe de Guerre du Commonwealth* will indicate their presence in France, while in Belgium they are marked with the additional words *Oorlogsgrave van het Gemenebest*. French military cemeteries are usually marked by the French national flag, whilst those which are contained within communal cemeteries are often marked by a sign at the cemetery entrance bearing the words: *Carre Militaire, Tombes de Soldats, Morts pour la France*. In Belgium those with military graves are sometimes marked with a white signpost bearing the words: *Belgische Militaire Begraafplaats*.

Visitors will find Belgian war cemeteries are often marked like this one at De Panne.

Tour 1

The Dunkerque Perimeter

Start: Bastion 32 Museum
Finish: Bergues
Distance: Approximately 30 miles

This tour takes in the majority of the Dunkerque Perimeter with the exception of De Panne, which is looked at in more detail by a walk around the town. It includes visits to Furnes (Veurne), Nieuport (Nieuwpoort) and Bergues, as well as a number of the battalion and regimental command centres, such as those at Les Möeres and De Moeren. In addition, directions and details are given for twelve cemeteries. Apart from Nieuport, the author has not provided a map for the tour - the French and Belgian IGN maps are more than adequate - as visitors may wish to be more selective in their choice of sites.

Bastion 32 Memorial Museum

We begin at the Bastion 32 Museum in Dunkerque, which is situated on Rue des Chantiers. The entrance to the museum is through the last remaining vestiges of the Bastion 32 curtain wall that stretched along the sea wall towards the East Mole. During the battle of Dunkerque Bastion 32 was the command post for **Admiral Abrial** and **Général Falgade**, and later for Alexander and Tennant. The buildings were kept intact until 1978, when Dunkerque's shipyards were extended, leaving only the section of curtain wall containing the museum. At the time of writing the museum is open every day from March until the end of November; confirmation of the price of entry and opening times can always be obtained from the Dunkerque Tourist Office, situated at Le Beffroi, Rue de l'Admiral Ronarc'h, or by email: accueil.dunesdeflandre @ot-dunkerque.fr. The museum is well worth a visit and tells the story of the evacuation in 1940, beginning with a short film and allows the visitor to explore its collection of weapons, models, uniforms, photographs and artefacts. Apart from toilets, there is also a shop selling a number of publications in French and English.

Outside, on Rue des Chantiers, close to the museum entrance, is the final resting place of the memorial to **Georges Guynemer,** the First

The entrance to the Bastion 32 Museum at Dunkerque.

The final resting place of the Georges Guynemer Memorial.

World War flying ace, which was originally erected in front of the Casino at Malo-lés-Bains and then, after the storms of 1935, in front of Avenue de la Mer on the Malo promenade. The monument was destroyed by the Germans in 1941 and the bronze bust – all that remained – was finally installed in 1989 where you see it today. It is likely that the formal surrender of Dunkerque to Friedrich-Carl Cranz, commanding the German 18th Division, was made in this vicinity.

The Hourglass Memorial with the structure of the Passerelle du Grand Large in the left background.

The Hourglass Memorial

Designed by Séverine Hubard, the monument to the soldiers killed or missing during Operation Dynamo, is actually called *Le Sablier*. Situated a few yards from the Bastion 32 Museum, it was dedicated in July 2017 and symbolises the possibility of defeat turning into victory and is an analogy between the measurement of time and the evacuation of allied soldiers caught in the Dunkirk pocket.

The East and Western Mole

From the Bastion 32 Museum you can either choose a circular walk of around three miles, which takes in the East Mole, or elect to drive and park your vehicle at the beginning of the Mole. From the museum walk or drive towards the new foot bridge, [Passerelle du Grand Large] that crosses the canal to Malo-lés-Bains. Stay on the western side, keeping

Looking towards the Passerelle du Grand Large from the Bastion 32 Museum.

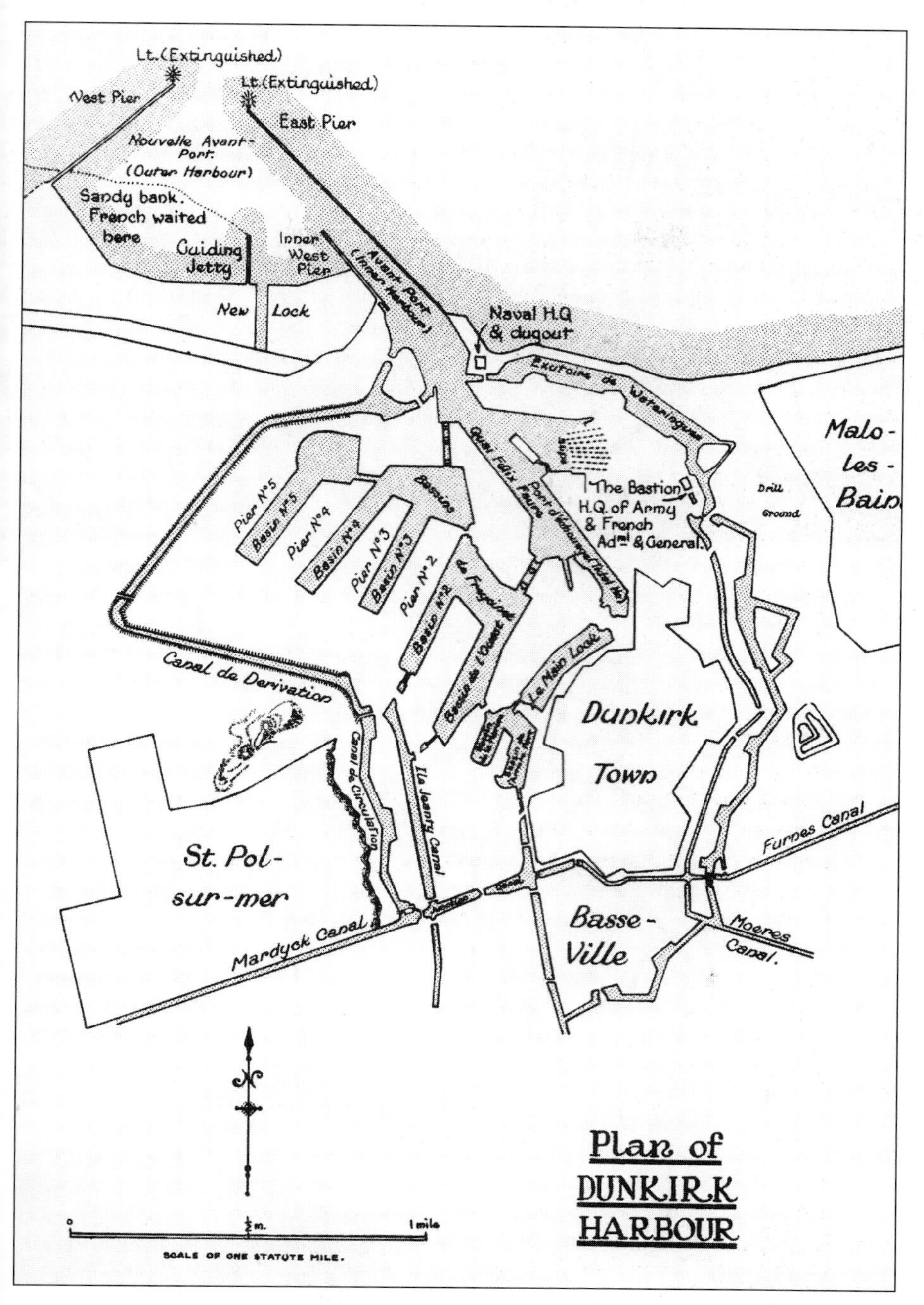

A contemporary map of Dunkerque Harbour in 1940, showing the Naval Headquarters and Bastion 32.

The East and West Mole at Dunkerque.

the canal on your right, and continue past the large FRAC building to the point where the pathway climbs to a viewing point on the right above the canal lock. From this viewing point the East and Western Mole can be seen clearly, while behind you can be seen the dock area and the Dunkerque Hôtel de Ville. In 1940 the East Mole was the point of evacuation for more than two thirds of the BEF and was formed from a stone jetty running out to the harbour entrance, with the final section being made of wood. This section was lost in a storm in the 1970s. The Royal Naval Headquarters was situated in a dugout at the shore end of the East Mole, somewhere near the German blockhouse. If you wish you can cross the canal via the road bridge across the lock gates and walk the half mile along the Mole to the metal fence.

The Malo-lés-Bains Memorial

If you are walking, continue over the Passerelle du Grand Large footbridge and, after crossing the canal, the **Malo-lés-Bains Memorial** is almost straight in front of you. The memorial was created by Maurice Ringot in 1962 using the cobblestones from one of the Dunkerque quays. From the

The Malo-lés-Bains Memorial, the structure of the Passerelle du Grand Large can be seen behind.

memorial you can walk along the promenade at Malo-lés-Bains for three-quarters of a mile until you reach the point where Avenue de la Mer joins the promenade opposite a restaurant. This is where the statue of **Georges Guynemer** was re-erected in 1935 and where **Major Charles Crawford** from 19/Field Regiment arranged to meet his colonel after he had embarked his men. Crawford, as you will remember, incorrectly assumed the memorial commemorated Louis Blériot.

The Georges Guynemer Memorial on the seafront at Malo-lés-Bains before it was destroyed by the Germans.

The SS *Princess Elizabeth*

Before you leave the port area of Dunkerque you may wish to visit the **SS *Princess Elizabeth*,** which is currently moored at Quai de L'Estacade and serves today as a tea rooms and restaurant. Built in 1927, she was taken over by the Admiralty and converted into a minesweeper (No.

SS *Princess Elizabeth* moored in the Dunkerque basin.

J111). A year later she was on her way to Dunkerque, where her first task was to clear the mines from the narrow channel off the beaches. Many of her sister ships, including the *Brighton Belle*, *Devonia* and *Gracie Fields,* were sunk at that time. On 29 May she and her fellow minesweepers embarked 3,415 troops; one of them, SS *Oriole*, had deliberately beached herself early that morning to allow 2,500 troops to pass over her decks to other ships, before she refloated on the next high tide. When *Princess Elizabeth* arrived back at Dunkerque on 1 June she docked in the middle of a furious air attack when, among others, the destroyers HMS *Keith* and *Basilisk* and the minesweepers *Skipjack* and *Brighton Queen* were sunk. She made a final trip in the night of 3/4 June, joining in the last desperate effort to rescue some of the remaining troops. Owned by the City of Dunkerque since 1999, she is one of the last surviving large ships involved in the evacuation that is still afloat.

The SS *Princess Elizabeth* in 1940.

Château Coquelle

Known by the troops as Chapeau Rouge – the red hat - and situated on Rue Belfort, the château is enclosed within a delightful public park and took its name from the rather strange hat-like roof on the tower. Designed by Jean Morel and Maurice Ringot, it was built between 1902 and 1907. The park appears to be open every day but the building, which is now the Rosendael Youth and Culture Centre, is governed by opening hours, although entrance is free. In May 1940 the château was home to 12/Field Ambulance, which arrived in 28 May, and was where **Major Phillip Newman** established an operating theatre in the large drawing room. The gardens surrounding the building were utilized by the CCS and the dead were buried in the grounds. Newman wrote that the house was packed full of wounded, as was the driveway, and the state of the wounded piling up in the grounds appeared to put the saving of life by surgical operation very much in the shade. The château was hit by at least one shell on 2 June, Newman writing that they were awakened by a 'terrific crash as a shell had come into the front room', Lieutenant Jimmy Langley remembered three shells landing on the lawn and a fourth in the lake, adding that he was shielded by the angle of the steps as the main doors were blown off their hinges by the second salvo. It was here that Langley first met **Lieutenant Lord Oswald Normanby**, 5/Green Howards, who had been wounded on 31 May at Houthem. The nearby Rosendael Cemetery on Quai des Maraichers contains only French war graves; the BEF casualties buried in the château grounds were eventually transferred to Dunkirk Town Cemetery.

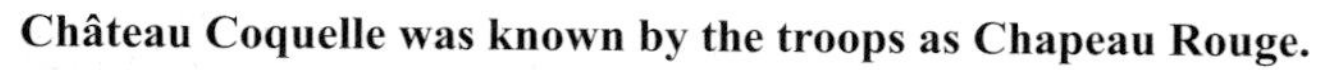

Château Coquelle was known by the troops as Chapeau Rouge.

Fort des Dunes

Général Louis Janssen.

Built and designed in 1880 at Leffrinckoucke as part of the Séré de Rivières line of fortifications, the site is best approached from the entrance on Rue du 2 Juin 1940. Spread over an area of 50,000 square metres, the fort could house 451 men in underground barracks in what were basic conditions even for the late 19th century. Five years after its completion it was virtually redundant and used as a barracks for the 110/ Regiment of Infantry. During the evacuation of the BEF in 1940, the fort became the headquarters of the 12th Mechanized Infantry Division, commanded by 56-year-old **Général Louis Janssen**. Arriving around 30 May, Janssen was killed during an air raid on 2 June, along with **Captains Robert Helle** and **Charles Michet de Varine-Bohan**. All three men are buried together in the adjacent National French Cemetery. Another bombing raid on 3 June hit the fort with six bombs, heavily damaging the superstructure and killing six more officers. With a total of between 150 and 200 killed during both raids and the subsequent heavy damage, the division left the confines of the fort. With Janssen at the time of his death was his faithful servant, **Louis Bouleau**, who returned to the fort each year on the anniversary of Janssen's death until his own death in 2015. A memorial to both men is on display close to where Jannsen was killed. On 27 May a number of searchlight batteries, including those from 3/Searchlight Regiment, were ordered to break up their equipment and move to the Fort des Dunes prior to embarkation.

The memorial to Janssen and Bouleau in the Fort des Dunes.

The fort is now under the control of the tourist office at Leffrinckoucke; entrance can be arranged in advance from the Secrétariat Culture-Tourisme-Patrimoine et Communication Ville de Leffrinckoucke, email: secretariat-ctp@ ville-leffrinckoucke.fr. The visit culminates at the fort museum, where a large model of the Dunkerque perimeter is on display with an audio commentary in English, together with a number of contemporary photographs. During the German occupation the fort was incorporated into the Atlantic Wall defences.

The French National Cemetery at Leffrinckoucke.

The French National Cemetery

This can be found just outside the Fort des Dunes compound, situated close to the railway line. An information board provides the French speaking visitor with details of the Battle of Dunkerque. In addition to the large memorial dedicated to the unknown French soldiers killed at the fort during June 1940, you will find Jannsen, Helle and Varine-Bohan's graves next to the railway line. The cemetery is in a poor condition compared to those maintained by the CWGC and is hardly a fitting tribute for the officers and men buried within.

Zuydcoote

From Leffrinckoucke the small seaside town of Zuydcoote is just under three miles along the D60. Pass Zuydcoote First World War Military Cemetery on the right, turning left at the crossroads along the D302 for 180 yards, where another right turn will take you onto Rue de Valenciennes. The seafront and parking is half a mile ahead. On the right, near the car park, are a number of information boards providing the visitor with details of the wreck of the *Crested Eagle* and *Devonia*, both of which are visible at low tide. The author suggests that a visit to these

The hospital at Zuydcoote seen from the beach.

two wrecks is made from Bray-Dunes while a visit to the hospital building is made from this point. A short walk of some 400 yards will bring you to the beach access to the front of the hospital. The original 1940 building has been reduced to the central entrance area, with two modern flanking wings replacing those which were damaged in 1944. The first wounded arrived on 10 May after the German invasion and five operating theatres worked around the clock. From 20 May more than 600 soldiers were admitted daily. During the evacuation some 1,400 men were treated here by the RAMC, who commandeered the hospital. After the war the hospital fell into disrepair and twenty-five years later was almost completely rebuilt and appeared in the Belmondo film, *A Weekend in Zuydcoote*. Today it is a civilian hospital.

This is where **Lieutenant Jimmy Langley** had his arm amputated by **Phillip Newman** after the wounded from 12/CCS was moved to the hospital by the Germans and is also where **Signalman Terry Nolan**, 63/Telegraph Operating Section, first arrived at the beach and walked down the beach to the East Mole at Dunkerque, from where he boarded the *Crested Eagle*. Surviving the air attack and subsequent beaching of the ship, he found himself back at Zuydcoote and sheltered in one of the corridors of the hospital.

Bray-Dunes

Continue into Bray-Dunes and turn down Avenue du Général de Gaulle where parking by the seafront is almost directly opposite the Bray-Dunes Memorial to the 12th Division of Infantry. Commissioned by **Lieutenant Colonel Etienne Anzemberger**, who commanded the 8/Zouaves, it is the only memorial within the Dunkerque perimeter dedicated to a French

The French 12th Division Memorial at Bray-Dunes.

division. Taken prisoner in 4 June, Anzemberger remained a prisoner at Oflag XXIB until he was repatriated in 1943. The memorial is flanked by two plaques recording the loss of two French ships: one to the French minesweeper *Bourrasqé*, which was sunk on 30 May 1940, and the other to the *Étendard*, sunk in April 1917.

The Shipwrecks

From the 12th Division memorial it is only 600 yards down to the western end of the Bray-Dunes Promenade, where an information board provides further detail of the *Crested Eagle* and *Devonia*, which can be seen to your left at low tide. A short walk along the beach will take you first to the *Devonia* and secondly to the *Crested Eagle*. The *Crested Eagle* was not unlike the *Princess Elizabeth,* which you may have visited at Dunkerque. It is possible to drive down to the slipway at Bray-Dunes by following the Boulevard Georges Pompidou, which runs parallel to the beach, and park by the information board. The *Devonia* was beached at La Panne and drifted down the coast to its present position.

As you return along Avenue du Général de Gaulle drive slowly, as just before you reach the major crossroads with the D60 there is a car park on the left. Park here and walk along the road for a few yards to find the former Bray-Dunes railway station, which is now disused and marked only by the railway lines. In May 1940, like many of the streets in the

The wreck of the *Crested Eagle* at Bray-Dunes can only be seen at low tide.

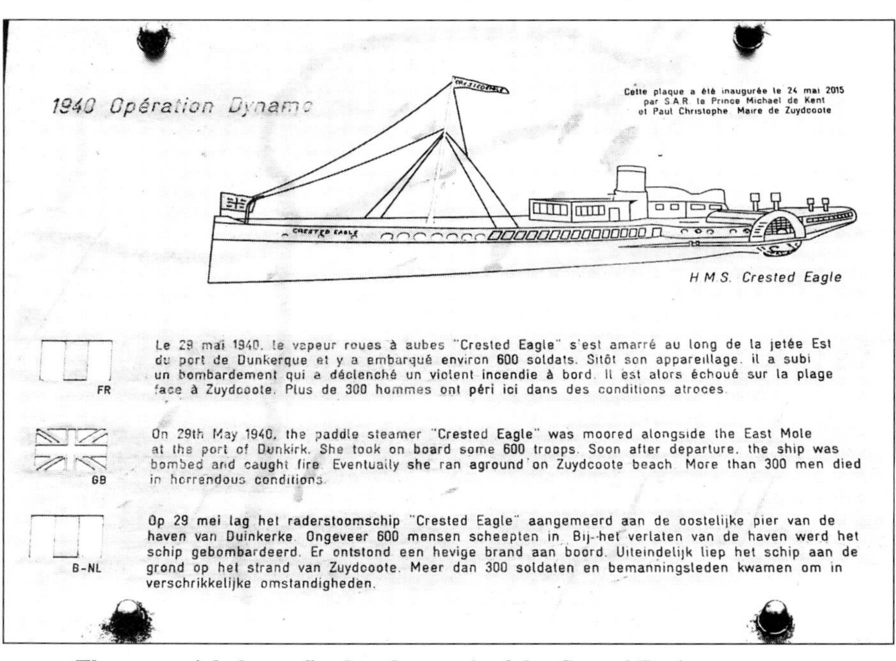

1940 Opération Dynamo
Cette plaque a été inaugurée le 24 mai 2015
par S.A.R. le Prince Michael de Kent
et Paul Christophe Maire de Zuydcoote
H.M.S. Crested Eagle
FR
Le 29 mai 1940, le vapeur roues à aubes "Crested Eagle" s'est amarré au long de la jetée Est du port de Dunkerque et y a embarqué environ 600 soldats. Sitôt son appareillage, il a subi un bombardement qui a déclenché un violent incendie à bord. Il est alors échoué sur la plage face à Zuydcoote. Plus de 300 hommes ont péri ici dans des conditions atroces.
GB
On 29th May 1940, the paddle steamer "Crested Eagle" was moored alongside the East Mole at the port of Dunkirk. She took on board some 600 troops. Soon after departure, the ship was bombed and caught fire. Eventually she ran aground on Zuydcoote beach. More than 300 men died in horrendous conditions.
B-NL
Op 29 mei lag het raderstoomschip "Crested Eagle" aangemeerd aan de oostelijke pier van de haven van Duinkerke. Ongeveer 600 mensen scheepten in. Bij het verlaten van de haven werd het schip gebombardeerd. Er ontstond een hevige brand aan boord. Uiteindelijk liep het schip aan de grond op het strand van Zuydcoote. Meer dan 300 soldaten en bemanningsleden kwamen om in verschrikkelijke omstandigheden.

The memorial plaque fixed to the wreck of the *Crested Eagle*.

area, the station was full of abandoned BEF vehicles, the occupants making their way down to the beach.

Adinkerke

From Bray-Dunes follow the N39 to Adinkerke, crossing the border into Belgium. The **Cabour WWII and 2/4 Lancers Military Museum** is at the junction of Moeresteenweg and Kromfortstraat on the south western edge of Adinkerke. The museum, marked by a post-war Leopard tank, is on the former site of a First World War Belgian Military Hospital, which was opened in April 1915. Only a small section of the museum is devoted to the siege of Dunkerque in 1940 and opening times appear to be on every first Saturday in the month and in school holidays.

Nieuport (Nieuwpoort)

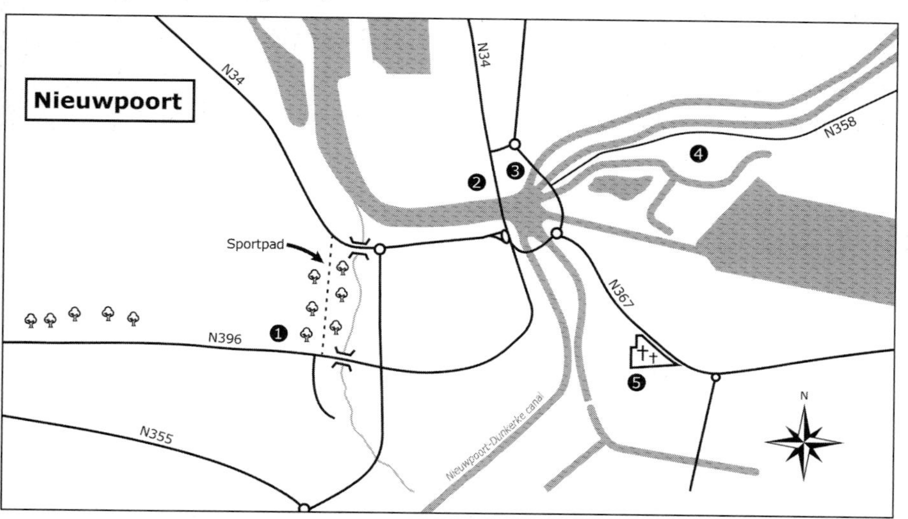

A modern map of Nieuwpoort, showing the myriad of waterways and the principal sights remaining from May 1940.

I have prepared a map of the principal sights in Nieuport. It is best to approach the town via the N396, past the triangular section of woodland on the left, which still contains a number of blockhouses of First World War vintage. The observant amongst you will notice some of the later constructions are of a German coastal flak battery. Drive slowly until you reach a bridge crossing one of the numerous drainage canals, called the **Bridge of Sighs,** by the troops in the First World War. To your left is a strip of woodland running at right angles to the road where there is parking along the roadside. ❶ A pathway – Sportpad – marked by a zebra crossing, will take you through the woods west of the Leopold II Park. It is thought that somewhere in this woodland **Lieutenant Colonel Allen** of the 2/Royal Fusiliers was killed. Continue into Nieuport and park your vehicle in the canal side car park ❷ near the Langebrug, from where you will see the circular Albert Memorial on the far side. ❸

The 1/East Lancs were to your left, their positions stretching down towards the sea, while the Royal Fusiliers and the 1/6 East Surreys were to your right. On 31 May a concerted German attack on both flanks of the town saw their troops attempting to cross through the 1/East Lancs and the 1/6 East Surreys. Although the German 256th Division were driven back by counter attack, the situation remained extremely precarious.

As you know, the initial German advance guard was prevented from crossing the bridge on 28 May by the troop of 12/Lancers, commanded by **Second Lieutenant Miller-Mundy**. In fact Miller-Mundy was involved in a fairly intense fire fight and after securing the crossing had taken up position some 300 yards from the bridge. Fortunately, **Second Lieutenant Henderson** arrived with the remainder of B Squadron and the situation was restored. The construction of the bridge began shortly after the conclusion of the First World War and was initially made of wood, thus the bridge that was the main focus of the German attack in May 1940 was still of a wooden construction. It was not until the 1950s that the bridge you see today was completed. The bridge was prepared for demolition by **13/Field Survey Company**, Royal Engineers, but when the time came to demolish the structure the leads were found to be

The Langebrug at Nieuport in 1928.

on the German side. The bridge therefore remained intact and was eventually blocked on the British side by the Royal Fusiliers' carriers.

Walk across the bridge on the footpath and look across to your right. This expanse of water, which was constructed in the 19th century, is called the Ganzepoot (or Goose Foot) and was occasional referred to as Piccadilly Circus by troops in the Second World War. The drainage canal linking Nieuport to Ostende, Brugge, Ieper and Dunkerque all converge at the Ganzepoot and these once played a vital part in the region's economy. It was these sluices that were opened in 1914 to flood the entire region between Nieuport and Diksmuide by 51-year-old **Hendrik Geeraert,** an act which effectively stopped the German advance. They were opened again in May 1940 but the flooding was not nearly as successful as in 1914.

Continue across the bridge to the **Albert Memorial,** which was dedicated in 1938 and designed by Julian de Ridder; the rather striking figure of Albert on horseback is by the artist Karel Aubroeck. It is possible to climb to the top of the structure, from where a superb view of the Ijzer Estuary can be obtained and the ground to the east. Down the steps from the Albert Memorial is the British Memorial to the Missing of the First World War.

The Albert Memorial at Nieuport.

Now look almost directly east along the line of the N358, running on the southern bank of the Plassendale Canal. A new housing estate can be glimpsed – the view is better from the top of the Albert Memorial – which is where the former site of the **Brickworks ❹** was situated and the scene of the counter attack by the 1/East Surreys. Nieuwpoort Communal

Cemetery ❺ is situated on the N367 and, from here, a short drive down to the seafront at Nieuport-Bad will bring you to the Mole, which is still intact and offers an insight into what the Mole at Dunkerque used to look like in 1940.

Wulpen

Take the N35a out of Nieuport, following the line of the Nieuport-Furnes Canal to Wulpen, which was part of the Dunkerque Perimeter. As you reach Wulpen you will be on what was the German side of the canal and it was where the bridge is today that **Second Lieutenant Robin Medley**, 2/Beds and Herts, was dug in with his platoon on the far side of the canal. Medley writes that a machine gun company of the 2/Middlesex was on his right flank.Wulpen was also where **Brigadier Clifton** initially established his headquarters. Continue along the N39a, crossing over the N330, into Furnes (Veurne).

Furnes (Veurne)

Today there is very little remaining to indicate the short stay by 7 Guards Brigade. Indeed, apart from the Communal Cemetery Extension, little is left of the original town, which suffered from almost continual German bombing and shelling as well as the strategic flooding in 1940. Remember Wednesday is market day. You can find the Tourist Information Office in the Grote-Markt, from which point visitors can see the church of Sint Walburga and the close where **Lieutenant Colonel Lloyd** and **Captain Jeffreys** were initially buried, before being moved to the communal cemetery. The actual spot where Lloyd and his two company commanders were gunned down remains elusive, but it was probably somewhere along

The Grote-Markt at Veurne.

the section of canal that runs between the road bridge on Zuidstraat and the bridge on Duinkerkestraat. **Lieutenant Colonel Prescott** established the 1/Grenadier Headquarters in Sint-Walburgapark, north of the Grote-Markt, while **Major Colvin** established his Battalion Headquarters in a house in the Grote-Markt itself. The sharp eyed amongst you will have noticed the memorial to **Hendrik Geeraert,** on the corner of Noordstraat, leading out of the Grote-Markt.

92/Field Regiment Windmill

The best approach to the windmill is via Adinkerke and then south on Debarkstraat. The latter part of the route is on narrow roads running alongside drainage canals. Satnav users will find the device more than helpful here. It was from the observation post in the mill that **Captain Richard Austin**, 368/Battery, fired on the church steeple in nearby Bulskamp, which you can see clearly from the windmill. **Major Dereck Cragg-Hamilton,** commanding 365/Battery, was also killed here. The windmill is, at the time of writing, undergoing extensive renovation.

The windmill used by 92/Field Regiment as an observation post.

Château Sint-Flora

Three quarters of a mile further along the road, a left turn onto Kasteellaan - note the information board on the roadside – will take you to the Château Sint-Flora, where the Belgian Royal Family were housed from the summer of 1917 until the end of the war. For a few days in May 1940 it was the headquarters of the 8 and 9/DLI and was where **Captain Rutherford** and **Lieutenant Wilkinson**, the two medical officers, established a RAP in the cellars. The château was almost completely destroyed in the battle and was rebuilt post-war.

1/Duke of Wellington's Headquarters

Continue across country towards Les Moëres to find the narrow Chemin Vicinal N1 dit de l'Octogne**.** It was in the farm along this road that **Lieutenant Colonel Beard** established Battalion Headquarters. Nicknamed 'The Piggery', the farm soon came under severe shelling. The RAP was also at the farm and was where the battalion medical officer, **Captain Cullen**, was crawling about amidst the shellfire, dressing wounds and administering morphine. Our next port of call is the Ringsloot, a small drainage canal representing the line to which the

The farm used by the 1/Duke of Wellington's Regiment as seen from Chemin N6 dit de la Dutchess.

1/Dukes were withdrawn to on 31 May. The rising flood water, caused by the opening of the canal gates at Nieuport, prompted Lieutenant Colonel Beard to withdraw his men north. The Ringsloot is approximately half a mile from Pont aux Cerfs, with the bridge situated just beyond the hamlet of La Cartonnerie on the perimeter canal. This was where C Company, under the command of **Major Waller,** were positioned and from where the bridge was blown at 11.00am on 30 May. The Belgian border is another mile to the east; and, if you follow the canal side road through Broek Straete you will come to a large blockhouse on the right side of the road, surrounded by trees. This is thought to have been used by Temple Force.

The bridge at Pont aux Cerfs was defended by C Company, 1/Duke of Wellington's Regiment.

2/Coldstream Guards

From La Cartonniere the D3 heads west along the German side of the perimeter canal. Stop at the junction with Voie Communale Smeet Straate. There is a farm to your left and across the canal you will see the modernized building that is now known as Langley's Cottage. The

Langley's Cottage.

battalion arrived on the canal on 29 May and their line ran from the right flank of the 1/Dukes to the bridge at Le Mille Brugge. Number 3 Company, under the command of **Major McCorquodale**, was in the centre – where you are standing now. Langley writes that they were only thirty-seven men strong and the fields behind them were flooded past the line of the Canal des Glaises, although the level of the water never reached the point where they had to abandon their positions. Company headquarters was in a trench fifty yards to the rear of the cottage and **Lieutenant Ronnie Speed** and Number 1 Company were positioned on the canal further to the left. Numbers 2 and 4 Company were further to your right, which was where **Second Lieutenant Charles Blackwell** was positioned. The cottage is where Langley was injured and evacuated in a wheelbarrow and the 34-year-old McCorquodale was killed while dressed in his best uniform. According to Howard and Sparrow, in their history of the Coldstream Guards, Battalion Headquarters was in a windmill at Krommenhoeck; but in Quilter's account Bootle-Wilbraham states his headquarters was north of Krommenhouck in a farmhouse on Rue Albert Poidevin, a few yards south of the mill. Bootle-Wilbraham tells us the windmill - on Rue Georges Dereudre - was initially used as an observation post, but by 31 May the position had become untenable. Today it still stands but has been converted into a private house.

The 2/Coldstream Battalion Headquarters was at or near to this windmill.

Benkies Mille

Stay on the D3 and in just over one mile further west from Langley's cottage you will come to the turning for the D403 on the right. This road will take you to Warhem, where you will find the communal cemetery.

Turn right along Rue Abel Vermersch to find the cemetery on your left. The British graves are just inside the entrance. Retrace your steps to the D3 and turn left; in approximately three quarters of a mile you will come to a drainage canal running at right angles to the road on your right. The canal is about 130 yards before the crossroads at Benkies Mille and runs north towards a cluster of farm buildings. The ground to the left, about 170 yards north from the road where you are standing, is the approximate position of B Company, 1/East Lancs. Contemporary aerial photographs show a barn north of the farm, near to the drainage canal, which may or may not have been Captain Ervine-Andrews Headquarters. Previously thought to have been destroyed by fire, local opinion is adamant that the now repaired barn was where B Company conducted their last stand. However, barn or not, the ground in front of you is where the last Victoria Cross of the campaign was won.

Recent 'on the ground research' has indicated that this barn is thought to be where Ervine-Andrews and B Company fought their rearguard action.

Bergues

Continue into Bergues, entering the town by Pont d'Honschoot and park in Place de la Republique. Bergues was devastated in the First World War and again during1940, when some eighty percent of the buildings were destroyed before the Germans entered the town on 2 June. Today the belfry is the town's most celebrated attraction, although it has had a chequered history, being rebuilt twice before it was damaged by fire in May 1940 and destroyed by the Germans in 1944. It was not until 1961 that it was finally rebuilt again. The Tourist Office can be found at the foot of the Belfry. Like Furnes, there is very little to see with regard to the defence of Bergues, although the various gates into the walled town have remained intact. Close to the Railway Gate the old barracks, where C Company, 2/Royal Warwicks and a composite company of stragglers were stationed, has remained intact on Rue de la Gare. Nevertheless, the town is worth a visit, if only as a lunch stop or to walk around the ramparts – a ramparts map is available from the Tourist Office. If you are intending to return to Dunkerque it is best to leave by the Dunkerque Gate, via Rue de Pont Saint Jean and Rue de Port.

The Belfry Tower at Berques.

The Dunkerque Gate at Bergues.

Cemeteries

Malo-lés-Bains Communal Cemetery

The cemetery can be found on Rue de Roubaixm. There are ninety-seven identified casualties buried here, sixty-three being from the Second World War, of whom all were killed in 1940. The Second World War graves are clustered around the Cross of Sacrifice in the top left hand corner of the cemetery. **Major William 'Archie' Smellie** (II.B.49) was 45-years-old when he was killed by a shell burst on HMS *Vanquisher* on 1 June. Commissioned into the 1/Dorsets in 1915, he survived the war to be called up in 1939 as a regular reservist. He was acting as ship's adjutant on the Isle of Man ferry, *Mona's Queen,* when she hit a mine off Dunkerque, broke in two and sank within two minutes. He and some of the crew were picked up by HMS *Vanquisher* and it was on board this vessel that he was killed. His elder brother, Lieutenant John Smellie, died of wounds received while serving with the Machine Gun Corps in August 1917.

Malo-lés-Bains Communal Cemetery.

21-year-old **Second Lieutenant Graham Berryman** (II.B.52), 6/Gordon Highlanders, died between 29 May and 1 June and is also remembered on the memorial at Christ's College, Blackheath. Berryman and his battalion may have been supporting the 1/Loyals and was killed during the retreat from Bergues.

25-year-old **Sub-Lieutenant Derrick King** (II.A.13), RNVR, was a member of the Devonia's crew and recorded by the CWGC as missing after the ship was beached at La Panne on 31 May. It is likely he was killed during the subsequent shelling of the ship.

North Londoner **Second Lieutenant Cecil 'Bot' Botibol** (II.B.58) was commissioned into the Leicestershire Regiment in 1939. By May 1940 he was serving as the battalion intelligence officer in the 2/5 Leicesters when he was badly wounded by shell fragments near Carvin on 26 May. Evacuated to a French hospital near Dunkirk, he died of his wounds on 28 May. A Sephardi Jew, he was a member of the highly regarded Bevis Marks Synagogue in London.

26-year-old **Lieutenant Donald Bird** (II.A.2) was medical officer to the 1/East Surrey Regiment. As the 1/East Surreys marched down the beach from La Panne towards Dunkerque, a number of men were killed and wounded. Lieutenant Bird was last seen devoting himself to the wounded men and it is assumed he was wounded while doing so. The CWGC has his date of death as 18 June, so we can presume he died of wounds.

24-year-old **Edgar Webb** (II.A.54) was one of eight crewmen lost when the *Lorina* was caught in a dive bombing attack and suffered a direct hit. Despite the efforts of her captain to beach the ship at Bray-Dunes, she went down in shallow water.

Flying Officer John Baird (II.A.30) was flying a Blenheim Mk IV on 1 June from 254 Squadron (Coastal Command) when his aircraft was attacked by eleven ME109s off Dunkerque. Baird was killed along with 21-year-old Sergeant Richard Roskrow, but the observer, Pilot Officer Spiers, was picked up alive by a British ship. Roskrow is commemorated on the Runnymede Memorial. **Flight Lieutenant Richard Meredith** (II.A.60) was the pilot of a Hurricane I from 17 Squadron on a routine patrol over the beaches when he was shot down on 3 June over Dunkerque.

46-year-old **Squadron Leader Maurice Gurney** (II.A.16) was aboard the SS *Abukir* on its way from Ostend to England when she was torpedoed by the German motor torpedo boat S-34 on 28 May. Maurice Gurney served in the First World War and was called up again in 1939, joining the RAFVR as part of the No. 3 Air Ministry Military and Air Mission and was in France in 1940 when the Germans invaded. Although the date of his death is given as 28 May, it would appear his body was washed up later at Dunkerque.

Dunkirk Town Cemetery and Memorial

Situated on Route de Furnes, this large cemetery contains 1042 burials, of which 592 identified casualties are from the Second World War. There is limited parking by the main entrance, much more by the entrance to

The Dunkirk Memorial and Town Cemetery.

the civilian cemetery. The memorial contains the names of 4,505 missing officers and men of the BEF, most of whom fell prior to and during the fighting around Dunkerque. Those named on the memorial include the BEF servicemen who died on SS *Abukir*, a British steamship that was torpedoed and sunk in the North Sea while evacuating Ostend. [See Squadron Leader Maurice Gurney, Malo-lés-Bains Communal Cemetery.] The missing military personnel lost when the RMS *Lancastria* was sunk are also commemorated here. On entering the cemetery through the columns of the Dunkirk Memorial, two war graves sections will be seen: Plots IV and V from the First World War and Plots I and II from the Second World War.

A large number of officers and men from the Royal Artillery are buried in the cemetery, including one of the youngest serving soldiers in the BEF, 17-year-old **Gunner Ralph Macdonald** (II.17.3), who was born in Edinburgh and lived in London. He died of wounds whilst in captivity on 14 June. The most senior officer is 45-year-old **Lieutenant Colonel Purves Kirsop** (II.17.2), MC and bar. In 1915 Lieutenant Kirsop had been a lucky survivor of the Gretna, Quintinshill railway disaster, which killed well over a hundred Royal Scots on their way to France. He was a passenger on the northbound sleeper which collided at full speed with the burning wreckage of the southbound (Royal Scots) express, which had run into a stationery goods train. Kirsop fell through the wooden floor of his compartment, suffering two broken legs and was trapped under the carriage. He survived, although his three travelling companions in the same compartment all died. In 1939 Kirsop was recalled from the reserves to be the commanding officer of the 58/Light Anti-Aircraft Regiment, and was subsequently killed at Dunkerque on 27 May. His name appears on one of the three stained glass windows located in New Kilpatrick Church. Seven other members of his regiment appear on the Dunkirk Memorial.

According to the 33/Field Regiment war diaries, 21-year-old **Second Robert Lieutenant Corbett-Winder** (I.1.34) was sent to Dunkirk on the 24 May along with two NCOs to return to England and pass on valuable lessons learnt from fighting in France and Flanders. The diary is quite hard to read but it appears Corbett-Winder's party was in Dunkirk when the Luftwaffe were bombing the town and he was killed on 27 May. The remaining members of the party were wounded but made it back to England. Corbett-Winder shares a headstone with **Corporal Harold Thompson**, RASC, who was also killed on 27 May. 25-year-old **Bombardier Frederick Camp** (II.12.8), serving with 226/Battery, 57/Anti-Tank Regiment, was killed on 25 May while the regiment was fighting near Merville; another nineteen members of his regiment are recorded on the Dunkirk Memorial. 29-year-old **Second Lieutenant Donald Waterman** (I.1.51), 140/Field Regiment, was 29-years-old when he was killed between 28 and 31 May. His father, Bertie Waterman, was a well known Dartford Auctioneer, while his mother helped raise funds for a Comfort Fund for troops in Wilmington. Donald was married to Chloe and working as a chartered surveyor. His name appears on the Wilmington War Memorial and also the memorial at St John the Baptist Church in Sutton-at-Home.

There are fifty-nine officers and men of the Royal Engineers from over twenty-five different companies buried here, one of which is 23-year-old **Lieutenant Robert Nigel Barge** (I.1.19), who was killed on 4 June. Said to be an outstanding officer, he came top of his intake at Woolwich and helped to prepare and map the defences around Dunkerque. He also assisted in repairing small craft to help his comrades escape. A licensed pilot, Nigel was a keen athlete who ran for Maryhill Harriers and to this day the Harriers still stage the Nigel Barge Road Race, first held in his memory in 1943. **Sappers John West** (II.13.31) and **Joseph Tracey** (II.15.22) of 7/Field Company were both killed on 1 June on the East Mole and, like Sapper Albert Wood, who was killed at La Panne on 29 May, little more is known of their deaths. **Major Ronald**

Thomas MC (I.1.53) was an elderly 54-year-old when he was badly wounded at Mont des Cats on 29 May while in command of 62/Chemical Warfare Company. Moved by ambulance to Dunkerque, he died of wounds later in the day. Killed at the same time was 27-year-old **Captain Cyril Pugh**, who is commemorated on the Dunkirk Memorial.

46-year-old **Colonel Vincent 'Marino' Brown** (II 16.4), Royal Marines, was Chief of Staff to the British 3rd Division, commanded by Major General Montgomery. During the night of 28/29 May, 'Marino' was on his way to II Corps HQ when he encountered vehicles from the French 2 DLM [Division Légère Mécanique] blocking the road. Apparently, after getting out of his vehicle, a French sentry shot him dead. 22-year-old **Seaman Albert North** (II.19.31), RNR, was a member of the crew of the *Crested Eagle* when he died on 30 May. It is more than likely that he succumbed to his wounds, as the ship was beached west of Bray beach on 28 May, two days before his death.

Of the 125 allied aircrew buried here, only three were victims of the air battle over Dunkerque. Canadian born 31-year-old **Sergeant Evan Jones** (II.17.15) was the wireless operator/air gunner flying in a Defiant I from 264 Squadron when the aircraft was badly damaged by a ME 110 on 2 June. Jones baled out but was hit and killed. The pilot, Pilot Officer Desmond Kay, returned to Manston only to discover that Jones was missing from the rear seat. 26-year-old **Sergeant Ronald Kidman** (II.7.21) was flying a Spitfire I from 266 Squadron on 2 June when he was shot down during an engagement with German fighters, while 25-year-old **Flying Officer Henry Dixon** (II.13.16) of 145 Squadron was shot down over Dunkirk on 1 June flying a Hurricane I and died of burns on 3 June. The combat was witnessed by his brother, Major John Dixon RA, who was on a ship leaving the Mole and did not realise that it was his brother on the end of a parachute which was on fire. Henry Dixon was one of the first who flew a Gladiator on the first patrol of the war on 3 September 1939. During the Phoney War he shot down three enemy aircraft.

Bray-Dunes Communal Cemetery

The cemetery lies just off the D60, directly opposite the *Mairie* on Rue Auguste Coolen. The three BEF burials are on the right of the entrance in two plots. The first contains 23-year-old **Private Joseph Lacey**, 1/9 Manchester Regiment, who was killed prior to the battalion embarking at Malo-lés-Bains on 31 May and 30-year-old **Lance Corporal George Smith**, 2/Wiltshires, killed on 28 May while the battalion was fighting at Oosttaverne. Next to them is ***Capitaine* Etienne Bazin**, the Adjutant-Chef of the 8/Zoauvres; an information board gives further details of this officer. Further along there is another group of six headstones that includes 26-year-old **Gunner Edwin Stone,** who was killed serving with 3/Battery, 4/Heavy Anti-Aircraft Regiment on 28 May.

Adinkerke Military Cemetery

The cemetery can be found just before a large roundabout on the N39. Directions to the cemetery are by the familiar green and white signpost, which takes the visitor down a narrow road to the entrance on the left. Access is via a grass pathway. There are 359 identified casualties buried here, of which eighty-nine are from the Second World War. Amongst the casualties incurred in 1944, visitors will find a large number of graves from the Czechoslovakian Obrena Brigade. For those of you who are struggling with the different rank descriptions, the following may be of some use here, as well as at De Panne Communal Cemetery and Veurne Communal Cemetery and Extension:

Vojin	Private
Svobodnik	Private First Class
Desátnik	Corporall
Četař	Sergeant
Rotmistr	Sergeant First Class
Poručik	Second Lieutenant

31-year-old **Captain Charles Threfall** (G.12) was serving with C Company, 2/Royal Northumberland Fusiliers, near Les Moëres on 31 May when heavy enemy shellfire, accompanied by a determined attempt by the enemy to cross the canal, resulted in severe casualties. During the engagement Captain Threfall was killed by shellfire along with 34-year-old **Captain Leslie Johnson**, who is buried at Veurne Communal Cemetery Extension. The two other Northumberland Fusiliers, **William Walker** (F.15) and **John Cook** (D.28), were members of the 4th Battalion and probably killed while the battalion was withdrawing to La Panne.

24-year-old Australian, **Flying Officer Keith Hynes** (E.23), and 25-year-old **Squadron Leader Desmond Kay** (E.22) [pilot] were both members of 109 Squadron when their Mosquito XV1 crashed near Adinkerke while returning from a nuisance raid on Pforzheim in southern Germany. Kay was an experienced pilot who had flown at least eighty-four operational sorties. 23-year-old **Squadron Leader John Mungo Park** (E.17), DFC and bar, was amongst the three Spitfire Vs from 74 Squadron shot down by Me 109s on 27 June 1941 but Park, who was commanding the squadron, was the only casualty.

Squadron Leader Mungo Park.

Mungo Park's father was a private serving with the 7/Royal Sussex Regiment, in October 1918, just seven months after his son's birth, Lance Corporal Colin Park was killed in action during the Hundred Days Offensive. He is buried in Valenciennes (St Roch) Military Cemetery in France.

De Panne Communal Cemetery

Located south of the town on the N34, the site is limited by normal cemetery opening hours. The cemetery benefits from nearby parking and the entrance can be found after crossing the tram lines. In August 1940 more than 200 casualties were moved here from the surrounding battlefields and the nearby beaches. The cemetery, which is next to the Belgian War Cemetery, contains a plot with 259 identified war graves from the Second World War and two from the First World War. Sadly, seventy-nine remain unidentified. There are also eight Czechoslovakian war graves and fourteen French war graves from the Second World War. Visitors will find a memorial dedicated to political prisoners who died in concentration camps and, in 1989, the ashes of nameless prisoners from nine different concentration camps were placed in the tomb.

19-year-old **Alfred Adams** (I.A.5) was the Radio Officer aboard HMS *Grive* when she was damaged in an air raid on Dunkerque harbour on 31 May and sunk the next morning by striking a mine. Adams was killed along with twenty-four of the crew, including 30-year-old **Seaman John Cooke** (I.C.23) from Rock Ferry in Cheshire. 28-year-old **Captain Geoffrey Onslow,** 2/Beds and Herts, (II.C.23) was one of six children; his father, Colonel Cranley Onslow, fought in the First World War and was decorated with the DSO. Geoffrey Osnslow was badly wounded in the head by shrapnel whilst bringing up the rear of his company on the march up to the beach and it was while he was being attended to at the CCS at La Panne that he was hit again by strafing German aircraft on 1 June and killed instantly. The eight other men of his regiment that have headstones in the cemetery were all killed on 31 May and evidence from the war diary suggests they may have been victims of German aircraft while on the beaches.

49-year-old **Major Hambleton Bousfield** (III.A.59), 1/East Surreys, was unfortunate enough to be travelling in the commanding officer's car when it was hit at La Panne. Wounded, he was transferred to an ambulance and killed when the vehicle was struck by a shell. The date of his death in the CWGC database is 31 May; but as the battalion was not ordered to withdraw until dawn on 1 June, we can safely assume date of death to be a day later.

41-year-old **Lieutenant Colonel John Le Sueur** (I.B.8) was the 5th

Division CRA and was killed on the beach at La Panne on 31 May while building a lorry pier along with 20-year-old **Second Lieutenant John Barrow** (I.B.21), 38/Field Company, 25-year-old **Captain Angus Galloway** (III.A.31), 59/Field Company and 28-year-old **Captain Paul Hodgson** (I.A 33). **Sappers Percival Chuter** (I.A.24), **Frederick Hall** (2.B.5) and **Driver Knowles** (I.A.31), were amongst the eighteen sappers killed alongside them. 20-year-old **Pilot Officer Clifford Dearden** (I.A.7) was the pilot of a reconnaissance Lysander from 2 Squadron who survived a twenty minute battle with nine ME109s before being shot down and killed on 21 May.

Coxyde Military Cemetery

Coxyde is just south of De Panne and the Military Cemetery is situated on the N396. Parking can be found in the nearby supermarket car park. The cemetery is the largest of its type on the Flemish coast and there is an information board for visitors at the beginning of the entrance avenue. The Second World War headstones are to the left of the entrance in Plots 4 and 5 and to the right, in Plot 6. There are 1,507 casualties from the two world wars buried here; and of the 155 Second World War burials, twenty-two remain unidentified. Buried here are men who took part in the Dieppe Raid in August 1942 and those who were serving with the Allied forces from 1941 to1945.

Coxyde Communal Cemetery.

The most senior officer buried here is 42-year-old **Lieutenant Colonel Geoffrey Allen** (V.A.10), 2/Royal Fusiliers, who was killed on 30 May at Nieuport. Commissioned into the Royal Fusiliers, he became adjutant in 1924. Promoted to major in 1938, he took command of the battalion whilst in France and was killed by a sniper. On 30 May the 5/Northamptonshires were in the sand dunes near Oost-Dunkerque and under shellfire. It was probably here that 20-year-old **Private Frederick Elliot** (VI.C.2) was killed, along with Privates **Joseph Britten** (VI.B.1), **Claude Bishop** (VI.B.2) and 21-year-old **Lance Corporal Ronald Francis** (V.A.11).

Amongst the forty-three allied and commonwealth aircrew buried here are the crew of a 582 Squadron Lancaster III that was shot down on 15 June 1944. The highly decorated crew, who between them had been awarded four DFCs and three DFMs, fell victim to a night fighter, crashing south-west of Adinkerke. The crew are buried as follows: Pilot, **Flight Lieutenant John Hewitt** (V.H.2-5), **Pilot Officer Denis Flynn,** Navigator (V.H.2-5), **Pilot Officer Harry Wilson,** Navigator (V.H.2-5), **Flight Sergeant Gilbert Cottrell**, Air Gunner, (V.H.2-5), **Flight Engineer, Vincent Crosby** (V.G.3), Tail Gunner, **Flight Sergeant Albert Bouch** (V.G.1), Air Bomber, **Pilot Officer Robert Clenahan** (V.H.6) and Wireless Operator, **Warrant Officer Walter Smith** (V.G.2). 19-year-old **Pilot Officer Guy Hickman** (IV.M.16) and **Leading Aircraftsman Alfred Fidler** (IV.M.15) were flying in a 264 Squadron Defiant I when they were shot down by a ME109 off the Belgian coast on 31 May 1940. The next day, 23-year-old **Sergeant Leslie White** (IV.F.1) suffered the same fate while flying a 222 Squadron Spitfire I. His was one of four aircraft shot down in an engagement over Dunkerque with ME109s and Me110s, of these, only Pilot Officer Roy Morant returned safely to England. It was during this time that Flight Lieutenant Douglas Bader was commanding a flight with the squadron.

OostDuinkerke Communal Cemetery

The cemetery is situated at the end of a long avenue – Kerkhofstraat – where there is plenty of parking. The entrance is on André Geryllaan and is open every day from 8.00am until sundown. There are now 180 burials from the Second World War, thirty-one of which remain unidentified. Apart from two casualties from the Dieppe raid and nine commonwealth aircrew, all the remaining casualties were buried in May and June 1940 and died in the heavy fighting along the Nieuwpoort-Veurne-Dunkerque Canal or in the skies above. Visitors will recognise many of the II Corps battalions that were fighting along the perimeter.

20-year-old **Second Lieutenant Michael Fisher** (F.131) was killed on 31 May serving with the Royal Fusiliers at Nieuport . He was only three years old when his father, Captain George Fisher, was killed in Gaza in 1917 serving with the Norfolk Regiment. Both father and son are commemorated on the Fleggburgh St Margaret and Billockby War Memorial, which was unveiled in 1922 by Michael Fisher's mother. Also killed on 31 May at Nieuport was 21-year-old **Second Lieutenant Guy Reid** (C.67), 22/Field Regiment, who was hit by a shell as he was going into the RAP.

242 Squadron lost two Hurricanes on 28 May; one of them was piloted by **Pilot Officer Dale Jones** (B.50) who was shot down by a ME109. While little is known of the circumstances surrounding the death of 22-year-old **Flight Lieutenant Basil 'Wonky' Way** (C.53), who was shot down while flying a 54 Squadron Spitfire 1 by an ME109 over the Channel and even less is known about **Sergeant William Medway** (E.111), who was flying a Spitfire 1 from 610 Squadron on 27 May.

Nieuwpoort Communal Cemetery

The cemetery contains seventy casualties of the First World War, three of them unidentified, and thirty-one from the Second World War, four of which remain unidentified. These graves are largely collected in the far left hand corner of the cemetery. Visitors will find the entrance on Brugge Steenweg. Apart from **Private George MaClean**, Royal Regiment of Canada, who was killed at Dieppe in 1942, the casualties are largely from the Royal Fusiliers and South Lancashire Regiments who were fighting in and around the town. There are also twelve RASC casualties from II Corps Ammunition Park, who were fighting with Brazier Force. One of Brazier's officers was 23-year-old **Captain Bruce Thornton**, 53/Medium Regiment, who was killed on 29 May while trying to rescue a Bren gun from an impossibly exposed position at Nieuport . His death, along with the three gunners from 76/Field Regiment, **John Mayne**, **Robert McConnell** and **Frederick Howell**, illustrates the precarious nature of the initial defence of Nieuport. Also of note is the memorial to **Hendrik Geeraert** on the right hand wall of the cemetery.

Veurne Communal Cemetery and Extension

From the Grote Markt take the Ooststraat for approximately 290 yards to reach the major intersection. Turn left into Oude Vestingstraat to find the entrance located beyond the communal cemetery on the right hand side of the road. There is plenty of parking. Veurne Communal Cemetery contains burials of the First World War, while the adjoining extension contains seventy-seven burials of the Second World War, almost all of which date from the last two or three days of May 1940, of which eight

Veurne Communal Cemetery Extension.

remain unidentified. There are also two Czech war graves within the extension and a number of French and Belgians.

The twenty-seven men of the Guards Brigade include the three officers who undertook the initial Grenadiers' reconnaissance along the canal at Veurne. 42-year-old **Lieutenant Colonel John Lloyd** (G.1) and 32-year-old **Captain Christopher Jeffreys** (G.2), of the 2/Grenadier Guards, were both killed on 29 May. The third member of the party, 39-year-old **Major Hercules Pakenham**, was evacuated to England and died of wounds on 1 June. On 30 May the 1/Coldstream Guards lost 35-year-old **Major John Campbell** (A.2), 31-year-old **Captain Cecil Preston** (D.4), **Lieutenant Lionel Graham-Clarke** (F.11) and 21-year-old **Second Lieutenant Peter Allix** (F.3), along with nineteen other ranks.

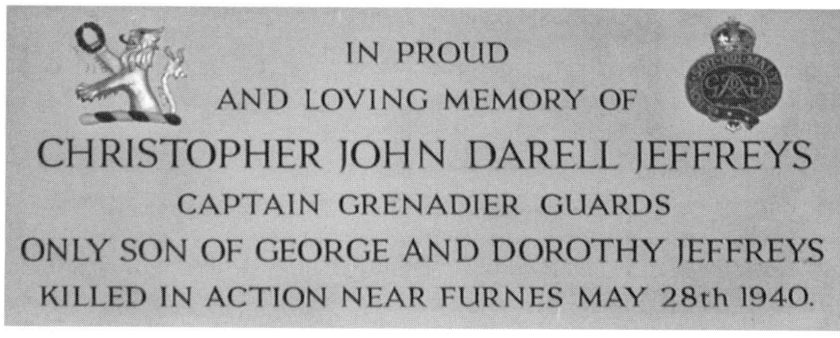

Captain Christopher Jeffreys is also commemorated at St Mary's Church, Bentworth in Hampshire.

31-year-old **Major Derek Cragg-Hamilton** (C.5), 92/Field Regiment, was commanding 365/Battery when he was killed on 31 May. The regiment was west of Bulskamp when German counter-battery shelling hit the Battery Headquarters, killing Cragg-Hamilton and four gunners, three of whom, **Gunners Charles Russell** (C.4), **Maurice Bull** (C.3) and **Arthur Palmer** (C.6), can be found nearby.

The Royal Engineers from 17 and 243/Field Companies were all killed on 30 and 31 May and were either involved in the withdrawal from the line of the canal along with the 4/Berkshires or killed by the heavy German shelling. 23-year-old **Second Lieutenant Douglas Evans** (A.3), 246/Field Company, may have been the officer who was shot by Second Lieutenant Jack Jones, 2/Grenadier Guards, but there is no evidence to support this.

Of the seven aircrew casualties, six were killed on 30 May when a 38 Squadron Wellington 1C, engaged in supporting the BEF, crashed at Veurne. **Sergeants John Knight**, **Dennis Spencer** and **AC2 James Adams** are buried next to each other in Row A; the pilot, **Flying Officer Vivian Rosewarne,** can be found in Row B, and **Pilot Officer Roy Baynes** and **Sergeant Dennis Spence** are in Row D. The letter that Rosewarne left for his mother was published in *The Times* in June 1940 (and later made into a short film), the text of which can be found in Appendix 1. Australian born 24-year-old **Pilot Officer James McFadyen** (G.7) was flying a 126 Squadron Spitfire IX during Ramrod 1398 on 8 December 1944 when he was hit by flak over Dunkerque and crashed near Nieuport. He was flying with Pilot Officer Kevin Loe, a New Zealander, who also failed to return after being hit by flak, who is commemorated on the Runnymede Memorial.

Flying Officer Vivian Rosewarne.

Les Moëres Communal Cemetery

The cemetery can be found behind the church on the D947. From the entrance turn right to find the Cross of Sacrifice, where you will find a line of headstones, twenty-seven of which are unidentified. The area was held by British units up until 1 June and was the scene of some heavy fighting. The nine identified men of the 1/Duke of Wellingtons Regiment were killed between 30 May and 1 June, a number which included 26-year-old **Captain Peter Skirrow**, who was killed when a shell landed in C Company Headquarters on 30 May. There are six men who fought with Temple Force, under the command of **Major Norman Temple** of the Sherwood Foresters, whose seven platoons formed a flank guard to the

1/Dukes. Temple died of wounds on 1 June and is buried at Calais Canadian War Cemetery, Leubringhen. Two men from 19/Field Regiment are also buried here; **Bombardier Edward Vanner and Gunner Lewis** were serving with 29/Battery.

Hondschoote Communal Cemetery

The Communal Cemetery is just north of the church on the D3, and the CWGC Plot is in the far left hand corner of the cemetery by the Cross of Sacrifice. Of the forty identified casualties, fourteen are unidentified. Buried here are twenty-four men of the 1/Duke of Wellingtons and four men who probably fought with Temple Force [see Les Moëres Communal Cemetery].

Warhem Communal Cemetery

Lance Corporal Eric Hughs.

There are nearly ninety Second World War casualties buried here, of which thirty remain unidentified. Marked by the Cross of Sacrifice, which can be seen from the road, the British graves are just inside the entrance. This is where you will find **Major Angus McCorquodale** (A.2) and 23-year-old **Second Lieutenant Charles Blackwell** (B.2), along with four identified other ranks from the 2/Coldstream Guards. Another guardsman was **Lance Corporal Eric Hughs** (A.19), 1/Welsh Guards, who was killed on 29 May, probably during the fighting around Vyfweg [now les Cinq Chemins] and West-Cappel. He was serving in the Signals Platoon, left a wife and daughter and is also commemorated at **St David's Parish Church, Blaenau Ffestiniog.** The most senior officer buried here is 39-year-old **Lieutenant Colonel Ronald Sharp** (A.45), commanding the 1/Fife and Forfar Yeomanry. He was standing with Brigadier Charles Norman at Regimental HQ near Vyfweg on 29 May when the building was hit by a shell, killing him and the regimental medical officer.

Tour 2

Ramsgate and Dover

Start: Military Road, Ramsgate
Finish: Waterloo Crescent, Dover

During the Second World War Ramsgate was a naval station and the principal port controlling the despatch of the little boats to the Dunkerque beaches. It was an obvious choice, given the sheltered nature of Ramsgate's harbour, its railway connections and proximity to Dunkerque. The fleet of small boats, capable of operating along the gently sloping shoreline of the Dunkerque beaches, began leaving on the night of 30 May 1940 for La Panne. By the afternoon of 31 May the line of boats stretched for five miles across the channel. As one skipper later wrote, 'the whole course from Ramsgate was like a main street in a busy town, traffic several abreast going each way'.

At Ramsgate the harbour area sprang into life, with boats constantly unloading their cargo of exhausted soldiers and being refuelled before they began the journey back to the beaches. Troops landed at the harbour and were required to hand over their weapons before being transported via a fleet of buses to the railway station on Station Approach Road, where they were whisked off to receiving stations around the country. Postcards were collected by local women's organizations and issued to the arriving troops so that their families could be informed of their safe arrival and there are several stories of local people and shopkeepers providing the troops with much needed food and clothing. Eighty-two trains left Ramsgate station over eight days, transporting some 39,848 returning troops from Dunkerque. Major Mark Henniker, writing home on 4 June 1940, was amazed at the reception that the returning troops received all along the line, but wondered if the cheering crowds really realized the true picture behind Dunkerque:

> *I suppose it will gradually dawn on the generous English people, who greeted us with food, socks, cigarettes and every sort of gift one could imagine, that it was no victory but a crashing defeat.*

I have not included a tour of the Ramsgate Tunnels on Marina Esplanade, as they are not strictly part of the story of the evacuation of the BEF, but

The RNLI Lifeboat Station.

they are worth a visit and details can be found online. Our walk along the Ramsgate harbour front begins at the large car park on Military Road, from where a short stroll will bring you to a turning on the right, opposite Jacob's Ladder - a flight of steps leading to the top of Westcliffe. A walk alongside the dock and a left turn will bring you to the start of the metal walkway running towards the RNLI lifeboat station. Badly damaged in August 1940 during one of the many bombing raids and reopened two months later, the lifeboat has been stationed here since 1865. One of the most outstanding periods in the history of the Ramsgate lifeboat was in May 1940 when the *Prudential* sailed for Dunkerque at 2.30pm on the 30 May towing eight wherries filled with water and supplies for the troops. Once the supplies had been unloaded, she towed the boats, laden with eight troops each, between the beaches and the larger vessels offshore. Operating for the most part off La Panne and under constant fire, she helped bring off some 2,800 men in thirty hours, a feat that was recognised by the award of the DSM to Coxswain Howard Knight. Inside the station is a plaque presented by the town of Dunkerque commemorating the *Prudential's* part in the evacuation.

Retrace your steps to Military Road to find the Sailor's Church and former home for Smackboys almost straight ahead. The home accommodated boys from the workhouse who worked on the fishing smacks between 1881 and 1915. Notice the plaque in memory of HMS *Fervent* on the wall before you enter. HMS *Fervent* was commissioned as a shore base on 10 October 1939, with the cliffs below Wellington Crescent used as an air raid shelter and storage for the ammunition

The *Prudential* in 1928.

The HMS *Fervent* plaque on the wall of the Sailor's Church.

A plaque presented to Ramsgate Lifeboat Station by the Town of Dunkerque.

supplying the two 6-inch naval guns that were based on the green near the present day bandstand. The harbour area was used by *Fervent* Motor Torpedo Boats, carrying out operations against enemy naval forces in the Channel and North Sea. The church contains a number of replica boats and plaques commemorating Ramsgate's maritime history in both world wars.

A plaque commemorating the work of 27 Air Sea Rescue.

Walk past the Harbour Office, with the monumental arches of Military Road forming the north-western edge of the harbour on your left. Keep bearing right to follow the line of the Royal Harbour, which dates back to the 18th century and was given its royal status in 1821 by George IV. You should be able to see the obelisk near the maritime museum commemorating George's trip to his native Hanover. Stop outside the Oak Hotel, where there is a plaque commemorating the officers and men of **27 Air Sea Rescue.** The RAF unit had its headquarters here and many of the crews were billeted in the hotel between 1942 and 1945.

Continue to the **Maritime Museum,** which you will see on your right. Built in 1817, the building was originally the harbour clock house and

The Maritime Museum at Ramsgate.

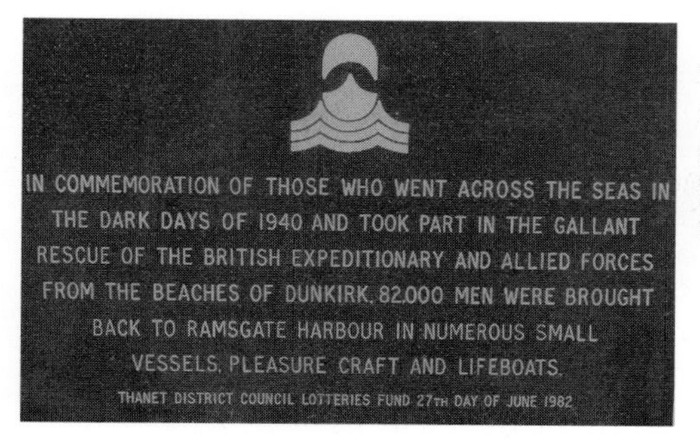

IN COMMEMORATION OF THOSE WHO WENT ACROSS THE SEAS IN
THE DARK DAYS OF 1940 AND TOOK PART IN THE GALLANT
RESCUE OF THE BRITISH EXPEDITIONARY AND ALLIED FORCES
FROM THE BEACHES OF DUNKIRK. 82,000 MEN WERE BROUGHT
BACK TO RAMSGATE HARBOUR IN NUMEROUS SMALL
VESSELS, PLEASURE CRAFT AND LIFEBOATS.
THANET DISTRICT COUNCIL LOTTERIES FUND 27TH DAY OF JUNE 1982

The plaque on the wall of the Maritime Museum commemorating the part played by Ramsgate in the evacuation.

still houses the unique Ramsgate Meridian. Outside the museum entrance is a plaque commemorating those who took part in the rescue of the BEF from the Dunkerque beaches. Inside there are four galleries of exhibits telling the maritime history of the area, including the evacuation from Dunkerque. The museum is closed on Mondays and open from June to September, 10.30am to 5.30pm. The entrance fee is currently £2.20, with children under twelve £1. There is a shop and toilets. The area in front of the museum contains the **Ramsgate Dunkirk Memorial**, which was opened by Dame Vera Lynne in 2000. The text on the memorial reads: *To commemorate the safe return to these shore of 228,226 men of the British Expeditionary Force, together with 120,000 French and Belgians from the beaches of Dunkerque by an armada of naval and civilian vessels of all types and sizes during Operation Dynamo, 26 May to 4 June 1940.* The **Channel Dash Memorial** to the men and machines of Operation Fuller, March 1941, is nearby.

The Ramsgate Dunkirk Memorial featuring the MY *Sundowner* and MV *Brittanic.*

The MY *Sundowner* tied up in the Inner Harbour, Ramsgate.

In the inner harbour, just in front of the museum, is the *Sundowner*, a fifty-eight foot motor yacht built in 1912 and one of the few remaining little ships that made the crossing to Dunkerque in May 1940. In 1929 the ship was bought by **Commander Charles Lightoller**, who was the most senior officer rescued from the *Titanic* disaster of April 1912. The 66-year-old Lightoller sailed the *Sundowner* across the channel with his son, Roger, bringing back 130 men to Ramsgate but was prevented from returning as by then only ships capable of maintaining twenty knots were allowed to continue.

Walk back to your vehicle and drive up to the church of **St George the Martyr**, marked by its tall bell tower. It is probably best to park in the car park on Staffordshire Street and walk the 200 or so yards to the church on Broad Street. It is also advisable to book your visit beforehand as the church is invariably locked. At the time of writing the telephone number is 01843 593593 and the email: enquiries@stgeorges churchramsgate. Inside the church is a stained glass window, which was installed in 1961 and depicts the little ships sailing from Ramsgate to Dunkerque and the troops being rescued from the beaches. It was unveiled by **Jack Hawkes**, one of the crew of the Lifeboat *Prudential*. Below the window is an oak box filled with sand taken from the beaches at Dunkerque, which was placed in the church in 1987.

The bell tower of the church of St George the Martyr.

The final stop is Ramsgate Cemetery, on Cecilia Road. There are a number of headstones scattered around the cemetery, some of which are CWGC headstones, but the main plots are to be found in the cemetery extension. To find them drive through the entrance gate and bear right until you reach the gate leading to the cemetery extension; the two CWGC plots are marked by the Cross of Sacrifice.

The Entrance to Ramsgate Cemetery.

Dover

The coastal town of Dover is approximately twenty miles from Ramsgate and while most books covering the evacuation focus upon the central role that Dover had during Operation Dynamo, it should be said that this was often at the expense of ports such as Ramsgate and Margate, where over 46,000 men of the BEF were landed. In many ways this is understandable, given that the planning and command structure was largely based in Dover and the bulk of the Royal Navy effort was centred on Dover. Admiral Ramsey set up headquarters in the casemate tunnels beneath Dover Castle and for some ten days in May and June these tunnels, which were originally intended as a shelter from air raids, were the command centre for what was possibly the greatest evacuation in military history.

During the evacuation Dover Harbour was crowded with vessels unloading their cargo of troops, often three abreast, to take on more fuel and supplies for the return journey across the channel. Ships of all shapes and sizes were tied up alongside the Eastern Arm, Admiralty Pier and Prince of Wales Pier, at whatever berths could be found. The spirit and morale among the returning troops was generally high, although some of the men who had lost contact with their units exhibited a lack of discipline and a number were seen throwing their weapons into the sea. Morale on the Eastern Pier was not helped by the stacking of bodies, many of which were badly mutilated, just outside the gun battery, which was located there. Troops were fed and put onto special troop trains to transport them to camps further inland for units to be re-organised and refitted. Southern Railway organised 327 of these to transport around 185,000 of the 200,000 allied troops landed at Dover. At the peak of the evacuation, a train left Dover Marine station every twenty minutes.

The castle is well worth a visit, the entrance being on Castle Hill. For English Heritage members entrance is free and, at the time of writing, the entry fee for non English Heritage members is:

Adult	£22.00
Child (5-17 years)	£13.20
Concession	£19.80
Family (2 adults plus (up to) 3 children)	£55.00

Once inside the large site you can immerse yourself in a history stretching from 1066 to the Cold War. Of particular interest to those of us interested in 1940 is the complex network of tunnels that housed the Operation Dynamo command centre, the Admiralty Casemate and the Admiralty Lookout. From this vantage point the whole of the Eastern Docks can be seen below you. There are two restaurants, at least one bookshop and other historical buildings to keep the whole family or group occupied for most of the day.

Dover Castle.

The Dunkirk Memorial at Dover.

The Admiralty Lookout in Dover Castle.

Before you leave Dover, take time to visit the Dunkerque Memorial, situated on the harbour front in front of the Best Western Hotel on Waterloo Crescent. If you look back towards the castle from the memorial you can see the Admiralty Lookout perched on the cliffs.

Cemeteries

Ramsgate Cemetery

This was mainly used by the General Hospital and nearby Manston Airfield. Most of the eighty-eight identified burials of the Second World War form the second CWGC plot. The ten German servicemen from the Air Force and Navy are all casualties who were killed or died of wounds between August 1940 and November 1943. Eleven soldiers evacuated from the beaches on 29 May died of their wounds and are buried in the cemetery; amongst them are **Private Thomas Brown**, 1/9 Manchesters, **Private Frederick Dennis**, 2/Northants, **Gunner Bernard Jones**, Royal Artillery, **Fusilier James McFarlane**, 2/Royal Scots Fusiliers and **Trooper Dennis Marritt**, 1/Fife and Forfar Yeomanry. Several Royal Naval and Merchant Seaman are also buried here, some of whom took part in the evacuation. Two of those served on the same ship; **Lieutenant Anthony Mainwairing** RN, the Executive Officer on board HMS *Mosquito,* and **Stoker Ronald Gorton** were badly injured when *Mosquito* was hit on 1 June off Dunkerque by a German bomb, damaging her beyond repair. Both men died of wounds the next day.

Looking across to the First World War plot from the Second World War burials at Ramsgate Cemetery.

Dover (St James) Cemetery

Situated on Old Charleton Road, this is the largest cemetery in the town. Once through the main entrance a cemetery map will indicate where the CWGC plots are located. Most of the 341Second World War burials are contained in a special war graves plot known as the **Dunkirk Plot** at the far end of the cemetery. Twenty-two of these burials are unidentified. A casual glance around the headstones will reveal at least 125 serving soldiers died of wounds on the sea crossing to Dover or shortly afterwards. One of these men, 36-year-old **Major Eric 'Pop' Wyatt**, 2/Coldstream Guards, was hit by a shell on 2 June at Malo-lés-Bains while leading his company on their way to the Mole. Pop Wyatt died on the boat on his way to Dover. Of the naval casualties, **Able Seaman Harry Andrews** was killed on 28 May serving on HMS *Gallant*, 20-year-old **Able Seaman Arthur Wean** was killed on 1 June while serving on HMS *Worcester* and **Petty Officer George Collins** died on 31 May after HMS *Bideford* was hit by a German bomb on 29 May, blowing forty feet of the ship's stern away. It was towed back to Dover on 31 May. The minesweeper HMS *Pangbourne* was holed on both sides above and below the waterline on 29 May and **Leading Seaman Percy Merrett** was one of twenty-three crew killed and injured. He died two days later at Dover. Another killed on HMS *Pangbourne* was 37-year-old **Petty Officer William Hoare**, who died on 30 May. **Able Seaman Charles Bushnell** died on 28 May whilst serving aboard the armed boarding vessel *Mona's Isle* when she suffered badly from the gun batteries at Gravelines and air attack.

Walk 1

De Panne

Start and Finish: Car Park on Koningsplein
Distance: Two miles
Maps: Street map of De Panne

Further information and a street map of De Panne can be obtained from the Tourist Office email – toerisme@depanne.be – situated near to the Stadhuis on Zeelaan. Park your vehicle in the large car park on Koningsplein and walk up to the roundabout. Turn left into Koninklijke Baan, keeping to the left hand side of the road. After 200 yards you will be able to see the Tram Depot on the left, which, like the surrounding streets, was used as a dumping ground for BEF vehicles. Continue to the next roundabout, passing the Hotel Donny on the right, from where you

The yard in front of the Tram Depot was used as a dumping ground for BEF vehicles.

A poor quality contemporary photograph showing the Tram Depot in May 1940.

The archway at the top of Leopold Esplanade.

will see a large sculpture in the form of an archway in front of you, marking the beginning of Leopold Esplanade. Using the numerous pedestrian crossings and mindful of the trams, cross the road and walk along the Esplanade towards the far end. After 180 yards you will come to Kapelleslaan on your right and a short walk up the road for eighty yards will bring you to the small Royal Chapel, which was often visited by the Royal Family during the First World War. The chapel is all that is left of the original buildings. Retrace your steps and continue to the end of the Esplanade.

Kapellalaan in May 1940.

Leopold's arrival in Belgium in 1830 began at Calais and he is said to have ridden along the beach from Dunkerque to La Panne accompanied by a squadron of French cavalry, having met numerous dignitaries at the border. The statue marks the spot where Leopold entered the country and is based on a design by Victor Martiny and was commissioned by the National Committee of the Leopold Monument in De Panne. On 5 October 1958, Mayor Gevaert inaugurated the monument in the presence of King Baudouin and Prime Minister Gaston Eyskens. To the left of the statue is the ground on which the three royal villas were built and where the Royal Family lived for part of the First World War. This is where Gort received Wake-Walker for dinner and presumably where he resided during the days prior to his evacuation. Damage incurred during 1940 forced the demolition of the buildings after the Second World War.

The Statue of Leopold I overlooks the beach.

Visitors should be aware that the town has seen considerable development during the post-war years and is largely unrecognizable from the seaside town of May 1940. Before the Second World War, for example, Leopold Esplanade was called the Royal Route, which became Route de Furnes (Veurnestraat) after it crossed Avenue de la Mer (Zeelaan), while the multitude of apartment blocks have dwarfed almost everything else. Nevertheless, the beach area remains much as it was in May 1940, although the journey through the town to the beach would have been fraught with danger from shellfire and a myriad of burning buildings.

The Memorial to Allied Forces.

Turn right to walk along the promenade, taking care not to miss the Memorial to the Allied Forces on the left. Two information boards provide the visitor with further information. Almost opposite the Leopold I Restaurant is what can only be described as a viewing platform, which is an excellent place to view the beach and the former lorry piers that were constructed in May 1940. The idea of using lorries as makeshift

The beach at La Panne in June 1940 after the BEF had been evacuated. The remains of at least one lorry pier can still be seen near the Geitenweg, while the flooring from the roller skating arena (bottom right) has been removed to provide a walkway on one of the piers.

piers is said to have come from Sub Lieutenant Edmund Croswell on 29 May, who had been landed from HMS *Harvester* at La Panne. The platform is almost on the line of Lorry Pier Number 3 and reportedly had little or no anti-aircraft protection. From the platform the shallow nature of the beach can be seen and the reason for the piers becomes clear, for they provided jetties that allowed ship's boats to come alongside and ferry men out to the waiting larger ships.

The gently shelving nature of the beaches to the east of Dunkerque is seen at La Panne. The Witteberg flats with the pointed turrets can be seen on the left. In the far distance the tall arch surrounding the Leopold I statue is visible.

Lorry Pier Number 2 was constructed approximately where Vuurtorenplein meets the promenade and Lorry Pier Number 1 – probably the first of the three piers to be built – was constructed opposite Geitenweg, next to the Witteberg flats. This pier was most probably constructed by vehicles driven into the sea in a nose to tail fashion and was destroyed by the tide quite early in the evacuation. Evidence supplied by **Lieutenant Ludlow-Hewitt**, a gunner officer with the 3/Medium Regiment, certainly supports this, as he remembered a lorry pier constructed of vehicles driven into the sea 'end to end.' The demise of this pier forced the engineers to build a stronger version next to it with vehicles lashed together sideways on. It was on this sector of the beach, at one of the lorry piers, that **Lieutenant Colonel John Le Sueur** was killed by a stick of four bombs, along with **Second Lieutenant John Barrow, Captain Angus Galloway** and **Captain Paul Hodgson.** Also killed were seven sappers from 7/Field Company, with nine others wounded.

Having passed the Witteberg flats, walk along the promenade for approximately 180 yards, turning right along Visserslaan. Cross over the main road and take the continuation of Visserslaan almost straight ahead. At the time of writing the road was marked by a no entry sign and a small

British dead at La Panne. A Bren gun lies in the foreground and three soldiers, possibly dispatch riders, lie close to their motorcycles.

hotel on the right. Continue for 500 yards past residential houses to find yourself facing an ornamental square. This open space may have been yet another vehicle scrap yard organized by the Germans when clearing up the debris left behind by the BEF, although there is a lack of photographic evidence supporting this.

Turn right along Zeelaan, where you will find plenty of cafes and restaurants should you feel the need for refreshments. Follow the road for a further 350 yards until you come to the Stadhuis on your right. This modern building is almost directly opposite the former site of the BEF Headquarters at La Panne, which was situated where numbers 16 to 18

The Stadhuis on Zeelaan.

The new flats opposite the Stadhuis that have replaced the former BEF HQ.

Zeelaan are today. If you sit on the bench provided by the Dunkerque Veterans Association, Lord Gort's Headquarters was almost directly in front of you; compare this to the photograph of the former *Mairie* in Chapter 2. Inside the Stadhuis – which you are able to visit - are two plaques, one erected by the citizens of De Panne and the Dunkirk Veteran's Association in memory of the evacuation and another of Lord Gort, which presumably was previously on the wall of the former headquarters building. In the glass cabinet, opposite the plaques, are a number of items connected to the evacuation. BEF Headquarters at La Panne was closed down at 6.00pm on 31 May after Gort had embarked for England. The building was initially Sir Robert Adam's Headquarters

The plaque erected by the citizens of De Panne and the Dunkirk Veteran's Association.

before it was taken over as the final GHQ of the BEF and was where the order of to evacuate was issued. It is likely that it was also the building where **Major General Alexander** was told he was to command the BEF rearguard. BEF Headquarters on Zeelaan is approximately half a mile from the sea and may possibly lead to the 'lane' referred to by **Brigadier Lawson** in his account.

The plaque which once adorned the exterior wall of BEF HQ.

Continue for a few yards to Poststraat, which is the next road on the right. On the corner is – at the time of writing – a health insurance building; this was the former site of the Post Office building, where the submarine cable joining England and La Panne could be accessed. There was a constant stream of messages being transmitted back and forth to London from here before it was closed down.

In sixty yards you will come to the former Royal Road – Koninklijke Baan; cross straight over and continue along Kerkstraat to reach the T-Junction with the N34. Standing at the junction you will see a new block of flats straight ahead and to your left the church of Sint Elizabeth. Across the road, where the block of flats stands today, there was a large German motorcycle scrap yard, comprising hundreds of motorcycles left behind by the BEF. There was another on the N34 Adinkerke road, about 800 yards before the entrance to De Panne Communal Cemetery. Turn right at the junction, following Westhoeklaan for approximately 120 yards and turn right again into Koningsplein, where the car park and your vehicle can be found on the left.

A German soldier stands by the tree surveying the motorcycle scrap yard opposite the church of Sint Elizabeth.

Selected Bibliography

The National Archives
Unit War Diaries in WO 166 and 167.
Personal accounts and Diaries in CAB 106 and WO 217.
POW Reports in WO 344, WO 373.

The Imperial War Museum Sound Archive
The Imperial War Museum Department of Documents
The National Army Museum
The Liddell Hart Military Archive, London
The RUSI Library
Daily Telegraph Archive
The Surrey History Centre

Published Sources
Barclay, C N, *The History of the Duke of Wellington's Regiment 1919-1952*, Clowes 1953
Baxter, I, *Blitzkrieg in the West*, Pen and Sword 2010
Blaxland, G, *Destination Dunkirk: The Story of Gort's Army*, William Kimber 1973
Blight, G, *The History of The Royal Berkshire Regiment 1920-1947*, Staples 1953
Boardman, C J, *Tracks in Europe*, Royal Inniskilling Dragoon Guards 1990
Chaplin, H D, *Queen's Own Royal West Kent Regiment 1920-50*, Michael Joseph 1954
Dean, C G, *The Loyal Regiment 1919-1953*, The Regiment 1955
Ellis, L.F, *The War in France and Flanders*, HMSO 1953
Farndale, M, *History of the Royal Regiment of Artillery*, Brasseys 1996
Foster, R, The *History of the Queen's Royal Regiment, Volume VIII 1924-1948*, Gale and Polden 1953
Frieser, K-H, *The Blitzkrieg Legend*, Naval Institute Press 2012
Godfrey, E G, *History of the Duke of Cornwall's Light Infantry 1939-45*, Gale and Polden 1966
Guderian, H, *Panzer Leader*, Michael Joseph 1952
Hart, L, *The Rommel Papers*, Collins 1953
Jackson, J, *The Fall of France,* OUP 2003
Lynch, T, *Dunkirk 1940 'Whereabouts Unknown'*, History Press 2010
Murland, J, *Retreat and Rearguard: Dunkirk 1940*, Pen and Sword 2015
Nicholson, W N, *The History of the Suffolk Regiment 1928-1946*, East Anglian Ltd 1948
Philson, A, *The British Army 1939-1945 Organization and Order of Battle Volume 6*, Military Press 2007
Quilter DC, *No Dishonourable Name*, Willian Cloves & sons 1947
Stanley-Clarke E & Tillott A, *From Kent to Kohima*, Gale and Polden 1951
Sebag-Montefiore, H, *Dunkirk – Fight to the Last Man*, Viking 2006
Synge, W, *The Story of the Green Howards*, The Regiment 1954
Underhill, W, *The History of The Royal Leicester Regiment*, Rowe 1957
Usher, K, *Charles 'Dougie' Usher*, Createspace 2014
White, G, *Straight on for Tokyo, The War History of the 2nd Battalion Dorsetshire Regiment*, Gale and Polden 1948
Younger, T, *Blowing Our Bridges*, Pen and Sword 2004

Appendix 1

The Rosewarne letter

Dearest Mother:

Though I feel no premonition at all, events are moving rapidly and I have instructed that this letter be forwarded to you should I fail to return from one of the raids that we shall shortly be called upon to undertake. You must hope on for a month, but at the end of that time you must accept the fact that I have handed my task over to the extremely capable hands of my comrades of the Royal Air Force, as so many splendid fellows have already done.

First, it will comfort you to know that my role in this war has been of the greatest importance. Our patrols far out over the North Sea have helped to keep the trade routes clear for our convoys and supply ships, and on one occasion our information was instrumental in saving the lives of the men in a crippled lighthouse relief ship. Though it will be difficult for you, you will disappoint me if you do not at least try to accept the facts dispassionately, for I shall have done my duty to the utmost of my ability. No man can do more, and no one calling himself a man could do less.

I have always admired your amazing courage in the face of continual setbacks; in the way you have given me as good an education and background as anyone in the country: and always kept up appearances without ever losing faith in the future. My death would not mean that your struggle has been in vain. Far from it. It means that your sacrifice is as great as mine. Those who serve England must expect nothing from her; we debase ourselves if we regard our country as merely a place in which to eat and sleep.

History resounds with illustrious names who have given all; yet their sacrifice has resulted in the British Empire where there is a measure of peace, justice and freedom for all, and where a higher standard of civilization has evolved, and is still evolving, than anywhere else. But this is not only concerning our own land. Today we are faced with the greatest organized challenge to Christianity and civilization that the world has ever seen, and I count myself lucky and honoured to be the right age and fully trained to throw my full weight into the scale. For this I have to thank you. Yet there is more work for you to do. The home front will still have to stand united for years after the war is won. For all that can be said against it, I still maintain that this war is a very good thing: every individual is having the chance to give and dare all for his principle like the martyrs of old. However long the time may be, one thing can never be altered – I shall have lived and died an Englishman. Nothing else matters one jot nor can anything ever change it.

You must not grieve for me, for if you really believe in religion and all that it entails that would be hypocrisy. I have no fear of death; only a queer elation ... I would have it no other way. The universe is so vast and so ageless that the life of one man can only be justified by the measure of his sacrifice. We are sent to this world to acquire a personality and a character to take with us that can never be taken from us. Those who just eat and sleep, prosper and procreate, are no better than animals if all their lives they are at peace. I firmly believe that evil things are sent into the world to try us; they are sent deliberately by our Creator to test our mettle because He knows what is good for us. The Bible is full of cases where the easy way out has been discarded for moral principles.

I count myself fortunate in that I have seen the whole country and known men of every calling. But with the final test of war I consider my character fully developed. Thus at my early age my earthly mission is already fulfilled and I am prepared to die with just one regret: that I could not devote myself to making your declining years more happy by being with you; but you will live in peace and freedom and I shall have directly contributed to that, so here again my life will not have been in vain.

Appendix 2

An abridged list of large ships which took part in Operation Dynamo with those sunk, beached or abandoned (dates in brackets).

Type	Number involved	Troops Evacuated	Sunk	Lost or abandoned
Cruiser	1	1,856	nil	nil
Destroyers	41	96,197	6	nil
Ships sunk: HMS *Basilisk* (1/6), HMS *Grafton* (29/5), HMS *Grenade* (29/5), HMS *Havant* (1/6), HMS *Keith* (1/6), HMS *Wakeful* (29/5).				
Corvettes	6	1,100	nil	nil
Sloops & Gunboats	3	3,512	1	nil
Ships sunk: HMS *Mosquito* (1/6)				
Paddle Minesweepers	36	46,434	5	1
Ships sunk: HMS *Brighton Belle* (28/5), HMS *Brighton Queen* (1/6), HMS *Devonia* (31/5), HMS *Gracie Fields* (30/5), HMS *Skipjack* (1/6), HMS *Waverley* (29/5).				
Trawlers	52	5,396	12	nil
Ships sunk: *Argyllshire* (1/6), *Blackburn Rovers* (2/6), *Calvi* (29/5), *Comfort* (29/5), *Nautilus* (29/5), *Ocean Reward* (28/5), *Polly Johnston* (29/5), *St Achilleus* (1/6), *Stella Dorado* (1/6), *Thomas Bartlett* (28/5), *Thuringia* (28/5), *Westella* (2/6).				
Drifters	61	12,370	2	3
Ships sunk: *Boy Roy* (27/5), *Fair Breeze* (1/6), *Girl Pamela* (28/5), *Lord Cavan* (1/6), *Paxton* (27/5).				
Special Service Vessels	3	4,408	1	nil
Ships sunk: *Crested Eagle* (29/5)				
Motor Torpedo Boats	6	20	nil	nil
Armed Boarding Vessels	3	4,848	1	nil
Ships sunk: *King Orry* (30/5).				
Skoots (Coasters)	40	22,698	3	1
Alice (28/5) , *Horst* (31/5), *Lena* (4/6), *Sursum-Corda* (31/5)				
Motor Yachts	26	4,681	2	1
Alumree (1/6), *Grive* (1/6), *Pellag II* (1/6).				
General Cargo Ships	45	87,810	8	nil
Ships sunk: *Clan Macalister* (29/5), *Fenella* (29/5), *Lorina* (29/5), *Mona's Queen* (29/5), *Normannia* (29/5), *Queen of the Channel* (28/5), *Sequacity* (27/5), *Scotia* (1/6).				
Hospital Ships	8	3,006	1	nil
Ships sunk: *Paris (3/6).*				
Tugs	40	3,164	2	1
Ships sunk: *Fossa* (2/6), *St Abbs* (1/6), *St Fagan* (1/6).				
Steam Hopper Barges	7	2,166	nil	nil
Auxillary Barges	8	1,256	1	nil
Ships sunk: *Lady Rosebery* (1/6).				
Sailing Barges	25	886	3	6
Ships sunk: *Aidia* (1/6), *Barbara Jean* (1/6), *Doris* (1/6), *Duchess* (1/6), *Ethel Everard* (1/6), *Lark* (1/6), *Royalty* (1/6), *Warrior (date of loss not known).*				
RNLI Life Boats	19	323	1	nil
Ships sunk: *The Viscountess of Wakefield* (31/5).				

Appendix 3

Evacuation Figures – Summary

Date	Beaches	Dunkerque Harbour
26 May	Nil	Nil
27 May	Nil	7,669
28 May	5,930	11,874
29 May	13,752	33,585
30 May	29,512	24,311
31 May	22,942	45,072
1 June	17,348	47,081
2 June	6,695	19,561
3 June	1,870	24,876
4 June	622	25,553
Total	**98,780**	**239,446**

* * *

Appendix 4

Nationality of Ships with Number of Troops Evacuated

Nationality	Beaches	Dunkerque Harbour	Total
British	98,754	210,134	308,888
French	7	22,153	22,160
Belgian	Nil	3,464	3,464
Dutch	Nil	214	214
Norwegian	Nil	3,500	3,500
Total	98,761	239,465	338,226

Index